NATIVE AMERICANS

OPPOSING VIEWPOINTS®

Other Books of Related Interest:

American History Series

African Americans
The American Frontier
The American Revolution
Asian Americans
The Bill of Rights
The Civil Rights Movement
The Civil War
The Cold War
The Creation of the Constitution
The Great Depression
Immigration
The Industrial Revolution
Isolationism
The 1960s
Puritanism
Reconstruction
Slavery
The Vietnam War
The Women's Rights Movement
World War I
World War II

Opposing Viewpoints in American History

Volume I: From Colonial Times to Reconstruction
Volume II: From Reconstruction to the Present

NATIVE AMERICANS

O P P O S I N G   V I E W P O I N T S®

David L. Bender, *Publisher*
Bruno Leone, *Executive Editor*

William Dudley, *Series Editor*
John C. Chalberg, Ph.D., professor of history,
   Normandale Community College, *Consulting Editor*

William Dudley, *Book Editor*

AMERICAN HISTORY SERIES

Greenhaven Press, Inc.
San Diego, California

Library of Congress Cataloging-in-Publication Data

Native Americans : opposing viewpoints / William Dudley,
   book editor.
         p.   cm. — (American history series)
      Includes bibliographical references (p.   ) and index.
      ISBN 1-56510-705-5 (lib. : alk. paper) —
   ISBN 1-56510-704-7 (pbk. : alk. paper)
      1. Indians of North America—History. I. Dudley, William,
   1964–   . II. Series: American history series (San Diego, Calif.)
   E77.2.N37   1998
   973'.0497—dc21   97-38334
                                                                   CIP

©1998 by Greenhaven Press, Inc., PO Box 289009,
San Diego, CA 92198-9009

Printed in the U.S.A.

"America was born of revolt, flourished in dissent, became great through experimentation."

Henry Steele Commager, American Historian

Contents

Foreword   9

Introduction   14

Chapter 1: Early Encounters

Chapter Preface   26

1. Colonists Should Maintain Friendly Relations
   with the Indians   28
   Powhatan

2. Colonists Should Wage War Against the Indians   30
   Virginia Company of London

3. A Captive's Account of the Cruelty of Indians   35
   Peter Williamson

4. A Captive's Account of the Kindness of Indians   45
   Mary Jemison

Chapter 2: Removal and Resistance: The Conflict over Land in the Early Nineteenth Century

Chapter Preface   59

1. Indians Should Join Together in War Against
   the Americans   62
   Tecumseh

2. Indians Should Live in Peace with the Americans   67
   Pushmataha

3. The Cherokee Are Creating a Civilized Society   73
   Elias Boudinot

4. The Cherokee Are Not Creating a Civilized
   Society   84
   Wilson Lumpkin

5. Indians Should Be Removed to the West   92
   Andrew Jackson

6. Indians Should Be Allowed to Remain in Their
   Homeland   101
   Cherokee Nation

Chapter 3: American Indians and the Western Frontier

Chapter Preface   112

1. The Federal Government Should Pursue Peace with the Indians   115
   James Henderson

2. The Federal Government Must Wage War on the Indians   126
   Samuel J. Crawford

3. Indians Are Cruel and Unchangeable Savages   131
   George Armstrong Custer

4. Indians Are Victims of American Injustice   137
   Helen Hunt Jackson

5. The White Takeover of Indian Land Was Unjust   143
   Chief Joseph

6. The White Takeover of Indian Land Was Inevitable   157
   Theodore Roosevelt

Chapter 4: Native Traditions Versus Assimilation: The Conflict over Culture

Chapter Preface   165

1. Indian Tribal Land Should Be Divided and Distributed to Individuals   167
   Carl Schurz

2. Indian Tribal Land Should Not Be Divided and Distributed to Individuals   175
   Minority Members of the House Committee on Indian Affairs

3. Indian Education Should Emphasize American Culture   183
   Thomas J. Morgan

4. Indian Education Should Not Destroy Indian Culture   191
   Luther Standing Bear

Chapter 5: Twentieth-Century Debates on American Indian Issues

Chapter Preface   203

1. New Deal Reforms Will Harm American Indians   206
   Flora Warren Seymour

2. New Deal Reforms Have Helped American Indians 216
John Collier

3. The Federal Government Should Terminate Its Trust Relationship with American Indians 224
Arthur V. Watkins

4. The Federal Government Should Not Terminate Its Trust Relationship with American Indians 232
Ruth Muskrat Bronson

5. Indians Who Have Moved to Cities Have Fared Well 237
O.K. Armstrong and Marjorie Armstrong

6. Indians Who Have Moved to Cities Have Not Fared Well 243
Ruth Mulvey Harmer

7. The American Indian Movement Has Helped Native Americans 252
Dennis Banks

8. The American Indian Movement Has Had Limited Effectiveness 258
Gerald Vizenor

Chapter 6: Two Historians Examine the Indian Removal Policy

Chapter Preface 264

1. The U.S. Policy of Indian Removal Was Intended to Subjugate Indians 265
Francis Jennings

2. The U.S. Policy of Indian Removal Was Intended to Protect Indians 277
Francis Paul Prucha

For Discussion 290
Chronology 293
Annotated Bibliography 302
Index 313

Foreword

Aboard the *Arbella* as it lurched across the cold, gray Atlantic, John Winthrop was as calm as the waters surrounding him were wild. With the confidence of a leader, Winthrop gathered his Puritan companions around him. It was time to offer a sermon. England lay behind them, and years of strife and persecution for their religious beliefs were over, he said. But the Puritan abandonment of England, he reminded his followers, did not mean that England was beyond redemption. Winthrop wanted his followers to remember England even as they were leaving it behind. Their goal should be to create a new England, one far removed from the authority of the Anglican church and King Charles I. In Winthrop's words, their settlement in the New World ought to be "a city upon a hill," a just society for corrupt England to emulate.

A Chance to Start Over

One June 8, 1630, John Winthrop and his company of refugees had their first glimpse of what they came to call New England. High on the surrounding hills stood a welcoming band of fir trees whose fragrance drifted to the *Arbella* on a morning breeze. To Winthrop, the "smell off the shore [was] like the smell of a garden." This new world would, in fact, often be compared to the Garden of Eden. Here, John Winthrop would have his opportunity to start life over again. So would his family and his shipmates. So would all those who came after them. These victims of conflict in old England hoped to find peace in New England.

Winthrop, for one, had experienced much conflict in his life. As a Puritan, he was opposed to Catholicism and Anglicanism, both of which, he believed, were burdened by distracting rituals and distant hierarchies. A parliamentarian by conviction, he despised Charles I, who had spurned Parliament and created a private army to do his bidding. Winthrop believed in individual responsibility and fought against the loss of religious and political freedom. A gentleman landowner, he feared the rising economic power of a merchant class that seemed to value only money. Once Winthrop stepped aboard the *Arbella*, he hoped, these conflicts would not be a part of his American future.

Yet his Puritan religion told Winthrop that human beings are fallen creatures and that perfection, whether communal or individual, is unachievable on this earth. Therefore, he faced a paradox: On the one hand, his religion demanded that he attempt to live a perfect life in an imperfect world. On the other hand, it told him that he was destined to fail.

Soon after Winthrop disembarked from the *Arbella*, he came face-to-face with this maddening dilemma. He found himself presiding not over a utopia but over a colony caught up in disputes as troubling as any he had confronted in his English past. John Winthrop, it seems, was not the only Puritan with a dream of a heaven on earth. But others in the community saw the dream differently. They wanted greater political and religious freedom than their leader was prepared to grant. Often, Winthrop was able to handle this conflict diplomatically. For example, he expanded participation in elections and allowed the voters of Massachusetts Bay greater power.

But religious conflict was another matter because it was grounded in competing visions of the Puritan utopia. In Roger Williams and Anne Hutchinson, two of his fellow colonists, John Winthrop faced rivals unprepared to accept his definition of the perfect community. To Williams, perfection demanded that he separate himself from the Puritan institutions in his community and create an even "purer" church. Winthrop, however, disagreed and exiled Williams to Rhode Island. Hutchinson presumed that she could interpret God's will without a minister. Again, Winthrop did not agree. Hutchinson was tried on charges of heresy, convicted, and banished from Massachusetts.

John Winthrop's Massachusetts colony was the first but far from the last American attempt to build a unified, peaceful community that, in the end, only provoked a discord. This glimpse at its history reveals what Winthrop confronted: the unavoidable presence of conflict in American life.

American Assumptions

From America's origins in the early seventeenth century, Americans have often held several interrelated assumptions about their country. First, people believe that to be American is to be free. Second, because Americans did not have to free themselves from feudal lords or an entrenched aristocracy, America has been seen as a perpetual haven from the troubles and disputes that are found in the Old World.

John Winthrop lived his life as though these assumptions were true. But the opposing viewpoints presented in the American History Series should reveal that for many Americans, these assumptions were and are myths. Indeed, for numerous Americans, liberty has not always been guaranteed, and disputes have been an integral, sometimes welcome part of their life.

The American landscape has been torn apart again and again by a great variety of clashes—theological, ideological, political, economic, geographical, and social. But such a landscape is not necessarily a hopelessly divided country. If the editors hope to prove anything during the course of this series, it is not that the United States has been destroyed by conflict but rather that it has been enlivened, enriched, and even strengthened by Americans who have disagreed with one another.

Thomas Jefferson was one of the least confrontational of Americans, but he boldly and irrevocably enriched American life with his individualistic views. Like John Winthrop before him, he had a notion of an American Eden. Like Winthrop, he offered a vision of a harmonious society. And like Winthrop, he not only became enmeshed in conflict but eventually presided over a people beset by it. But unlike Winthrop, Jefferson believed this Eden was not located in a specific community but in each individual American. His Declaration of Independence from Great Britain could also be read as a declaration of independence for each individual in American society.

Jefferson's Ideal

Jefferson's ideal world was composed of "yeoman farmers," each of whom was roughly equal to the others in society's eyes, each of whom was free from the restrictions of both government and fellow citizens. Throughout his life, Jefferson offered a continuing challenge to Americans: Advance individualism and equality or see the death of the American experiment. Jefferson believed that the strength of this experiment depended upon a society of autonomous individuals and a society without great gaps between rich and poor. His challenge to his fellow Americans to create—and sustain—such a society has itself produced both economic and political conflict.

A society whose guiding document is the Declaration of Independence is a society assured of the freedom to dream—and to disagree. We know that Jefferson hated conflict, both personal and political. His tendency was to avoid confrontations of any sort, to squirrel himself away and write rather than to stand up and speak his mind. It is only through his written words that we can grasp Jefferson's utopian dream of a society of independent farmers, all pursuing their private dreams and all leading lives of middling prosperity.

Jefferson, this man of wealth and intellect, lived an essentially happy private life. But his public life was much more troublesome. From the first rumblings of the American Revolution in the 1760s to the North-South skirmishes of the 1820s that ultimately produced the Civil War, Jefferson was at or near the center of American political history. The issues were almost too many—and too crucial—for one lifetime: Jefferson had to choose between sup-

11

porting or rejecting the path of revolution. During and after the ensuing war, he was at the forefront of the battle for religious liberty. After endorsing the Constitution, he opposed the economic plans of Alexander Hamilton. At the end of the century, he fought the infamous Alien and Sedition Acts, which limited civil liberties. As president, he opposed the Federalist court, conspiracies to divide the union, and calls for a new war against England. Throughout his life, Thomas Jefferson, slaveholder, pondered the conflict between American freedom and American slavery. And from retirement at his Monticello retreat, he frowned at the rising spirit of commercialism he feared was dividing Americans and destroying his dream of American harmony.

No matter the issue, however, Thomas Jefferson invariably supported the rights of the individual. Worried as he was about the excesses of commercialism, he accepted them because his main concern was to live in a society where liberty and individualism could flourish. To Jefferson, Americans had to be free to worship as they desired. They also deserved to be free from an over-reaching government. To Jefferson, Americans should also be free to possess slaves.

Harmony, an Elusive Goal

Before reading the articles in this anthology, the editors ask readers to ponder the lives of John Winthrop and Thomas Jefferson. Each held a utopian vision, one based upon the demands of community and the other on the autonomy of the individual. Each dreamed of a country of perpetual new beginnings. Each found himself thrust into a position of leadership and found that conflict could not be avoided. Harmony, whether communal or individual, was a forever elusive goal.

The opposing visions of Winthrop and Jefferson have been at the heart of many differences among Americans from many backgrounds through the whole of American history. Moreover, their visions have provoked important responses that have helped shape American society, the American character, and many an American battle.

The editors of the American History Series have done extensive research to find representative opinions on the issues included in these volumes. They have found numerous outstanding opposing viewpoints from people of all times, classes, and genders in American history. From those, they have selected commentaries that best fit the nature and flavor of the period and topic under consideration. Every attempt was made to include the most important and relevant viewpoints in each chapter. Obviously, not every notable viewpoint could be included. Therefore, a selective, annotated bibliography has been provided at the end of each book to aid readers in seeking additional information.

The editors are confident that as this series reveals past conflicts, it will help revitalize the reader's views of the American present. In that spirit, the American History Series is dedicated to the proposition that American history is more complicated, more fascinating, and more troubling than John Winthrop or Thomas Jefferson ever dared to imagine.

John C. Chalberg
Consulting Editor

Greenhaven Press anthologies primarily consist of previously published material taken from a variety of sources, including periodicals, books, scholarly journals, newspapers, government documents, and position papers from private and public organizations. These original sources are often edited for length and to ensure their accessibility for a young adult audience. The anthology editors also change the original titles of these works in order to clearly present the main thesis of each viewpoint and to explicitly indicate the opinion presented in the viewpoint. These alterations are made in consideration of both the reading and comprehension levels of a young adult audience. Every effort is made to ensure that Greenhaven Press accurately reflects the original intent of the authors included in this anthology.

Introduction

"Since its beginning as a nation, the United States has faced the question of just what place Native Americans have in the American body politic."

The first Americans, archaeologists believe, migrated in various waves across a now-submerged land bridge from Asia to Alaska between ten and seventy thousand years ago. Their descendants subsequently spread into both North and South America; by 1500, more than three hundred distinct societies existed throughout North America. Historian Jason Silverman writes in *The Peopling of America: A Synoptic History* that each group "constituted a separate and distinct cultural entity with its own name, language, traditions and government." These diverse Native American societies, he states, ranged

> from small, nomadic bands of the Great Basin to the large, sedentary pueblos of the southwest; from the seasonal coastal villages of the Pacific northwest to the semipermanent, fortified communities of the central Plains; from the tribal confederations of the northeast (notably that of the Iroquois) to the complex chiefdoms of the southeast.

All of these various cultures shared at least one characteristic—they had developed in virtual isolation from the peoples of Europe, Asia, and Africa. This isolation ended in 1492 when Italian navigator Christopher Columbus, attempting to find a western route to Asia, stumbled on a continent previously unknown to Europeans. (Columbus, thinking he had arrived at his intended destination, the East Indies, called the people he found there Indians.) Columbus's voyage brought about great changes for both Europeans and the peoples of the Western Hemisphere. Reports of a "New World" sparked a wave of exploration and colonization by various European powers who sought economic riches and lands for settlement. The colonies they founded later became independent nations, the first being the United States in 1783. Historian James Merrell has stated that developments after

Columbus's voyage created a "New World" for Native Americans as well. Indians had to adapt to extensive changes the newcomers introduced to the land, including new diseases, animals (such as the horse), material goods, trade relationships, and ideas about religion, political authority, and property ownership.

This collision of previously separate populations raised fundamental and perennial questions for both Europeans and Indians. Native Americans faced the challenge of how to respond to and cope with the changes brought about by contact with whites and whether to retain traditional cultural values or discard them. Europeans confronted questions of what relationship should be established with the native peoples in lands they wished to colonize and whether the taking of occupied land was justified. Similar dilemmas would later face citizens and officials of the United States.

Since its beginning as a nation, the United States has faced the question of just what place Native Americans have in the American body politic—a question that has persisted to the present day. At various times in U.S. history, Indians were treated as members of sovereign nations, as dependent wards of the federal government, as U.S. citizens, or as some combination of these. The following discussion reveals the complexity of the evolving political status of Native Americans in the United States.

Indian Land and International Law

The initial relationship between the United States and Native Americans had its legal roots in concepts of international law recognized and used by European colonial powers, but unknown to Native Americans. European nations such as Great Britain employed these concepts to support their claims of vast stretches of the North American continent. The "right of discovery" entitled Christian European governments to claim possession of lands of so-called savage peoples. The "right of conquest" allowed a European power to win through war the land discovered and claimed by another power. Theda Perdue and Michael D. Green explain in *The Cherokee Removal* that under these international laws the British government

> recognized and accepted the rights of [American] colonists and Indians to own and use their lands, govern themselves, shape their societies, and develop local economies, [but] the ultimate and overarching authority was always the sovereign authority of England. When England lost the Revolutionary War, the United States won, by right of conquest, England's rights, which included sovereign authority over all the land and people within its domain.

When the United States won its independence from Great Britain in 1783, it not only inherited territorial claims stretching across the Appalachian Mountains to the Mississippi, but also conflicts over Indian policy and land claims. During colonial times, the British government and the colonial governments had struggled over who should have final authority in dealing with the Indians. Following independence, the U.S. government had to reconcile its conflict with state governments over control of Indian policy and to settle disputes between whites and Indians over land.

Merciless Savages, Conquered Subjects, Sovereign Nations

For some Americans, the solution to disputed land claims was simple: Indians were "merciless savages" (a description found in the Declaration of Independence) and as such had no rights of ownership to the land on which they lived. "They have the shapes of men," argued Hugh Henry Brackenridge, a writer and resident of Pittsburgh, Pennsylvania, in 1782, "but certainly in their present shape they approach nearer the character of devils." Settlers also asserted that Indians did not have any right to claim land because they did not farm or develop it. "I am so far from thinking the Indians have a right to the soil," Brackenridge maintained, "that not having made a better use of it for many hundred years, I conceive they have forfeited all pretence to claim, and ought to be driven from it."

Some historians consider this view an accurate representation of what motivated U.S. actions against Indians throughout its history—actions they claim amounted to the physical and cultural genocide of Native Americans. Lyman H. Legters, a professor emeritus at the School of International Studies at the University of Washington, argues that "the policies and practices of the colonies and of the United States [toward Native Americans] qualify easily [as genocide] under provisions of the [United Nations] Genocide Convention." However, an examination of official U.S. Indian policy from the time of the American Revolution to the present casts doubt on charges of deliberate mass extermination.

During the American Revolution, the United States sought to form alliances with Indian tribes on its western borders. However, most Native American tribes, viewing the Americans as the greater threat, allied themselves with Great Britain. After winning its independence in 1783, the United States attempted to treat the various Indian tribes as conquered subjects who had forfeited legal claims to their land by virtue of their alliance with the losing side. Nevertheless, many Indian tribes continued to resist American encroachments into territory they still considered their own. In 1790 and 1791, Little Turtle, a Miami chief, led several tribes in inflicting serious defeats on U.S. armies in the Ohio Valley. These defeats, and the financial and military costs of attempting to impose military control over the western territories, caused the United States to abandon its efforts to treat Indians as conquered subjects.

George Washington, the first president of the United States, and his secretary of war, Henry Knox, devised a new Indian policy that, according to Perdue and Green, was based on the assumption that "tribes were sovereign independent nations and that the United States should recognize and respect their rights to autonomous self-government within their borders." Indian-white conflict, Knox wrote in 1794, was caused not by warlike Indians, but rather resulted from "the desire of too many frontier white people, to seize, by force or fraud, upon the neighboring Indian lands." Washington and Knox did not intend to forgo U.S. expansion, however. Perdue and Green write that they

> fully concurred with the general American view that as the population of the United States grew, Indians must surrender their lands to accommodate the increased numbers. These views added up to a policy aptly described by one historian as "expansion with honor," the central premise of which was that the United States Indian policy should make expansion possible without detriment to the Indians.

The instrument used by the U.S. government to implement Indian policy was the treaty. The practice of negotiating treaties with Native American nations dated to the Revolutionary War, when Americans sought Indian support against Great Britain. The first U.S. treaty with Native Americans was negotiated by the Continental Congress in 1778 with the Delaware Indians. In 1790, the process of negotiating treaties was formalized when Congress passed the Federal Indian Trade and Intercourse Act. This act required Indian land purchases to be accomplished by Senate-ratified treaties negotiated between tribal leaders and commissioners appointed by the president. Between 1778 and 1871, 371 treaties were negotiated between the federal government and Indian tribes and were ratified by the Senate. In most of these treaties, tribes ceded land in exchange for various goods, services, and promises by the U.S. government. In such treaties, the U.S. government in many instances promised instruction in agriculture techniques, stock raising, and other skills with the intent of helping Indian tribes adapt to white society. For example, in the 1794 agreement between the Oneidas and the United States, the Oneida tribe exchanged territory in what is now New York for guaranteed instruction "in the arts of the miller and sawyer" as well as annual payments of cash and goods.

The policy established by Washington and Knox rested on the belief that obtaining land from Indians by treaty and purchase was more desirable than seizing the land by force. However, U.S.

policy on Indian sovereignty changed during the nineteenth century as the political and military power of Indian nations eroded. The U.S. government consistently broke previous treaties with Indians, either by taking land promised to tribes or by failing to prevent encroachment by white settlers, prospectors, and other trespassers. Eventually, Native Americans found themselves being driven from their traditional homelands and confined to reservations, where they were treated as legal and dependent wards of the U.S. government.

Indian Removal

Events of the early nineteenth century, including the 1804 Louisiana Purchase, the War of 1812, and the U.S. purchase of Florida from Spain, all contributed to two general trends: the expansion of the United States and the weakening of the political and military position of Native American nations. The latter occurred partly as a result of lost military and diplomatic support from Great Britain, Spain, and other European powers. State and local authorities, desirous of Indian land, increasingly pressed Indians within their borders to give up their land and their status as sovereign nations. In the 1830s, the United States embarked on a program of removing all remaining Indian tribes east of the Mississippi to territories in the west.

The impact of these developments on the political status of Native Americans can be seen in an important early U.S. Supreme Court case involving the Cherokee Indians. In an attempt to resist removal from their traditional homeland in Georgia—and to maintain their status as a sovereign independent nation—the Cherokee nation created its own constitution and challenged the removal policy in court. However, in *Cherokee Nation v. Georgia* in 1831, the Court concluded that Indian tribes were not really independent foreign nations. The decision written by Chief Justice John Marshall stated that

> the Indians are acknowledged to have a . . . right to the lands they occupy, until that right shall be extinguished by a voluntary cession to our government; yet it may well be doubted whether those tribes which reside within the acknowledged boundaries of the United States can, with strict accuracy, be denominated foreign nations. They may, more correctly, perhaps, be denominated domestic, dependent nations. They occupy a territory to which we assert a title independent of their will, which must take effect in point of possession when their right of possession ceases. Meanwhile, they are in a state of pupilage. Their relation to the United States resembles that of a ward to his guardian.

> They look to our government for protection; rely upon its kindness and its power; appeal to it for relief to their wants; and ad-

dress the president as their great father. They and their country are considered by foreign nations, as well as by ourselves, as being . . . completely under the sovereignty and dominion of the United States.

Between 1830 and 1890, the United States defeated all Indian tribes who attempted to fight to preserve their land and lifestyle, and U.S. Indian policy shifted closer to the "pupilage" described by Marshall. Indians were confined to reservations on land that they did not own but that was held "in trust" for them by the federal government. In 1871, Congress abolished the treaty-making process with Indian tribes. In 1885, it passed legislation giving the federal government jurisdiction over murder and other crimes committed by Indians against other Indians. In *United States v. Kagama*, the Supreme Court in 1886 upheld Congress's authority to take this action, ruling that Indians were members "not [of] a State or nation" but of "local dependent communities." In the 1903 case *Lone Wolf v. Hitchcock*, the Supreme Court held that Congress was not bound by previous treaties in exercising its "plenary powers" over all aspects of Indian life.

Assimilation and the Dawes Act

As the U.S. government exercised more and more control over the lives of its Indian wards, increasing efforts were made to force Native Americans to abandon traditional cultural practices and adopt the ways of white society. Assimilation was the central focus of U.S. Indian policy from the 1880s through the early decades of the twentieth century.

Assimilation—or civilization, as it was often called—had actually been part of American Indian policy since at least 1819, when Congress established an annual "civilization fund." That fund appropriated money for Christian missionaries to establish schools for teaching Native Americans agriculture, reading, writing, and arithmetic "for the purpose of providing against the further decline and final extinction of the Indian tribes . . . and for introducing among them the habits and arts of civilization." Many Americans considered the private ownership of land to be a key to civilization and therefore sought to introduce the concept to Native Americans. Commissioner of Indian Affairs T. Hartley Crawford, in his report of 1838, maintained:

Unless some system is marked out by which there shall be a separate allotment of land to each individual . . . , you will look in vain for any general casting off of savagism. Common property and civilization cannot co-exist.

Such opinions were central to the passage of the 1887 General Allotment Act (also called the Dawes Act), which parceled out Indian reservation lands to individual families in the hope that they would become successful farmers.

Supporters of assimilation often criticized past U.S. Indian policy and decried broken treaties and mistreatment of Indians. They did not argue for the reinstatement of treaties or for the restoration of the sovereign status of Indian nations, however. Instead, they supported Indian assimilation within white society, which they believed was the only way for Native Americans to survive. Senator Henry L. Dawes, sponsor of the 1887 act, argued that "we may cry out against the violation of treaties, denounce flagrant disregard of inalienable rights and the inhumanity of our treatment of the defenseless . . . but the fact remains. . . . Without doubt these Indians are to be somehow absorbed into and become a part of the 50,000,000 of our people. There does not seem to be any other way to deal with them."

Some reformers saw the General Allotment Act as a means to eliminate Indian tribal society. President Theodore Roosevelt, in his annual message to Congress in 1901, argued that the law, by dividing up tribal properties into individual lots, served as "a mighty pulverizing engine to break up the tribal mass." He praised this as a positive development that fostered assimilation and prevented Indian tribal separatism: "The Indian should be treated as an individual—like the white man."

The result of the General Allotment Act and the reforms it spawned was an increase in federal government control over every aspect of Indian life. The Bureau of Indian Affairs (BIA), the federal government agency established in 1832 to oversee U.S. Indian policy, supervised the allotting of land to individual Indians and the leasing and selling of Indian land to mine and timber interests. In addition, it provided education and health care, policed the Indian reservations, and regulated all Indian trade. The BIA ran boarding schools, often forcing Indian children to live away from their families and adopt white ways. Indian feasts, languages, religious ceremonies, dances, and other cultural practices were banned by BIA officials. Many BIA officials considered the resultant weakening of tribal authority a forward step toward their goal of Indian assimilation.

The Question of U.S. Citizenship

The ultimate goal of most reformers who advocated assimilation was to enable all Indians to become citizens, with all the rights, privileges, and responsibilities of other citizens. The central dilemma of America's "Indian problem," argued Unitarian minister Jonathan Benjamin Harrison in 1887, was to determine "how the Indians shall be brought to a condition of self-support, and of equal rights before the law, in which they will no longer require the special protection and control of the Government."

Whether Native Americans were U.S. citizens and whether they possessed the same legal rights as other Americans was a long-standing political, legal, and constitutional question. The Constitution makes direct references to American Indians, but in ways that imply separate status. The Constitution explicitly excludes "Indians not taxed" in counting the population of the states for the purpose of apportioning representatives and taxes. It also empowers Congress "to regulate commerce with foreign nations . . . and with the Indian tribes." The Fourteenth Amendment, adopted after the Civil War and aimed primarily at securing citizenship for former slaves, bestows U.S. citizenship on all "persons born or naturalized in the United States, and subject to the jurisdiction thereof." However, in several cases the Supreme Court ruled that the amendment was not applicable to Indians. In *Elk v. Wilkins* in 1884, it denied citizenship status to John Elk, an Indian who had voluntarily forsaken his tribe and resettled with whites. Congress would have to pass specific legislation in order for Indians to become U.S. citizens, the Court concluded.

Given this power, Congress in the late nineteenth and early twentieth centuries made conditional U.S. citizenship an essential component of its assimilationist Indian policy. The Dawes Act decreed that all Indians who accepted an individual allotment of land or who left their tribal residence to live among whites would thereby become U.S. citizens. From this point on, they would be subject to federal, state, and local laws and taxes. (Indians remained exempt from property taxes as long as their land was held in trust for them by the federal government.) However, accepting citizenship under these terms also severed Native Americans from their respective tribes and thus from their rights to lands the U.S. government had guaranteed in past treaties—a fact not lost on many Indians. As famed western novelist Larry McMurtry points out in the *New York Review of Books*, ironically

> American citizenship, dream and hope of millions of immigrants, was, for the real natives who were being forced to accept it, a tool of destruction. Citizenship was the legal crowbar which would be used to pry them off their land, since, once they were citizens, their land could be bought and sold like that of any other citizens.

In 1924 Congress ended its policy of giving conditional citizenship to Indians by enacting legislation that granted automatic citizenship to all Native Americans. This did not automatically end their status as wards of the federal government, however. As the Supreme Court ruled in 1916 in *United States v. Nice*, citizenship "is not incompatible with tribal existence or continued guardianship, and so may be conferred without completely emancipating the Indian or placing them beyond the reach of congressional regulations adopted for their protection." Even after 1924, the federal government still continued to govern most aspects of life on Indian reservations and to hold their land in trust.

The Resurgence of Sovereignty

During the nineteenth and early twentieth centuries, American Indian tribes and nations lost much of their political sovereignty. Since the 1930s, however, that trend has been reversed. Recent decades have seen the resurgence of sovereignty—the idea that Native Americans, unlike other American ethnic minorities, are members of separate and sovereign organizations possessing a special political relationship with the U.S. government. This development has been the product both of changes in U.S. Indian policy and of Native American responses to U.S. government actions.

Many important changes in U.S. government policy occurred under the leadership of John Collier, an anthropologist and social worker, who served as commissioner of Indian affairs from 1933 to 1945. The direction and effectiveness of his long administration is still debated today, but it is generally recognized as a crucial turning point in the history of American Indian policy. Unlike many of his predecessors, Collier professed a deep admiration for Native American cultures and sought to strengthen Indian tribalism rather than destroy it. The tribe, he believed, could be restored and refashioned in the form of a modern business and political corporation. In 1934 Collier pushed through the Indian Reorganization Act (IRA), which ended land allotment, returned remaining reservation properties to tribal ownership, and gave Indian tribes the option of creating and voting for new tribal government constitutions (subject to the final approval of the secretary of the interior).

Collier sought to combine Indian sovereignty with federal guardianship, arguing that by creating new Indian governments under the auspices of the BIA, tribes would be "surrounded by the protective guardianship of the federal government and clothed with the authority of the federal government." In this way, Collier believed, the tribal structures damaged by past U.S. government policies could gradually be strengthened and restored. However, some Native American critics, both in the 1930s and after, objected that these new tribal governments remained financially and legally dependent on the U.S. government. Collier's reforms, they contended, actually increased the role of the BIA in controlling the internal affairs of Indian tribes. The tribal governments and business councils incorporated under the IRA, critics asserted, were merely tools of the federal government.

Collier's reforms were also criticized by those who felt they gave Indian tribes too much autonomy rather than too little.

Members of Congress sharply attacked Collier's reforms for promoting the "un-American" idea that Indians were different from other citizens. Federal government policy underwent a dramatic shift following Collier's resignation in 1945, shortly after World War II. Echoing many of the ideas of nineteenth-century reformers, the federal government in the 1950s sponsored several initiatives designed to assimilate Native Americans within mainstream society and to end the federal government's responsibility for managing Indian affairs. The government sponsored programs to relocate Indians away from reservations, to transfer federal responsibilities over Indians to state governments, and to terminate the federal trust status of tribes deemed capable of managing their own affairs without federal supervision and financial support—a cluster of policies known collectively as "termination."

However, the federal government's termination initiatives received political opposition from Native Americans who lobbied against termination and argued for recognition of their sovereign status. Tribal government leaders and lawyers worked aggressively to extend the scope and authority of Indian government on reservation lands. Native Americans both inside and outside the reservation system formed intertribal organizations such as the National Congress of American Indians and the American Indian Movement in order to challenge laws and practices they believed violated past treaties and to create public awareness of discrimination against Native Americans.

Native American political activism, aided and inspired by the 1960s civil rights movement, succeeded in blocking termination policies and led to the passage of laws giving Native Americans greater authority to govern themselves. Legislation such as the 1972 Indian Education Act and the 1975 Indian Self-Determination Act gave Indian tribes greater autonomy in administering housing, education, and other services previously managed by the BIA.

Native American sovereignty and tribal self-government were also expanded by a series of important Supreme Court decisions. In *Williams v. Lee* in 1959, the Court upheld the authority of tribal courts to make decisions involving non-Indians on reservation territory. A 1968 case, *Menominee Tribe v. United States*, ruled that states could not invalidate Native American hunting and fishing rights attained through past treaty agreements. In *Morton v. Mancari* in 1974, the Supreme Court defended preferential treatment practices that favored Indians over whites in BIA hirings and promotions. The Court said that such practices did not violate civil rights laws against racial discrimination because the preferential treatment of Indians was based not on their race, but on their membership in tribal entities that had a political relationship with the federal government. "It is no accident," argues lawyer Alvin

J. Ziontz in *The Aggressions of Civilization*, "that following *Mancari* the Interior Department began describing the relationship between the tribes and the United States government as one of 'government to government.'" Not all Supreme Court decisions in recent decades have favored Native Americans, leaving the legal extent of Indian sovereignty a complex and controversial issue. For example, one area in which state, federal, and tribal authorities have recently clashed over Native American sovereignty is whether Indian tribes can operate gambling casinos free of state and federal taxes and regulations.

One of the most remarkable developments of recent times is the renewed importance of the Trade and Intercourse Act of 1790. The long-ignored law states that the United States cannot take land from Indian nations without federal treaties. In 1972, the Penobscot and Passamaquoddy Indians of Maine filed a federal lawsuit seeking the return of land taken from them in violation of the 1790 law. A federal court ruled in their favor, paving the way for a 1980 settlement in which the two tribes received an $81.5 million settlement. Their success has inspired other Native American tribes to pursue similar legal actions.

A Complex History

In a way, the legal victory for the Indians of Maine suggests that American policy toward Native Americans has come full circle. Despite the loss of their sovereign status during a period when the U.S. government pursued a policy of assimilation, Native Americans have reestablished a "government to government" relationship that would surprise most nineteenth-century observers. The evolving status of Native Americans in the United States constitutes but one part of a multifaceted debate that has endured throughout American history. The viewpoints in this volume, taken from a variety of Native American and non-Indian sources, document the complex cultural and legal history that gives Native Americans a unique status among American ethnic minority groups.

CHAPTER 1

Early Encounters

Chapter Preface

The known history of Native Americans prior to European contact is limited to information obtained from such sources as oral tradition and archaeological evidence. From this information, present-day historians and anthropologists have concluded that these peoples descended from migrants from Asia, who arrived on the continent between ten and seventy thousand years ago. At the time of European contact, Native Americans lived in diverse societies ranging from small hunting bands to large and highly structured communities. They had developed complex religious and ritualistic beliefs and practices. Many Indian societies were linked together in extensive trade networks and political alliances established for protection against enemies.

Little of this was known by the English and European colonizers of the Atlantic coast of North America, whose activities during the seventeenth and eighteenth centuries greatly altered the lives of Native Americans. Most white colonists were unaware of the history and diversity of Indian culture; many simply categorized the various indigenous peoples they encountered as savages who needed to be taught Christianity and European civilization. Likewise, most Indians had very little knowledge about the history and ideas of the new settlers they encountered. Such mutual ignorance hampered efforts by both whites and Indians to create and maintain peaceful relations with each other.

Three important agents of change that the Europeans brought about in Native American life were new diseases, new trade relationships, and war. Ironically, one of the most devastating effects of the European presence in North America was inadvertent. European explorers and settlers brought with them infectious diseases, such as smallpox and yellow fever, to which most Native Americans had no immunities. The diseases spread quickly, often affecting tribes who had yet to set eyes on Europeans. The resulting epidemics wiped out entire tribes of Indians; others lost up to 90 percent of their populations. Furthermore, this massive depopulation caused the loss of much communal knowledge that perished with the deaths of elders, leaders, and storytellers.

The arrival of Europeans also changed Indian trade practices. Many tribes eagerly established relations with Europeans in order to obtain guns, metal goods, woolen clothing, and other items in exchange for beaver furs and deerskins. This trade had a mixed effect on Native American life. Many Indians sought and appreciated the new goods. However, the increased demand for furs and skins resulted in the depletion of animal populations they had once relied on for food and clothing. Warfare increased between Indian tribes as they competed for more hunting territory. European trade also introduced alcohol to Native Americans, often resulting in widespread alcoholism and its related effects.

Warfare between Indians and whites was common during the colonial period. Much of the initial warfare between Europeans and Indians arose from simple conflicts over resources and land. For instance, hogs and cattle, allowed by European colonists to roam freely, often destroyed Indian cornfields. When the offending animals were killed, colonists retaliated against local Indians, and conflict quickly escalated. Colonists often condemned Indian tactics of warfare—such as surprise ambushes, scalping, and the killing of captives—as especially brutal. Solomon Stoddard, a Massachusetts minister, complained that Indians "are to be looked upon as thieves and murderers. They do acts of hostility, without proclaiming war. They don't appear openly in the field to bid us battle, they use those cruelly that fall into their hands." In response, many colonial forces not only adopted similar tactics but also deliberately waged campaigns of starvation by destroying Indian villages and food caches.

In addition to strife over land rights, an important contributing cause to Indian-white warfare was worldwide conflict between Spain, France, the Netherlands, and Great Britain that included a long-term struggle for control of North America. For instance, four times between 1689 and 1763, England and France waged wars over land between the Allegheny Mountains and the Mississippi River. During each of these wars, various Indian tribes allied themselves with either the English or the French. Thus, Indian-white warfare often had both local and global ramifications.

However, the history of Indian peoples during this period was not just one of warfare and disease. For some Indians it was also a time of friendly coexistence and cultural exchange with the newcomers. The first colonists at Jamestown, Virginia, and Plymouth, Massachusetts, depended for survival on their Indian neighbors' willing assistance with food and farming techniques. A few Indians in New England and other places responded to the efforts of missionaries by converting to Christianity. William Penn, the founder of the colony of Pennsylvania, avoided the Indian-white conflict endemic in other colonies throughout his lifetime by purchasing lands from local Delaware Indian chieftains in fair negotiations, prohibiting the sale of alcohol to Indians, and earning their respect as an honest man. His policies encouraged other Indian tribes to move to Pennsylvania.

The following viewpoints provide a sampling of how Europeans and Native Americans viewed each other during the European colonization of North America.

VIEWPOINT 1

"You see us unarmed, and willing to supply your wants, if you will come in a friendly manner."

Colonists Should Maintain Friendly Relations with the Indians

Powhatan (ca. 1550–1618)

Powhatan was the name given by the English to Wahunsonacock, the leader of a confederacy of American Indian tribes that lived in what is now the state of Virginia. Powhatan was one of the first Indian leaders to have extensive contact with European colonists in North America. The following viewpoint is taken from a 1609 speech he made to John Smith, the leader of the Virginia Company settlement of Jamestown. Smith later wrote down Powhatan's call for peaceful relations between the two peoples, which stresses the importance of Indian food assistance to Jamestown's survival. Despite occasional skirmishes and confrontations, the Indians of the Powhatan Confederacy and the English settlers maintained a general truce until 1622 (a truce aided in part by the marriage of Powhatan's daughter, Pocahontas, to English settler John Rolfe in 1614).

Excerpted from *Biography and History of the Indians of North America*, by Samuel B. Drake (Boston: Antiquarian Bookstore, 1841).

I am now grown old, and must soon die; and the succession must descend, in order, to my brothers, *Opitchapan*, *Opekankanough*, and *Catataugh*, and then to my two sisters, and their two daughters. I wish their experience was equal to mine; and that your love to us might not be less than ours to you. Why should you take by force that from us which you can have by love? Why should you destroy us, who have provided you with food? What can you get by war? We can hide our provisions, and fly into the woods; and then you must consequently famish by wronging your friends. What is the cause of your jealousy? You see us unarmed, and willing to supply your wants, if you will come in a friendly manner, and not with swords and guns, as to invade an enemy. I am not so simple, as not to know it is better to eat good meat, lie well, and sleep quietly with my women and children; to laugh and be merry with the English; and, being their friend, to have copper, hatchets, and whatever else I want, than to fly from all, to lie cold in the woods, feed upon acorns, roots, and such trash, and to be so hunted, that I cannot rest, eat, or sleep. In such circumstances, my men must watch, and if a twig should but break, all would cry out, *"Here comes Capt. Smith;"* and so, in this miserable manner, to end my miserable life; and, Capt. *Smith*, this *might* be soon your fate too, through your rashness and unadvisedness. I, therefore, exhort you to peaceable councils; and, above all, I insist that the guns and swords, the cause of all our jealousy and uneasiness, be removed and sent away.

VIEWPOINT 2

"The way of conquering them is much more easy than of civilizing them by fair means, for they are a rude, barbarous, and naked people."

Colonists Should Wage War Against the Indians

Virginia Company of London

A few years after the death of American Indian leader Powhatan (see the preceding viewpoint), his brother Opekankanough (Opachankano), the new leader of the Powhatan Confederacy, launched a surprise attack on English households in and around Jamestown, Virginia, the first permanent English settlement in North America. The 1622 assault, one of the first major violent conflicts between English colonists and American Indians, was partly a response to continuing seizures of Indian land—especially cleared fields—by the colonists. The attackers killed 347 people, about one quarter of Jamestown's population, and destroyed many houses and farms before they were stopped. Among those killed was John Rolfe, the widower of Powhatan's daughter Pocahontas.

The following viewpoint contains an account of the attack and its ramifications. It was written by officials of the Virginia Company, which had sponsored the Jamestown settlement, and was in part meant to explain why the colony had yet to show any profit for its investors. The officials argue that the Indians have revealed themselves to be treacherous and cruel but that campaigns of extermination against them will allow the colony to prosper. In subsequent years the colonists repeatedly attacked Indian villages and destroyed their food supplies; by the 1640s the Powhatan Indians were virtually eliminated as a threat to the colony.

Reprinted from *The Records of the Virginia Company of London,* edited by Susan Kingsbury, vol. 3 (Washington, DC: GPO, 1933).

That all men may see the impartial ingenuity of this discourse, we freely confess, that the country is not so good, as the natives are bad, whose barbarous selves need more cultivation then the ground itself, being more overspread with incivility and treachery, than that with briars. For the land, being tilled and used well by us, deceive not our expectation but rather exceeded it far, being so thankful as to return a hundred for one. But the savages, though never a nation used so kindly upon so small desert, have instead of that harvest which our pains merited, returned nothing but briars and thorns, pricking even to death many of their benefactors. Yet doubt we not, but that as all wickedness is crafty to undo itself, so these also have more wounded themselves than us, God Almighty making way for severity there, where a fair gentleness would not take place. The occasion whereof thus I relate from thence.

The last May [1622] there came a letter from Sir Francis Wiat [Wyatt] Governor in Virginia, which did advertise that when in November last [1621] he arrived in Virginia and entered upon his government, he found the country settled in a peace (as all men there thought), sure and unviolable, not only because it was solemnly ratified and sworn, but as being advantageous to both parts; to the savages as the weaker, under which they were safely sheltered and defended; to us, as being the easiest way then thought to pursue and advance our projects of buildings, plantings, and effecting their conversion by peaceable and fair means. And such was the conceit [conception] of firm peace and amity as that there was seldom or never a sword worn. . . . The plantations of particular adventurers and planters were placed scatteringly and stragglingly as a choice vein of rich ground invited them, and the further from neighbors held the better. The houses generally set open to the savages, who were always friendly entertained at the tables of the English, and commonly lodged in their bedchambers. The old planters (as they thought now come to reap the benefit of their long travels) placed with wonderful content upon their private lands, and their familiarity with the natives, seeming to open a fair gate for their conversion to Christianity.

A Surprise Attack

The country being in this estate, an occasion was ministered of sending to Opachankano, the King of these savages, about the middle of March last, what time the messenger returned back with these words from him, that he held the peace concluded so firm as the sky should sooner fall than it dissolve. Yea, such was the treacherous dissimulation of that people who then had contrived our destruction, that even two days before the massacre, some of our men were guided through the woods by them in safety. . . . Yea, they borrowed our own boats to convey themselves across the river (on the banks of both sides whereof all our plantations were) to consult of the devilish murder that ensued, and of our utter extirpation, which God of His mercy (by the means of themselves converted to Christianity) prevented. And as well on the Friday morning (the fatal day) the twenty-second of March, as also in the evening, as on other days before, they came unarmed into our houses, without bows or arrows, or other weapons, with deer, turkey, fish, fur, and other provisions to sell and trade with us for glass, beads, and other trifles. Yet in some places, they sat down at breakfast with our people at their tables, whom immediately with their own tools and weapons either laid down, or standing in their houses, they basely and barbarously murdered, not sparing either age or sex, man, woman, or child, so sudden in their cruel execution that few or none discerned the weapon or blow that brought them to destruction. In which manner they also slew many of our people then at their several work and husbandries in the fields, and without their houses, some in planting corn and tobacco, some in gardening, some in making brick, building, sawing, and other kinds of husbandry, they well knowing in what places and quarters each of our men were, in regard of their daily familiarity and resort to us for trading and other negotiations, which the more willingly was by us continued and cherished for the desire we had of effecting that great masterpiece of works, their conversion. And by this means that fatal Friday morning, there fell under the bloody and barbarous hands of that perfidious and inhuman people, contrary to all laws of God and men, of nature and nations, three hundred forty seven men, women, and children, most by their own weapons. And not being content with taking away life alone, they fell after again upon the dead, making as well as they could, a fresh murder, defacing, dragging, and mangling the dead carcasses into many pieces, and carrying some parts away in derision, with base and brutish triumph. . . .

That the slaughter had been universal, if God had not put it into the heart of an Indian belonging to one Perry to disclose it, who living in the house of one Pace, was urged by another Indian his brother (who came the night before and lay with him) to kill Pace. Telling further that by such an hour in the morning a number would come from different places to finish the execution, who failed not at the time, Perry's Indian rose out of his bed and revealed it to Pace, that used him as a son. And thus the rest of the colony that had warning given them by this means was saved. Such was (God be thanked for it) the good fruit of an infidel converted to Christianity. For though three hundred and more of ours died by many of these pagan infidels, yet thousands of ours were saved by the means of one of them alone which was made a Christian. Blessed be God forever, whose mercy endureth forever. . . .

Lessons of the Massacre

Thus have you seen the particulars of this massacre, wherein treachery and cruelty have done their worst to us, or rather to themselves; for whose understanding is so shallow, as not to perceive that this must needs be for the good of the plantation after, and the loss of this blood to make the body more healthful, as by these reasons may be manifest.

First, because betraying innocence never rests unpunished. . . .

The 1622 attack by Indians on Jamestown was graphically depicted in this 1634 picture.

Secondly, because our hands, which before were tied with gentleness and fair usage, are now set at liberty by the treacherous violence of the savages, not untying the knot, but cutting it. So that we, who hitherto have had possession of no more ground than their waste, and our purchase at a valuable consideration to their own contentment gained, may now, by right of war and law

33

of nations, invade the country, and destroy them who sought to destroy us. Whereby we shall enjoy their cultivated places, possessing the fruits of others' labors. Now their cleared grounds in all their villages (which are situated in the fruitfulest places of the land) shall be inhabited by us, whereas heretofore the grubbing of woods was the greatest labor.

Thirdly, because those commodities which the Indians enjoyed as much or rather more than we, shall now also be entirely possessed by us. The deer and other beasts will be in safety, and infinitely increase, which heretofore not only in the general huntings of the King, but by each particular Indian were destroyed at all times of the year, without any difference of male, dame, or young.

There will be also a great increase of wild turkeys, and other weighty fowl, for the Indians never put difference of destroying the hen, but kill them whether in season or not, whether in breeding time, or sitting on their eggs, or having new hatched, it is all one to them. . . .

Fourthly, because the way of conquering them is much more easy than of civilizing them by fair means, for they are a rude, barbarous, and naked people, scattered in small companies, which are helps to victory, but hindrance to civility. Besides that, a conquest may be of many, and at once; but civility is in particular and slow, the effect of long time, and great industry. Moreover, victory of them may be gained many ways: by force, by surprise, by famine in burning their corn, by destroying and burning their boats, canoes, and houses, by breaking their fishing wares, by assailing them in their huntings, whereby they get the greatest part of their sustenance in winter, by pursuing and chasing them with our horses and bloodhounds to draw after them, and mastiffs to tear them.

VIEWPOINT 3

"Terrible and shocking to human nature were the barbarities daily committed by these savages!"

A Captive's Account of the Cruelty of Indians

Peter Williamson (d. 1799)

White settlers' accounts of being taken into captivity by Indians were a popular form of American literature in colonial times. Many of these captivity narratives emphasized the cruel and barbaric nature of the Indian captors.

The following viewpoint is excerpted from one such narrative by Peter Williamson, who was held captive for several months in the winter of 1754. First published in 1757, his story was later reprinted in a somewhat abridged form in 1794 in a collection of captivity narratives; it is the later version that appears here.

Williamson begins his narrative by briefly recapping his early life, including his childhood in Scotland, his forced passage to and indentured servitude in America, and his marriage and establishment of a farm on the western Pennsylvania frontier. On October 2, 1754, at the start of the French and Indian War, he was captured by a band of Indians (probably Shawnee or Delaware). Williamson describes his travels with his captors, the acts of cruelty he witnessed, and his eventual escape.

Williamson later joined the British army and was captured by the French. He was taken to Montreal, Canada, and sent with other prisoners to England. He died in Edinburgh, Scotland, in 1799.

From "The Sufferings of Peter Williamson . . . ," by Peter Williamson, in *The Affecting History of the Dreadful Distresses of Frederic Manheim's Family* . . . (Philadelphia: Carey, 1794).

I was born within ten miles of the town of Aberdeen, in the north of Scotland; of reputable parents; at eight years of age, being a sturdy boy, I was taken notice of by two fellows belonging to a vessel, employed (as the trade then was) by some of the worthy merchants of Aberdeen, in that villainous and execrable practice, of stealing young children from their parents, and selling them as slaves in the plantations abroad, and on board the ship easily cajoled by them, where I was conducted between decks, to some others they had kidnapped in the same manner, and in about a month's time set sail for America. When arrived at Philadelphia, the captain sold us at about sixteen pounds per head. What became of my unhappy companions I never knew; but it was my lot to be sold for seven years, to one of my countrymen, who had in his youth been kidnapped like myself, but from another town.

Having no children of his own, and commiserating my condition, he took care of me, indulged me in going to school, where I went every winter for five years, and made a tolerable proficiency. With this good master, I continued till he died, and, as a reward for my faithful service, he left me two hundred pounds currency, which was then about an hundred and twenty pounds sterling, his best horse, saddle, and all his wearing apparel.

Being now seventeen years old, and my own master, having money in my pocket, and all other necessaries, I employed myself in jobbing for near seven years; when I resolved to settle, and married the daughter of a substantial planter. My father-in-law made me a deed of gift of a tract of land that lay (unhappily for me, as it has since proved) on the frontiers of the province of Pennsylvania, near the forks of Delaware, containing about two hundred acres, thirty of which were well cleared and fit for immediate use, on which were a good house and barn. The place pleasing me well, I settled on it. My money I expended in buying stock, household furniture, and implements for out-of-door work; and being happy in a good wife, my felicity was compleat: but in 1754, the Indians, who had for a long time before ravaged and destroyed other parts of America unmolested, began now to be very troublesome on the frontiers of our province, where they generally appeared in small skulking parties, committing great devastations.

Attacked and Captured

Terrible and shocking to human nature were the barbarities daily committed by these savages! Scarce did a day pass but some unhappy family or other fell victims to savage cruelty. Terrible, indeed, it proved to me, as well as to many others; I that was now happy in an easy state of life, blessed with an affectionate and tender wife, became on a sudden one of the most unhappy of mankind: scarce can I sustain the shock which for ever recurs on recollecting the fatal second of October, 1754. My wife that day went from home, to visit some of her relations; as I staid up later than usual, expecting her return, none being in the house besides myself, how great was my surprize and terror, when about eleven o'clock at night, I heard the dismal war-whoop of the savages, and found that my house was beset by them. I flew to my chamber window, and perceived them to be twelve in number. Having my gun loaded, I threatened them with death, if they did not retire. But how vain and fruitless are the efforts of one man against the united force of so many blood thirsty monsters! One of them that could speak English, threatened me in return, 'That if I did not come out, they would burn me alive,' adding, however, 'That if I would come out and surrender myself prisoner, they would not kill me.' In such deplorable circumstances, I chose to rely on their promises, rather than meet death by rejecting them; and accordingly went out of the house, with my gun in my hand, not knowing that I had it. Immediately on my approach they rushed on me like tigers, and instantly disarmed me. Having me thus in their power, they bound me to a tree, went into the house, plundered it of every thing they could carry off, and then set fire to it, and consumed what was left before my eyes. Not satisfied with this, they set fire to my barn, stable, and out-houses, wherein were about 200 bushels of wheat, six cows, four horses, and five sheep, all which were consumed to ashes.

Having thus finished the execrable business, about which they came, one of the monsters came to me with a tomahawk and threatened me with the worst of deaths, if I would not go with them. This I agreed to, and then they untied me, and gave me a load to carry, under which I travelled all that night, full of the most terrible apprehensions, lest my unhappy wife should likewise have fallen into their cruel power. At day break, my infernal masters ordered me to lay down my load, when tying my hands again round a tree, they forced the blood out at my fingers' ends. And then kindling a fire near the tree to which I was bound, the most dreadful agonies seized me, concluding I was going to be made a sacrifice to their barbarity. The fire being made, they for some time danced round me after their manner, whooping, hollowing and shrieking in a frightful manner. Being satisfied with this sort of mirth, they proceeded in another manner; taking the burning coals, and sticks flaming with fire at the ends, holding them to my face, head, hands, and feet, and at the same time threatening to burn me entirely if I cried out: thus tortured as I was, almost to death, I suffered their brutalities, without being allowed to vent my anguish otherwise, than by shedding silent tears; and these being observed, they took fresh coals, and applied them near my eyes, telling me my face was wet, and that they would dry it for me, which indeed they cruelly did. How I underwent these tortures has been matter of wonder to me, but God enabled me to wait with more than common patience for the deliverance I daily prayed for.

This 1812 picture is typical of the illustrations that accompanied captive narratives published in the eighteenth and nineteenth centuries.

At length they sat down round the fire, and roasted the meat, of which they had robbed my dwelling. When they had supped, they offered some to me: though it may easily be imagined I had but little appetite to eat, after the tortures and miseries I had suffered, yet was I forced to seem pleased with what they offered me, lest by refusing it, they should re-assume their hellish practices. What I could not eat, I contrived to hide, they having unbound me till they imagined I had eat all; but then they bound me as before; in which deplorable condition I was forced to continue the whole day. When the sun was set, they put out the fire, and covered the ashes with leaves, as is their usual custom, that the white people might not discover any traces of their having been there.

Going from thence along the Susquehanna, for the space of six miles, loaded as I was before, we arrived at a spot near the Apalachian mountains, or Blue-hills, where they hid their plunder under logs of wood. From thence they proceeded to a neighbouring house, occupied by one Jacob Snider and his unhappy family, consisting of his wife, five children, and a young man his servant. They soon got admittance into the unfortunate man's house, where they immediately, without the least remorse, scalped both parents and children: nor could the tears, the shrieks, or cries of poor innocent children, prevent their horrid massacre: having thus scalped them, and plundered the house of every thing that was movable, they set fire to it, and left the distressed victims amidst the flames.

Thinking the young man belonging to this unhappy family, would be service to them in carrying part of their plunder, they spared his life, and loaded him and myself with what they had here got, and again marched to the Blue-hills, where they stowed their goods as before. My fellow sufferer could not support the cruel treatment which we were obliged to suffer, and complaining bitterly to me of his being unable to proceed any farther, I endeavoured to animate him, but all in vain, for he still continued his moans and tears, which one of the savages perceiving, as we travelled along, came up to us, and with his tomahawk gave him a blow on the head, which felled the unhappy youth to the ground, whom they immediately scalped and left. The suddenness of this murder shocked me to that degree, that I was in a manner motionless, expecting my fate would soon be the same: however, recovering my distracted thoughts, I dissembled my anguish as well as I could from the barbarians; but still, such was my terror, that for some time I scarce knew the days of the week, or what I did.

More Cruelties

They still kept on their course near the mountains, where they lay skulking four or five days, rejoicing at the plunder they had got. When provisions became scarce, they made their way towards Susquehanna, and passing near another house, inhabited by an old man, whose name was John Adams, with his wife and four small children, and meeting with no resistance, they immediately scalped the mother and her children before the old man's eyes. Inhuman and horrid as this was, it did not satisfy them; for when they had murdered the poor woman, they acted with her in such a brutal manner, as decency will not permit me to mention. The unhappy husband, not being able to avoid the sight, intreated them to put an end to his miserable being; but they were as deaf to the tears and entreaties of this venerable sufferer, as they had been to those of the others, and proceeded to burn and destroy his house, barn, corn, hay, cattle, and every thing the poor man, a few hours before, was master of. Having saved what they thought proper from the flames, they gave the old man, feeble, weak, and in the miserable condition he then was, as well as myself, burdens to carry, and loading themselves likewise with bread and meat, pursued their journey towards the Great Swamp. Here they lay for eight or nine days diverting themselves, at times, in barbarous cruelties on the old man: sometimes they would strip him naked, and paint him all over with various sorts of colours: at other times they would pluck the white hairs from his head, and tauntingly tell him, 'He was a fool for living so long, and that they should shew him kindness in putting him out of the world.' In vain were all his tears, for daily did they tire themselves with the various means they tried to torment him; sometimes tying him to a tree, and whipping him; at other times, scorching his furrowed cheeks with red-hot coals, and burning his legs quite to the knees. One night after he had been thus tormented, whilst he and I were condoling each other at the miseries we daily suffered, 25 other Indians arrived, bringing with them 20 scalps and 3 prisoners, who had unhappily fallen into their hands in Conogocheague, a small town near the river Susquehanna, chiefly inhabited by the Irish. These prisoners gave us some shocking accounts of the murders and devastations committed in their parts; a few instances of which will enable the reader to guess at the treatment the provincials have suffered for years past. This party, who now joined us, had it not, I found, in their power to begin their violences so soon as those who visited my habitation; the first of their tragedies being on the 25th of October, 1754, when John Lewis, with his wife and three small children, were inhumanly scalped and murdered; and his house, barn, and every thing he possessed burnt and destroyed. On the 28th, Jacob Miller, with his wife and six of his family, with every thing on his plantations, shared the same fate. The 30th, the house, mill, barn, 20 head of cattle, two teams of horses, and every thing belonging to George Folke, met with the like treatment, himself, wife, and all his miserable family, consisting of nine in number, being scalped, then cut in pieces and given to the swine. One of the substantial traders, belonging to the province, having business that called him some miles up the country, fell into the hands of these ruffians, who not only scalped him, but immediately roasted him before he was dead; then, like cannibals, for want of other food, eat his whole body, and of his head made, what they called, an Indian pudding.

From these few instances of savage cruelty, the deplorable situation of the defenceless inhabitants, and what they hourly suffered in that part of the globe, must strike the utmost horror, and cause in every breast the utmost detestation, not only against the authors, but against those who, through inattention, or pusillanimous or erroneous principles, suffered these savages at first, unrepelled, or even unmolested, to commit such outrages, depredations, and murders.

The three prisoners that were brought with these additional forces, constantly repining at their lot, and almost dead with their excessive hard treatment, contrived at last to make their escape; but being far from their own settlements, and not knowing the country, were soon after met by some others of the tribes, or nations at war with us, and brought back. The poor creatures, almost famished for want of sustenance, having had none during the time of their escape, were no sooner in the power of the barbarians, than two of them were tied to a tree, and a great fire made round them, where they remained till they were terribly scorched and burnt; when one of the villains with his scalping knife, ripped open their bellies, took out their entrails, and burned them before their eyes, whilst the others were cutting, piercing, and tearing the flesh from their breasts, hands, arms, and legs, with red-hot irons, till they were dead. The third unhappy victim was reserved a few hours longer, to be, if possible, sacrificed in a more cruel manner; his arms were tied close to his body, and a hole being dug, deep enough for him to stand upright, he was put into it, and earth rammed and beat in all round his body up to his neck, so that his head only appeared above ground; they then scalped him, and there let him remain for three or four hours, in the greatest agonies; after which they made a small fire near his head, causing him to suffer the most excruciating torments; whilst the poor creature could only cry for mercy by killing him immediately, for his brains were boiling in his head; inexorable to all he said, they continued the fire, till his eyes gushed out of their sockets; such agonizing torments did this unhappy creature suffer for near two hours before he was quite dead. They then cut off his head, and buried it with the other bodies; my task being to dig the graves; which, feeble and terrified as I was, the dread of suffering the same fate enabled me to do.

Winter with the Indians

A great snow now falling, the barbarians were fearful, lest the white people should, by their tracks, find out their skulking retreats, which obliged them to make the best of their way to their winter-quarters, about two hundred miles farther from any plantations or inhabitants. After a long and painful journey, being almost starved, I arrived with this infernal crew at Alamingo. There I found a number of wigwams, full of their women and children.

41

Dancing, singing, and shouting were their general amusements. And in all their festivals and dances, they relate what successes they have had, and what damages they have sustained in their expeditions; in which I now unhappily became part of their theme. The severity of the cold increasing, they stripped me of my cloaths for their own use, and gave me such as they usually wore themselves, being a piece of blanket, and a pair of mockasons, or shoes, with a yard of coarse cloth, to put round me instead of breeches.

At Alamingo I remained near two months, till the snow was off the ground. Whatever thoughts I might have of making my escape, to carry them into execution was impracticable, being so far from any plantations or white people, and the severe weather rendering my limbs in a manner quite stiff and motionless: however, I contrived to defend myself against the inclemency of the weather as well as I could, by making myself a little wigwam with the bark of the trees, covering it with earth, which made it resemble a cave; and, to prevent the ill effects of the cold, I kept a good fire always near the door. My liberty of going about, was, indeed, more than I could have expected, but they well knew the impracticability of my escaping from them. Seeing me outwardly easy and submissive, they would sometimes give me a little meat, but my chief food was Indian corn. At length the time came when they were preparing themselves for another expedition against the planters and white people; but before they set out, they were joined by many other Indians.

As soon as the snow was quite gone, they set forth on their journey towards the back parts of the province of Pennsylvania; all leaving their wives and children behind in their wigwams. They were now a formidable body, amounting to near 150. My business was to carry what they thought proper to load me with, but they never intrusted me with a gun. We marched on several days without any thing particular occurring, almost famished for want of provisions; for my part, I had nothing but a few stalks of Indian corn, which I was glad to eat dry: nor did the Indians themselves fare much better, for as we drew near the plantations they were afraid to kill any game, lest the noise of their guns should alarm the inhabitants.

When we again arrived at the Blue-hills, about thirty miles from the Irish settlements before-mentioned, we encamped for three days, though God knows, we had neither tents nor any thing else to defend us from the inclemency of the air, having nothing to lie on by night but the grass. Their usual method of lodging, pitching, or encamping, by night, being in parcels of ten or twelve men to a fire, where they lie upon the grass or brush, wrapped up in a blanket, with their feet to the fire.

During our stay here, a sort of council of war was held, when it was agreed to divide themselves into companies of about twenty men each; after which every captain marched with his party where he thought proper. I still belonged to my old masters, but was left behind on the mountains with ten Indians, to stay till the rest should return; not thinking it proper to carry me nearer to Conogocheague, or the other plantations.

Escape

Here I began to meditate an escape, and though I knew the country round extremely well, yet I was very cautious of giving the least suspicion of any such intention. However the third day after the grand body left us, my companions thought proper to traverse the mountains in search of game for their subsistence, leaving me bound in such a manner that I could not escape: at night when they returned, having unbound me, we all sat down together to supper on what they had killed, and soon after (being greatly fatigued with their day's excursion) they composed themselves to rest, as usual. I now tried various ways to try whether it was a scheme to prove my intentions or not; but after making a noise and walking about, sometimes touching them with my feet, I found there was no fallacy. Then I resolved, if possible, to get one of their guns, and, if discovered, to die in my defence, rather than be taken: for that purpose I made various efforts to get one from under their heads (where they always secured them) but in vain. Disappointed in this, I began to despair of carrying my design into execution: yet, after a little recollection, and trusting myself to the divine protection, I set forward, naked, and defenceless as I was. Such was my terror, however, that in going from them I halted, and paused every four or five yards, looking fearfully towards the spot where I had left them, lest they should awake and miss me; but when I was two hundred yards from them, I mended my pace, and made as much haste as I possibly could to the foot of the mountains; when, on a sudden, I was struck with the greatest terror at hearing the wood-cry, as it is called, which the savages I had left were making, upon missing their charge. The more my terror encreased the faster I pushed on, and, scarce knowing where I trod, drove through the woods with the utmost precipitation, sometimes falling and bruising myself, cutting my feet and legs against the stones in a miserable manner. But faint and maimed as I was I continued my flight till day-break, when, without having any thing to sustain nature, but a little corn left, I crept into a hollow tree, where I lay very snug, and returned my prayers and thanks to the divine being, that had thus far favoured my escape. But my repose was in a few hours destroyed at hearing the voices of the savages near the place where I was hid, threatening and talking how they would use me, if they got me again. However, they at last left the spot, where I heard them, and I remained in my apartment all that day without further molestation.

At night I ventured forwards again, frightened; thinking each twig that touched me a savage. The third day I concealed myself in like manner as before, and at night travelled, keeping off the main road as much as possible, which lengthened my journey many miles. But how shall I describe the terror I felt on the fourth night, when, by the rustling I made among the leaves, a party of Indians, that lay round a small fire, which I did not perceive, started from the ground, and, seizing their arms, ran from the fire amongst the woods. Whether to move forward or rest where I was, I knew not, when to my great surprize and joy, I was relieved by a parcel of swine that made towards the place where I guessed the savages to be; who, on seeing them, imagined that they had caused the alarm, very merrily returned to the fire, and lay again down to sleep. Bruised, crippled, and terrified as I was, I pursued my journey till break of day, when, thinking myself safe, I lay down under a great log, and slept till about noon. Before evening I reached the summit of a great hill, and looking out if I could spy any habitations of white people, to my inexpressible joy, I saw some which I guessed to be about ten miles distance.

In the morning I continued my journey towards the nearest cleared lands I had seen the day before, and, about four o'clock in the afternoon, arrived at the house of John Bell, an old acquaintance, where knocking at the door, his wife, who opened it, seeing me in such a frightful condition, flew from me, screaming, into the house. This alarmed the whole family, who immediately fled to their arms, and I was soon accosted by the master with his gun in his hand. But on making myself known, (for he before took me to be an Indian) he immediately caressed me, as did all his family with extraordinary friendship, the report of my being murdered by the savages having reached them some months before. For two days and nights they very affectionately supplied me with all necessaries, and carefully attended me till my spirits and limbs were pretty well recovered, and I thought myself able to ride, when I borrowed of these good people (whose kindness merits my most grateful returns) a horse and some cloaths, and set forward for my father-in-law's house in Chester county, about one hundred and forty miles from thence, where I arrived on the 4th day of January, 1755, (but scarce one of the family could credit their eyes, believing with the people I had lately left, that I had fallen a prey to the Indians) where I was received and embraced by the whole family with great affection; upon enquiring for my dear wife, I found she had been dead two months! This fatal news greatly lessened the joy I otherwise should have felt at my deliverance from the dreadful state and company I had been in.

"Notwithstanding all that has been said against the Indians, . . . it is a fact that they are naturally kind, tender and peaceable toward their friends, and strictly honest."

A Captive's Account of the Kindness of Indians

Mary Jemison (ca. 1743–1833)

Mary Jemison, the daughter of Irish immigrants who had settled in Pennsylvania, was fifteen years old when she and her family were captured by a Shawnee raiding party in 1758. Her parents were soon killed, but she was instead taken to a French fort. From there two Seneca Indian women brought her to their village and formally adopted her into their family. Jemison eventually married, had children, and became thoroughly assimilated into Indian society. Living most of her life in Genesee county in western New York—the Seneca heartland—she became known as the "white woman of the Genesee." Her experience was not unique; an unknown number of child and adult captives of Native Americans chose to remain with their captors, while other whites voluntarily left their settlements to live with Indians.

In 1824, at the age of eighty, Jemison dictated her life story to writer James E. Seaver. The following excerpts describe her capture, her adoption, and daily Indian life. Although Jemison relates some cruelties committed by Indians, she stresses that after her adoption into the tribe she was treated with compassion and kindness. Her account includes interesting details about Native American life and provides a striking contrast to the negative portrayal of American Indians that is found in many other captivity narratives.

From *A Narrative of the Life of Mary Jemison* by James Seaver (New York: Miller, Orton, and Mulligan, 1856).

I got home with the horse very early in the morning, where I found a man that lived in our neighborhood, and his sister-in-law who had three children, one son and two daughters. . . .

Immediately after I got home, the man took the horse to go to his house after a bag of grain, and took his gun in his hand for the purpose of killing game, if he should chance to see any.—Our family, as usual, was busily employed about their common business. Father was shaving an axe-helve at the side of the house; mother was making preparations for breakfast;—my two oldest brothers were at work near the barn; and the little ones, with myself, and the woman and her three children, were in the house.

Breakfast was not yet ready, when we were alarmed by the discharge of a number of guns, that seemed to be near. Mother and the women before mentioned, almost fainted at the report, and every one trembled with fear. On opening the door, the man and horse lay dead near the house, having just been shot by the Indians.

I was afterwards informed, that the Indians discovered him at his own house with his gun, and pursued him to father's, where they shot him as I have related. They first secured my father, and then rushed into the house, and without the least resistance made prisoners of my mother, Robert, Matthew, Betsey, the woman and her three children, and myself, and then commenced plundering.

My two brothers, Thomas and John, being at the barn, escaped and went to Virginia, where my grandfather Erwin then lived, as I was informed by a Mr. Fields, who was at my house about the close of the revolutionary war.

A Forced March

The party that took us consisted of six Indians and four Frenchmen, who immediately commenced plundering, as I just observed, and took what they considered most valuable; consisting principally of bread, meal and meat. Having taken as much provision as they could carry, they set out with their prisoners in great haste, for fear of detection, and soon entered the woods. On our march that day, an Indian went behind us with a whip, with which he frequently lashed the children to make them keep up. In this manner we travelled till dark without a mouthful of food or a drop of water; although we had not eaten since the night before. Whenever the little children cried for water, the Indians would make them drink urine or go thirsty. At night they encamped in the woods without fire and without shelter, where we were watched with the greatest vigilance. Extremely fatigued, and very hungry, we were compelled to lie upon the ground supperless and without a drop of water to satisfy the cravings of our appetites. As in the day time, so the little ones were made to drink urine in the night if they cried for water. Fatigue alone brought us a little sleep for the refreshment of our weary limbs; and at the dawn of day we were again started on our march in the same order that we had proceeded on the day before. . . .

Towards evening we arrived at the border of a dark and dismal swamp, which was covered with small hemlocks, or some other evergreen, and other bushes, into which we were conducted; and having gone a short distance we stopped to encamp for the night.

Here we had some bread and meat for supper: but the dreariness of our situation; together with the uncertainty under which we all labored, as to our future destiny, almost deprived us of the sense of hunger, and destroyed our relish for food. . . .

A Mother's Farewell

As soon as I had finished my supper, an Indian took off my shoes and stockings and put a pair of moccasins on my feet, which my mother observed; and believing that they would spare my life, even if they should destroy the other captives, addressed me as near as I can remember in the following words:—

"My dear little Mary, I fear that the time has arrived when we must be parted forever. Your life, my child, I think will be spared; but we shall probably be tomahawked here in this lonesome place by the Indians. O! how can I part with you my darling? What will become of my sweet little Mary? Oh! how can I think of your being continued in captivity without a hope of your being rescued? O that death had snatched you from my embraces in your infancy; the pain of parting then would have been pleasing to what it now is; and I should have seen the end of your troubles!—Alas, my dear! my heart bleeds at the thoughts of what awaits you; but, if you leave us, remember my child your own name, and the name of your father and mother. Be careful and not forget your English tongue. If you shall have an opportunity to get away from the Indians, don't try to escape; for if you do they will find and destroy you. Don't forget, my little daughter, the prayers that I have learned you—say them often; be a good child, and God will bless you. May God bless you my child, and make you comfortable and happy."

During this time, the Indians stripped the shoes and stockings from the little boy that belonged to the woman who was taken with us, and put moccasins on his feet, as they had done before on mine. I was crying. An Indian took the little boy and myself by the hand, to lead us off from the company, when my mother exclaimed, "Don't cry Mary—don't cry my child. God will bless you! Farewell—farewell!"

The Indian led us some distance into the bushes, or woods, and there lay down with us to spend the night. The recollection of parting with my tender mother kept me awake, while the tears constantly flowed from my eyes. A number of times in the night the little boy begged of me earnestly to run away with him and get clear of the Indians; but remembering the advice I had so lately received, and knowing the dangers to which we should be exposed, in travelling without a path and without a guide, through a wilderness unknown to us, I told him that I would not go, and persuaded him to lie still till morning.

Unhappy to Be Freed

Some white captives became attached to their Indian captors and were reluctant to leave them. This phenomenon was documented in a 1765 account of captives' being returned to a British military expedition during the French and Indian War.

Among the children who had been carried off young, and had long lived with the Indians, it is not to be expected that any marks of joy would appear on being restored to their parents or relatives. Having been accustomed to look upon the Indians as the only connexions they had, having been tenderly treated by them, and speaking their language, it is no wonder that they considered their new state in the light of captivity, and parted from the savages with tears.

But it must not be denied that there were even some grown persons who shewed an unwillingness to return. The Shawanese were obliged to bind several of their prisoners and force them along to the camp; and some women, who had been delivered up, afterwards found means to escape and run back to the Indian towns. Some, who could not make their escape, clung to their savage acquaintance at parting, and continued many days in bitter lamentations, even refusing sustenance.

Early the next morning the Indians and Frenchmen that we had left the night before, came to us; but our friends were left behind. It is impossible for any one to form a correct idea of what my feelings were at the sight of those savages, whom I supposed had murdered my parents and brothers, sister, and friends, and left them in the swamp to be devoured by wild beasts! But what could I do? A poor little defenceless girl; without the power or means of escaping; without a home to go to, even if I could be liberated; without a knowledge of the direction or distance to my former place of residence; and without a living friend to whom to fly for protection, I felt a kind of horror, anxiety, and dread, that, to me, seemed insupportable. I durst not cry—I durst not complain; and to inquire of them the fate of my friends (even if I could have mustered resolution) was beyond my ability, as I could not speak their language, nor they understand mine. My only relief was in silent stifled sobs.

The Fate of the Parents

My suspicions as to the fate of my parents proved too true; for soon after I left them they were killed and scalped, together with Robert, Matthew, Betsey, and the woman and her two children, and mangled in the most shocking manner.

Having given the little boy and myself some bread and meat for breakfast, they led us on as fast as we could travel, and one of them went behind and with a long staff, picked up all the grass and weeds that we trailed down by going over them. By taking that precaution they avoided detection; for each weed was so nicely placed in its natural position that no one would have suspected that we had passed that way. . . .

They made me to understand that they should not have killed the family if the whites had not pursued them.

Mr. Fields, whom I have before mentioned, informed me that at the time we were taken, he lived in the vicinity of my father; and that on hearing of our captivity, the whole neighborhood turned out in pursuit of the enemy, and to deliver us if possible: but that their efforts were unavailing. They however pursued us to the dark swamp, where they found my father, his family and companions, stripped and mangled in the most inhuman manner: That from thence the march of the cruel monsters could not be traced in any direction; and that they returned to their homes with the melancholy tidings of our misfortunes, supposing that we had all shared in the massacre.

The next morning we went on; the Indian going behind us and setting up the weeds as on the day before. At night we encamped on the ground in the open air, without a shelter or fire.

In the morning we again set out early, and travelled as on the two former days, though the weather was extremely uncomfortable, from the continual falling of rain and snow.

At night the snow fell fast, and the Indians built a shelter of boughs, and a fire, where we rested tolerably dry through that and the two succeeding nights. . . .

On account of the storm, we were two days at that place. On one of those days, a party consisting of six Indians who had been to the frontier settlements, came to where we were, and brought with them one prisoner, a young white man who was very tired and dejected. His name I have forgotten.

Misery certainly loves company. I was extremely glad to see him, though I knew from his appearance, that his situation was as deplorable as mine, and that he could afford me no kind of assistance. In the afternoon the Indians killed a deer, which they dressed, and then roasted it whole; which made them a full meal. We were each allowed a share of their venison, and some bread, so that we made a good meal also.

Having spent three nights and two days at that place, and the storm having ceased, early in the morning the whole company, consisting of twelve Indians, four Frenchmen, the young man, the little boy and myself, moved on at a moderate pace without an Indian behind us to deceive our pursuers.

In the afternoon we came in sight of Fort Pitt (as it is now called), where we were halted while the Indians performed some customs upon their prisoners which they deemed necessary. That fort was then occupied by the French and Indians, and was called Fort Du Quesne. . . .

At the place where we halted, the Indians combed the hair of the young man, the boy and myself, and then painted our faces and hair red, in the finest Indian style. We were then conducted into the fort, where we received a little bread, and were then shut up and left to tarry alone through the night. . . .

The night was spent in gloomy forebodings. What the result of our captivity would be, it was out of our power to determine or even imagine.—At times we could almost realize the approach of our masters to butcher and scalp us;—again we could nearly see the pile of wood kindled on which we were to be roasted; and then we would imagine ourselves at liberty; alone and defenceless in the forest, surrounded by wild beasts that were ready to devour us. The anxiety of our minds drove sleep from our eyelids; and it was with a dreadful hope and painful impatience that we waited for the morning to determine our fate.

The morning at length arrived, and our masters came early and let us out of the house, and gave the young man and boy to the French, who immediately took them away. Their fate I never learned; as I have not seen nor heard of them since.

I was now left alone in the fort, deprived of my former companions, and of everything that was near or dear to me but life. But it was not long before I was in some measure relieved by the appearance of two pleasant looking squaws of the Seneca tribe, who came and examined me attentively for a short time, and then went out. After a few minutes absence they returned with my former masters, who gave me to them to dispose of as they pleased.

The Indians by whom I was taken were a party of Shawanees, if I remember right, that lived, when at home, a long distance down the Ohio.

Journey down the Ohio River

My former Indian masters, and the two squaws, were soon ready to leave the fort, and accordingly embarked; the Indians in a large canoe, and the two squaws and myself in a small one, and went down the Ohio. . . .

At night we arrived at a small Seneca Indian town, at the mouth of a small river, that was called by the Indians, in the Seneca language, She-nan-jee, where the two Squaws to whom I belonged resided. There we landed, and the Indians went on; which was the last I ever saw of them.

Having made fast to the shore, the Squaws left me in the canoe while they went to their wigwam or house in the town, and returned with a suit of Indian clothing, all new, and very clean and nice. My clothes, though whole and good when I was taken, were now torn in pieces, so that I was almost naked. They first undressed me and threw my rags into the river; then washed me clean and dressed me in the new suit they had just brought, in complete Indian style; and then led me home and seated me in the center of their wigwam.

I had been in that situation but a few minutes, before all the Squaws in the town came in to see me. I was soon surrounded by them, and they immediately set up a most dismal howling, crying bitterly, and wringing their hands in all the agonies of grief for a deceased relative.

Their tears flowed freely, and they exhibited all the signs of real mourning. At the commencement of this scene, one of their number began, in a voice somewhat between speaking and singing, to recite some words to the following purport, and continued the recitation till the ceremony was ended; the company at the same time varying the appearance of their countenances, gestures and tone of voice, so as to correspond with the sentiments expressed by their leader:

"Oh our brother! Alas! He is dead—he has gone; he will never return! Friendless he died on the field of the slain, where his bones are yet lying unburied! Oh, who will not mourn his sad fate? No tears dropped around him; oh, no! No tears of his sisters were there! He fell in his prime, when his arm was most needed to keep us from danger! Alas! he has gone! and left us in sorrow, his loss to bewail: Oh where is his spirit? His spirit went naked, and hungry it wanders, and thirsty and wounded it groans to return! Oh helpless and wretched, our brother has gone! No blanket nor food to nourish and warm him; nor candles to light him, nor weapons of war;—Oh, none of those comforts had he! But well we remember his deeds!—The deer he could take on the chase! The panther shrunk back at the sight of his strength! His enemies fell at his feet! He was brave and courageous in war! As the fawn he was harmless: his friendship was ardent: his temper was gentle: his pity was great! Oh! our friend, our companion is dead! Our brother, our brother, alas! he is gone! But why do we grieve for his loss? In the strength of a warrior, undaunted he left us, to fight by the side of the Chiefs! His war-whoop was shrill! His rifle well aimed laid his enemies low: his tomahawk drank of their blood: and his knife flayed their scalps while yet covered with gore! And why do we mourn? Though he fell on the field of the slain, with glory he fell, and his spirit went up to the land of his fathers in war! Then why do we mourn? With transports of joy they received him, and fed him, and clothed him, and welcomed him there! Oh friends, he is happy; then dry up your tears! His spirit has seen our distress, and sent us a helper whom with pleasure we greet. Dickewamis has come: then let us receive her with joy! She is handsome and pleasant! Oh! she is our sister, and gladly we welcome her here. In the place of our brother she stands in our tribe. With care we will guard her from trouble; and may she be happy till her spirit shall leave us."

Adopted by the Indians

In the course of that ceremony, from mourning they became serene—joy sparkled in their countenances, and they seemed to rejoice over me as over a long lost child. I was made welcome amongst them as a sister to the two Squaws before mentioned, and was called Dickewamis; which being interpreted, signifies a pretty girl, a handsome girl, or a pleasant, good thing. That is the name by which I have ever since been called by the Indians.

I afterwards learned that the ceremony I at that time passed through, was that of adoption. The two squaws had lost a brother in [George] Washington's war [the French and Indian War], sometime in the year before, and in consequence of his death went up to Fort Pitt, on the day on which I arrived there, in order to receive a prisoner or an enemy's scalp, to supply their loss.

It is a custom of the Indians, when one of their number is slain or taken prisoner in battle, to give to the nearest relative to the dead or absent, a prisoner, if they have chanced to take one, and if not, to give him the scalp of an enemy. On the return of the Indians from conquest, which is always announced by peculiar shoutings, demonstrations of joy, and the exhibition of some trophy of victory, the mourners come forward and make their claims. If they receive a prisoner, it is at their option either to satiate their vengeance by taking his life in the most cruel manner they can conceive of; or, to receive and adopt him into the family, in the place of him whom they have lost. All the prisoners that are taken in battle and carried to the encampment or town by the Indians, are given to the bereaved families, till their number is made good. And unless the mourners have but just received the news of their bereavement, and are under the operation of a paroxysm of grief, anger and revenge; or, unless the prisoner is very old, sickly, or homely, they generally save him, and treat him kindly. But if their mental wound is fresh, their loss so great that they deem it irreparable, or if their prisoner or prisoners do not meet their approbation, no torture, let it be ever so cruel, seems sufficient to make them satisfaction. It is family, and not national, sacrifices amongst the Indians, that has given them an indelible stamp as barbarians, and identified their character with the idea which is generally formed of unfeeling ferocity, and the most abandoned cruelty.

It was my happy lot to be accepted for adoption; and at the time of the ceremony I was received by the two squaws, to supply the place of their brother in the family; and I was ever considered and treated by them as a real sister, the same as though I had been born of their mother.

During my adoption, I sat motionless, nearly terrified to death at the appearance and actions of the company, expecting every moment to feel their vengeance, and suffer death on the spot. I was, however, happily disappointed, when at the close of the ceremony the company retired, and my sisters went about employing every means for my consolation and comfort.

Being now settled and provided with a home, I was employed in nursing the children, and doing light work about the house. Occasionally I was sent out with the Indian hunters, when they went but a short distance, to help them carry their game. My situation was easy; I had no particular hardships to endure. But still, the recollection of my parents, my brothers and sisters, my home, and my own captivity, destroyed my happiness, and made me constantly solitary, lonesome and gloomy.

My sisters would not allow me to speak English in their hearing; but remembering the charge that my dear mother gave me at the time I left her, whenever I chanced to be alone I made a business of repeating my prayer, catechism, or something I had learned in order that I might not forget my own language. By practicing in that way I retained it till I came to Genesee flats, where I soon became acquainted with English people with whom I have been almost daily in the habit of conversing.

My sisters were diligent in teaching me their language; and to their great satisfaction I soon learned so that I could understand it readily, and speak it fluently. I was very fortunate in falling into their hands; for they were kind good natured women; peaceable and mild in their dispositions; temperate and decent in their habits, and very tender and gentle towards me. I have great reason to respect them, though they have been dead a great number of years.

The town where they lived was pleasantly situated on the Ohio, at the mouth of the Shenanjee: the land produced good corn; the woods furnished a plenty of game, and the waters abounded with fish. Another river emptied itself into the Ohio, directly opposite the mouth of the Shenanjee. We spent the summer at that place, where we planted, hoed, and harvested a large crop of corn, of an excellent quality. . . .

The corn being harvested, the Indians took it on horses and in canoes, and proceeded down the Ohio, occasionally stopping to hunt a few days, till we arrived at the mouth of Sciota river; where they established their winter quarters, and continued hunting till the ensuing spring, in the adjacent wilderness. While at that place I went with the other children to assist the hunters to bring in their game. The forests on the Sciota were well stocked with elk, deer, and other large animals; and the marshes contained large numbers of beaver, muskrat, &c. which made excellent hunting for the Indians; who depended, for their meat, upon their success in taking elk and deer; and for ammunition and clothing, upon the beaver, muskrat, and other furs that they could take in addition to their peltry.

The season for hunting being passed, we all returned in the spring to the mouth of the river Shenanjee, to the houses and fields we had left in the fall before. There we again planted our corn, squashes, and beans, on the fields that we occupied the preceding summer. . . .

We tended our cornfields through the summer; and after we had harvested the crop, we again went down the river to the hunting ground on the Sciota, where we spent the winter, as we had done the winter before.

Early in the spring we sailed up the Ohio river, to a place that the Indians called Wiishto, where one river emptied into the Ohio on one side, and another on the other. At that place the Indians built a town, and we planted corn.

Marriage and Family

We lived three summers at Wiishto, and spent each winter on the Sciota.

The first summer of our living at Wiishto, a party of Delaware Indians came up the river, took up their residence, and lived in common with us. . . .

Not long after the Delawares came to live with us, at Wiishto, my sisters told me that I must go and live with one of them, whose name was She-nin-jee. Not daring to cross them, or disobey their commands, with a great degree of reluctance I went; and Sheninjee and I were married according to Indian custom.

Sheninjee was a noble man; large in stature; elegant in his appearance; generous in his conduct; courageous in war; a friend to peace, and a great lover of justice. He supported a degree of dignity far above his rank, and merited and received the confidence and friendship of all the tribes with whom he was acquainted. Yet, Sheninjee was an Indian. The idea of spending my days with him, at first seemed perfectly irreconcilable to my feelings: but his good nature, generosity, tenderness, and friendship towards me, soon gained my affection; and, strange as it may seem, I loved him!—To me he was ever kind in sickness, and always treated me with gentleness; in fact, he was an agreeable husband, and a comfortable companion. . . .

In the second summer of my living at Wiishto, I had a child at the time that the kernels of corn first appeared on the cob. When I was taken sick, Sheninjee was absent, and I was sent to a small shed, on the bank of the river, which was made of boughs, where I was obliged to stay till my husband returned. My two sisters, who were my only companions, attended me, and on the second day of my confinement my child was born; but it lived only two days. It was a girl: and notwithstanding the shortness of the time that I possessed it, it was a great grief to me to lose it.

After the birth of my child, I was very sick, but was not allowed to go into the house for two weeks; when, to my great joy, Sheninjee returned, and I was taken in and as comfortably provided for as our situation would admit of. My disease continued to increase for a number of days; and I became so far reduced that my recovery was despaired of by my friends, and I concluded that my troubles would soon be finished. At length, however, my complaint took a favorable turn, and by the time that the corn was ripe I was able to get about. I continued to gain my health, and in the fall was able to go to our winter quarters, on the Sciota, with the Indians.

From that time, nothing remarkable occurred to me till the fourth winter of my captivity, when I had a son born, while I was at Sciota: I had a quick recovery, and my child was healthy. To commemorate the name of my much lamented father, I called my son Thomas Jemison. . . .

I had then been with the Indians four summers and four winters, and had become so far accustomed to their mode of living, habits and dispositions, that my anxiety to get away, to be set at liberty, and leave them, had almost subsided. With them was my home; my family was there, and there I had many friends to whom I was warmly attached in consideration of the favors, affection and friendship with which they had uniformly treated me, from the time of my adoption. Our labor was not severe; and that of one year was exactly similar, in almost every respect, to that of the others, without that endless variety that is to be observed in the common labor of the white people. Notwithstanding the Indian women have all the fuel and bread to procure, and the cooking to perform, their task is probably not harder than that of white women, who have those articles provided for them; and their cares certainly are not half as numerous, nor as great. In the summer season, we planted, tended and harvested our corn, and generally had all our children with us; but had no master to oversee or drive us, so that we could work as leisurely as we pleased. We had no ploughs on the Ohio; but performed the whole process of planting and hoeing with a small tool that resembled, in some respects, a hoe with a very short handle.

Indian Life

Our cooking consisted in pounding our corn into samp or hommany, boiling the hommany, making now and then a cake and baking it in the ashes, and in boiling or roasting our venison. As our cooking and eating utensils consisted of a hommany block and pestle, a small kettle, a knife or two, and a few vessels of bark or wood, it required but little time to keep them in order for use.

Spinning, weaving, sewing, stocking and knitting, and the like, are arts which have never been practised in the Indian tribes generally. After the revolutionary war, I learned to sew, so that I could make my own clothing after a poor fashion; but the other domestic arts I have been wholly ignorant of the application of, since my captivity. In the season of hunting, it was our business, in addition to our cooking, to bring home the game that was taken by the Indians, dress it, and carefully preserve the eatable meat, and prepare or dress the skins. Our clothing was fastened together with strings of deer skin, and tied on with the same.

In that manner we lived, without any of those jealousies, quarrels, and revengeful battles between families and individuals, which have been common in the Indian tribes since the introduction of ardent spirits amongst them.

The use of ardent spirits amongst the Indians, and the attempts which have been made to civilize and christianize them by the white people, has constantly made them worse and worse; increased their vices, and robbed them of many of their virtues; and will ultimately produce their extermination. I have seen, in a number of instances, the effects of education upon some of our Indians, who were taken when young, from their families, and placed at school before they had had an opportunity to contract many Indian habits, and there kept till they arrived to manhood; but I have never seen one of those but what was an Indian in every respect after he returned. Indians must and will be Indians, in spite of all the means that can be used for their cultivation in the sciences and arts.

One thing only marred my happiness, while I lived with them on the Ohio; and that was the recollection that I had once had tender parents, and a home that I loved. Aside from that consideration, or, if I had been taken in infancy, I should have been contented in my situation. Notwithstanding all that has been said against the Indians, in consequence of their cruelties to their enemies—cruelties that I have witnessed, and had abundant proof of—it is a fact that they are naturally kind, tender and peaceable towards their friends, and strictly honest; and that those cruelties have been practised, only upon their enemies, according to their idea of justice.

Chapter 2

Removal and Resistance: The Conflict over Land in the Early Nineteenth Century

Chapter Preface

At the close of the Seven Years' War in 1763, Great Britain received France's territory between the Appalachian Mountains and the Mississippi River. Many residents of Britain's thirteen colonies looked eagerly on the prospect of settling those lands, agreeing with Benjamin Franklin's prediction that "all the country from the St. Lawrence to the Mississippi will in another century be filled with British people."

This territory was the home of numerous Indian tribes, however, and the expense and effort of peacekeeping between the tribes and the colonial settlers who rushed to the area soon became burdensome to the British government. In an effort to tighten its administration of the region and to prevent Indians and settlers from attacking each other, Great Britain issued the Proclamation of 1763. Intended as a temporary measure to restore order to the region, the proclamation closed the lands west of the Appalachians to white settlement, placed the territory under direct British control, and forbade colonial governments and private citizens from acquiring land from the Indians.

The Proclamation of 1763 was one of the grievances against England that eventually drove the thirteen colonies to rebel in 1776. During the American Revolution, many Indians of the trans-Appalachian region viewed the rebelling colonies as a greater threat to their well-being than the British government and therefore chose to ally with Great Britain. Despite their efforts, the United States won its independence and in the 1783 Treaty of Paris received from Great Britain the territory between the Appalachians and the Mississippi. The new national government promptly revoked the Proclamation of 1763 and encouraged white settlers to move past the boundary; much of its early legislation dealt with how to incorporate these western lands within the United States. However, the territory in question was still home to approximately 150,000 Indians of various tribes—people who did not necessarily recognize Great Britain's transfer of their lands to the United States. The U.S. government found itself in much the same position as the royal British government it replaced. It officially possessed territory inhabited by Indians and desired by white settlers—a situation at constant risk of erupting into violence requiring expensive military intervention.

In an effort to maintain peaceful relations with Indians and to obtain land for white settlement, the federal government negotiated treaties with Indian tribes of the region. Tribal leaders ceded possession claims to land in return for money and material goods and for federal commitments to protect against further white encroachments. The federal government also established and administered trading posts to exchange manufactured goods with the Indians for furs. Part of the plan behind these government trading houses, President Thomas Jefferson wrote in a private 1803 letter to William Henry Harrison, then governor of Indiana Territory, was to enable Indian tribal leaders to run up debts that could then be settled by further land cessions.

In addition to acquiring land, the American government also hoped to reduce Indian-white conflict by encouraging Indians to adopt white customs and ways of life. Toward this end, the government provided financial assistance to religious societies that sponsored Christian missionaries and schools in Indian communities. In the same 1803 letter to Harrison, Thomas Jefferson stated his objectives for Indian assimilation. His goal, he wrote, was "to live in perpetual peace with the Indians, to cultivate an affectionate attachment from them," in the hopes that "our settlements will gradually circumscribe and approach the Indians, and they will in time either incorporate with us as citizens of the United States, or remove beyond the Mississippi."

At the time that Jefferson wrote this letter, the United States had just agreed to purchase from France vast expanses of territory west of the Mississippi River. Other American leaders soon latched onto the idea of moving tribes to this new land as a way of gaining more territory from the Indians and preventing further conflicts between Indians and whites. (The fact that such lands were already occupied by different Indian tribes did not dissuade advocates of Indian removal.) At first the federal government attempted to convince Indian tribes to move voluntarily. However, while some Indian leaders agreed to sign treaties and relocate, many sought to remain in their traditional homelands.

The Indian peoples who resisted removal chose one of two approaches—armed confrontation or cultural adaptation and accommodation. In the first decades after U.S. independence, Indians who attempted military resistance could often count on arms and aid from Spain and Great Britain, which still maintained presences on America's southern and western borders. One of the most famous Indian leaders to advocate armed resistance was the Shawnee leader Tecumseh, who tried to create an extensive pan-Indian alliance in the early 1800s. Traveling to various Indian tribes, Tecumseh pleaded with them to join together in fighting the Americans, arguing that unless they fought together, they would be driven away from their homes.

The War of 1812 between Great Britain and the United States marked an important turning point in the balance of power between Indians and whites. Tecumseh was killed in 1813 while fighting alongside the British; what remained of his following fell apart soon after his death. After the war, Great Britain withdrew from its forts on American soil and stopped aiding its former Indian partners. A short time later, Spain withdrew from Florida, leaving eastern Indians with no European allies to supply them with guns or otherwise aid their resistance.

Of the Indians who chose assimilation, perhaps the most famous were the Cherokee Indians. The Cherokee of the early nineteenth century adopted various aspects of white culture while maintaining a distinct and separate nation within the United States. They developed a written alphabet, opened schools, welcomed missionaries, adopted plantation agriculture (complete with black slaves), published a newspaper, and, in 1827, formally adopted a constitution. This last act was viewed with alarm by the state of Georgia, which soon thereafter passed laws declaring Cherokee political authority null and void. Georgia claimed political jurisdiction over the tribe and its lands and sought the expulsion of the Cherokee people. The state found an ally in Andrew Jackson, elected president in 1828. Jackson called on Congress to pass legislation providing for the forcible removal of all Indians in the area to an "Indian Territory" west of the Mississippi. After bitter debate, Congress passed the Indian Removal Act in 1830. Within ten years, the United States coerced the remaining eastern Indian tribes, including the Cherokee, into signing treaties ceding their lands to the U.S. government. U.S. soldiers enforced the relocation of more than sixty thousand Indians to lands across the Mississippi. Thousands more perished during the journey.

The Indian removal of the 1830s marked the culmination of the conflict between Native Americans and white settlers in the trans-Appalachian region that dated back to American dissatisfaction with Britain's Proclamation of 1763. The viewpoints in this chapter provide some of the opposing arguments made by American and Indian leaders during this time.

VIEWPOINT 1

"The annihilation of our race is at hand unless we unite in one common cause against the common foe."

Indians Should Join Together in War Against the Americans

Tecumseh (ca. 1768–1813)

Tecumseh, a Shawnee Indian chief, became one of the most famous Indian warriors and orators of the period following the American Revolutionary War. Born in what is now Ohio, Tecumseh grew up at a time when Indian tribes east of the Mississippi River were rapidly losing their territory through war and white settlement. Along with his brother Tenskwatawa, who was known as the Shawnee Prophet, Tecumseh led a religious and political crusade to unite American Indian tribes in an alliance to resist further loss of Indian land and to revitalize Indian culture. In 1808 the two brothers founded the community of Prophetstown, located in what is now Indiana at the juncture of the Wabash and Tippecanoe Rivers. From that base Tecumseh traveled to almost every tribe east of the Rocky Mountains, arguing that they should join together in fighting the white invaders.

The following viewpoint is taken from one such speech made in the spring of 1811 to a gathering of members of the Choctaw and Chickasaw tribes in the southern part of the United States. In his speech, Tecumseh asserts that the Choctaw and Chickasaw must join with other tribes in a fighting alliance against the Americans to prevent the repetition of the fate of the vanquished eastern Indian tribes.

Later in 1811, while Tecumseh was traveling among the Creek Indians, his vision of a grand Indian alliance suffered a major set-

From *History of Fort Wayne*, by Wallace A. Brice (Fort Wayne, IN: D.W. Jones, 1868).

back: In what became known as the Battle of Tippecanoe, American forces under William Henry Harrison attacked and destroyed Prophetstown. (Harrison later successfully ran for president of the United States based on his Tippecanoe victory.) Tecumseh joined the British to fight the Americans in the War of 1812, serving as a brigadier general. He was killed at the Battle of the Thames in 1813.

In view of questions of vast importance, have we met together in solemn council tonight. Nor should we here debate whether we have been wronged and injured, but by what measures we should avenge ourselves; for our merciless oppressors, having long since planned out their proceedings, are not about to make, but have and are still making attacks upon our race who have as yet come to no resolution. Nor are we ignorant by what steps, and by what gradual advances, the whites break in upon our neighbors. Imagining themselves to be still undiscovered, they show themselves the less audacious because you are insensible. The whites are already nearly a match for us all united, and too strong for any one tribe alone to resist; so that unless we support one another with our collective and united forces; unless every tribe unanimously combines to give check to the ambition and avarice of the whites, they will soon conquer us apart and disunited, and we will be driven away from our native country and scattered as autumnal leaves before the wind.

But have we not courage enough remaining to defend our country and maintain our ancient independence? Will we calmly suffer the white intruders and tyrants to enslave us? Shall it be said of our race that we knew not how to extricate ourselves from the three most dreadful calamities—folly, inactivity and cowardice? But what need is there to speak of the past? It speaks for itself and asks, Where today is the Pequod? Where the Narragansetts, the Mohawks, Pocanokets, and many other once powerful tribes of our race? They have vanished before the avarice and oppression of the white men, as snow before a summer sun. In the vain hope of alone defending their ancient possessions, they have fallen in the wars with the white men. Look abroad over their once beautiful country, and what see you now? Naught but the ravages of the pale face destroyers meet our eyes. So it will be with you Choctaws and Chickasaws! Soon your mighty forest trees, under the shade of whose wide spreading branches you have played in infancy, sported in boyhood, and now rest your wearied limbs after the fatigue of the chase, will be cut down to fence in the land which the white intruders dare to call their own. Soon their broad roads will pass over the grave of your fathers, and the place of their rest will be blotted out forever. The annihilation of our race is at hand unless we unite in one common cause against the common foe. Think not, brave Choctaws and Chickasaws, that you can remain passive and indifferent to the common danger, and thus escape the common fate. Your people, too, will soon be as falling leaves and scattering clouds before their blighting breath. You, too, will be driven away from your native land and ancient domains as leaves are driven before the wintry storms.

War or Extermination

Sleep not longer, O Choctaws and Chickasaws, in false security and delusive hopes. Our broad domains are fast escaping from our grasp. Every year our white intruders become more greedy, exacting, oppressive and overbearing. Every year contentions spring up between them and our people and when blood is shed we have to make atonement whether right or wrong, at the cost of the lives of our greatest chiefs, and the yielding up of large tracts of our lands. Before the palefaces came among us, we enjoyed the happiness of unbounded freedom, and were acquainted with neither riches, wants nor oppression. How is it now? Wants and oppression are our lot; for are we not controlled in everything, and dare we move without asking, by your leave? Are we not being stripped day by day of the little that remains of our ancient liberty? Do they not even kick and strike us as they do their black-faces? How long will it be before they will tie us to a post and whip us, and make us work for them in their corn fields as they do them? Shall we wait for that moment or shall we die fighting before submitting to such ignominy?

Have we not for years had before our eyes a sample of their designs, and are they not sufficient harbingers of their future determinations? Will we not soon be driven from our respective countries and the graves of our ancestors? Will not the bones of our dead be plowed up, and their graves be turned into fields? Shall we calmly wait until they become so numerous that we will no longer be able to resist oppression? Will we wait to be destroyed in our turn, without making an effort worthy of our race? Shall we give up our homes, our country, bequeathed to us by the Great Spirit, the graves of our dead, and everything that is dear and sacred to us, without a struggle? I know you will cry with me: Never! Never! Then let us by unity of action destroy them all, which we now can do, or drive them back whence they came. War or extermination is now our only choice. Which do you choose? I know your answer. Therefore, I now call on you, brave

Attack the Palefaces

A famous contemporary of Tecumseh was Black Hawk, a Sauk chief who also urged Indians to unite and retake their land from white settlers. The following passage is excerpted from Black Hawk's April 1832 speech to a group of Sauk warriors (the speech was heard and later recorded by a white prisoner). Shortly thereafter, Black Hawk crossed the Mississippi River into Illinois with four hundred families to reclaim land that had been ceded in a controversial 1804 treaty; in the subsequent Black Hawk War, most of his outnumbered followers were killed. Black Hawk died in 1838.

From the day when the palefaces landed upon our shores, they have been robbing us of our inheritance, and slowly, but surely, driving us back, back, back towards the setting sun, burning our villages, destroying our growing crops, ravishing our wives and daughters, beating our papooses with cruel sticks, and brutally murdering our people upon the most flimsy pretenses and trivial causes. . . .

They are now running their plows through our graveyards, turning up the bones and ashes of our sacred dead, whose spirits are calling to us from the land of dreams for vengeance on the despoilers. Will the descendants of Nanamakee and our other illustrious dead stand idly by and suffer this sacrilege to be continued? Have they lost their strength and courage, and become squaws and papooses? The Great Spirit whispers in my ear, no! Then let us be again united as a nation and at once cross the Mississippi, rekindle our watchfires upon our ancient watch-tower, and send forth the war-whoop of the again united Sauks, and our cousins, the Masquawkees, Pottawattamies, Ottawas, Chippewas, Winnebagoes and Kickapoos, will unite with us in avenging our wrongs upon the white pioneers of Illinois.

When we recross the Mississippi with a strong army, the British Father will send us not only guns, tomahawks, spears, knives and ammunition in abundance, but he will also send us British soldiers to fight our battles for us. Then will the deadly arrow and fatal tomahawk hurtle through the air at the hearts and heads of the pale faced invaders, sending their guilty spirits to the white man's place of endless punishment.

Choctaws and Chickasaws, to assist in the just cause of liberating our race from the grasp of our faithless invaders and heartless oppressors. The white usurpation in our common country must be stopped, or we, its rightful owners, be forever destroyed and wiped out as a race of people. I am now at the head of many warriors backed by the strong arm of English soldiers. Choctaws and Chickasaws, you have too long borne with grievous usurpation inflicted by the arrogant Americans. Be no longer their dupes. If there be one here tonight who believes that his rights will not sooner or later be taken from him by the avaricious American palefaces, his ignorance ought to excite pity, for he knows little of the character of our common foe.

And if there be one among you mad enough to undervalue the growing power of the white race among us, let him tremble in considering the fearful woes he will bring down upon our entire race, if by his criminal indifference he assists the designs of our common enemy against our common country. Then listen to the voice of duty, of honor, of nature and of your endangered country. Let us form one body, one heart, and defend to the last warrior our country, our homes, our liberty, and the graves of our fathers.

Grounds of Complaint

Choctaws and Chickasaws, you are among the few of our race who sit indolently at ease. You have indeed enjoyed the reputation of being brave, but will you be indebted for it more from report than fact? Will you let the whites encroach upon your domains even to your very door before you will assert your rights in resistance? Let no one in this council imagine that I speak more from malice against the paleface Americans than just grounds of complaint. Complaint is just toward friends who have failed in their duty; accusation is against enemies guilty of injustice. And surely, if any people ever had, we have good and just reasons to believe we have ample grounds to accuse the Americans of injustice; especially when such great acts of injustice have been committed by them upon our race, of which they seem to have no manner of regard, or even to reflect. They are a people fond of innovations, quick to contrive and quick to put their schemes into effectual execution no matter how great the wrong and injury to us; while we are content to preserve what we already have. Their designs are to enlarge their possessions by taking yours in turn; and will you, can you longer dally, O Choctaws and Chickasaws?

Do you imagine that that people will not continue longest in the enjoyment of peace who timely prepare to vindicate themselves, and manifest a determined resolution to do themselves right whenever they are wronged? Far otherwise. Then haste to the relief of our common cause, as by consanguinity of blood you are bound; lest the day be not far distant when you will be left singlehanded and alone to the cruel mercy of our most inveterate foe.

VIEWPOINT 2

"If we take up arms against the Americans we must of necessity meet in deadly combat our daily neighbors and associates in this part of the country near our homes."

Indians Should Live in Peace with the Americans

Pushmataha (1764–1824)

Pushmataha was a Choctaw Indian leader. Residing in what is now the state of Mississippi, the Choctaws were one of the "Five Civilized Tribes" of the region (the others were the Cherokee, Creek, Chickasaw, and Seminole). These tribes gained their appellation because they adopted many aspects of European culture, including European clothing and plantation agriculture. Pushmataha himself made numerous trips to Washington, D.C., in negotiations on behalf of his tribe and was on familiar terms with several presidents. In the War of 1812 he fought with Andrew Jackson and the Americans against the British.

The following viewpoint is taken from an 1811 speech made in response to Shawnee leader Tecumseh's call for the Choctaws and neighboring Chickasaws to join in a pan-Indian war against the Americans. Pushmataha argues that his own tribe has enjoyed friendly relations with the local whites and has no reason to wage war against them. Furthermore, he contends that the Choctaw are bound by treaty to maintain peace with the Americans.

Pushmataha died while visiting Washington, D.C., in 1824, and was buried there with military honors. Nevertheless, in 1831 the Choctaw became the first of the Five Civilized Tribes to be affected by the 1830 Indian Removal Act, a federal law that authorized the U.S. president to remove all Indians from the Southeast. Through bribes and coercion, the tribe signed a treaty ceding all of its lands in Mississippi and agreed to move west of the Missis-

Reprinted from *Indian Oratory: Famous Speeches by Noted Indian Chieftains*, edited by W.C. Vanderwerth (Norman: University of Oklahoma Press, 1971).

sippi River. Of the approximately twenty thousand Choctaws, nine thousand moved to what is now Oklahoma, four thousand perished during the journey, and seven thousand remained in Mississippi, where they ceased to be officially recognized as a tribe by the U.S. government.

Attention, my good red warriors! Hear ye my brief remarks.

The great Shawnee orator [Tecumseh] has portrayed in vivid picture the wrongs inflicted on his and other tribes by the ravages of the paleface. The candor and fervor of his eloquent appeal breathe the conviction of truth and sincerity, and, as kindred tribes, naturally we sympathize with the misfortunes of his people. I do not come before you in any disputation either for or against these charges. It is not my purpose to contradict any of these allegations against the white man, but neither am I here to indulge in any indiscreet denunciation of him which might bring down upon my people unnecessary difficulty and embarrassment.

The distinguished Shawnee sums up his eloquent appeal to us with this direct question:

"Will you sit idly by, supinely awaiting complete and abject submission, or will you die fighting beside your brethren, the Shawnees, rather than submit to such ignominy?"

These are plain words and it is well they have been spoken, for they bring the issue squarely before us. Mistake not, this language means war. And war with whom, pray? War with some band of marauders who have committed there depredations against the Shawnees? War with some alien host seeking the destruction of the Choctaws and Chickasaws? Nay, my fellow tribesmen. None of these are the enemy we will be called on to meet. If we take up arms against the Americans we must of necessity meet in deadly combat our daily neighbors and associates in this part of the country near our homes.

The Choctaws and the Americans

If Tecumseh's words be true, and we doubt them not, then the Shawnee's experience with the whites has not been the same as that of the Choctaws. These white Americans buy our skins, our corn, our cotton, our surplus game, our baskets, and other wares, and they give us in fair exchange their cloth, their guns, their tools, implements, and other things which the Choctaws need but do not make. It is true we have befriended them, but who will deny that these acts of friendship have been abundantly reciprocated? They have given us cotton gins, which simplify the spinning and sale of our cotton; they have encouraged and helped us in the production of our crops; they have taken many of our wives into their homes to teach them useful things, and pay them for their work while learning; they teach our children to read and write from their books. You all remember the dreadful epidemic visited upon us last winter. During its darkest hours these neighbors whom we are now urged to attack responded generously to our needs. They doctored our sick; they clothed our suffering; they fed our hungry; and where is the Choctaw or Chickasaw delegation who has ever gone to St. Stephens with a worthy cause and been sent away empty handed? So, in marked contrast with the experiences of the Shawnees, it will be seen that the whites and Indians in this section are living on friendly and mutually beneficial terms.

Forget not, O Choctaws and Chickasaws, that we are bound in peace to the Great White Father at Washington by a sacred treaty and the Great Spirit will punish those who break their word. The Great White Father has never violated that treaty and the Choctaws have never been driven to the necessity of taking up the tomahawk against him or his children. Therefore the question before us tonight is not the avenging of any wrongs perpetrated against us by the whites, for the Choctaws and Chickasaws have no such cause, either real or imaginary, but rather it is a question of carrying on that record of fidelity and justice for which our forefathers ever proudly stood, and doing that which is best calculated to promote the welfare of our own people. Yea, my fellow tribesmen, we are a just people. We do not take up the warpath without a just cause and honest purpose. Have we that just cause against our white neighbors, who have taken nothing from us except by fair bargain and exchange? Is this a just recompense for their assistance to us in our agricultural and other pursuits? Is this to be their gracious reward for teaching our children from their books? Shall this be considered the Choctaws' compensation for feeding our hungry, clothing our needy, and administering to our sick? Have we, O Choctaws and Chickasaws, descended to the low estate of ruthlessly breaking the faith of a sacred treaty? Shall our forefathers look back from the happy hunting grounds only to see their unbroken record for justice, gratitude, and fidelity thus rudely repudiated and abruptly abandoned by an unworthy offspring?

We Choctaws and Chickasaws are a peaceful people, making our subsistence by honest toil; but mistake not, my Shawnee brethren, we are not afraid of war. Neither are we strangers to war, as those who have undertaken to encroach upon our rights in the past may abundantly testify. We are thoroughly familiar with war in all its details and we know full well all its horrible consequences. It is unnecessary for me to remind you, O Choctaws and Chickasaws, veteran braves of many fierce conflicts in the past, that war is an awful thing. If we go into this war against the Americans, we must be prepared to accept its inevitable results. Not only will it foretoken deadly conflict with neighbors and death to warriors, but it will mean suffering for our women, hunger and starvation for our children, grief for our loved ones, and devastation of our beloved homes. Notwithstanding these difficulties, if the cause be just, we should not hesitate to defend our rights to the last man, but before that fatal step is irrevocably taken, it is well that we fully understand and seriously consider the full portent and consequences of the act.

War Is Wicked

In an 1830 council that included the warrior chief Black Hawk, Senachwine, a Potawatomi leader, argued that a war against the whites would be futile.

For more than seventy years I have hunted in this grove and fished in this stream, and for many years I have worshipped on this ground. Through these groves and over these prairies in pursuit of game our fathers roamed, and by them this land was left unto us as a heritage forever. No one is more attached to his home than myself, and none among you is so grieved to leave it. But the time is near at hand, when the red men of the forest will have to leave the land of their nativity, and find a home toward the setting sun. The white men of the east, whose numbers are like the sands of the sea, will overrun and take possession of this country. They will build wigwams and villages all over the land, and their domain will extend from sea to sea.

In my boyhood days I have chased the buffalo across the prairies, and hunted the elk in the groves; but where are they now? Long since they have left us; the near approach of the white man has frightened them away. The deer and the turkey will go next, and with them the sons of the forest.

Resistance to the aggression of the whites is useless; war is wicked and must result in our ruin. Therefore, let us submit to our fate, return not evil for evil, as this would offend the Great Spirit and bring ruin upon us. The time is near when our race will become extinct, and nothing left to show the world that we ever did exist. . . . My friends, do not listen to the words of Black Hawk for he is trying to lead you astray. Do not imbrue your hands in human blood; for such is the work of the evil one, and will only lead to retribution upon our heads.

The People's Decision

Hear me, O Choctaws and Chickasaws, for I speak truly for your welfare. It is not the province of your chiefs to settle these important questions. As a people, it is your prerogative to have either peace or war, and as one of your chiefs, it is mine simply to counsel and advise. Therefore, let me admonish you that this critical period is no time to cast aside your wits and let blind impulse sway; be not driven like dumb brutes by the frenzied harangue of this wonderful Shawnee orator; let your good judgment rule and ponder seriously before breaking bonds that have served you well and ere you change conditions which have brought peace and happiness to your wives, your sisters, and your children. I would not undertake to dictate the course of one single Choctaw warrior. Permit me to speak for the moment, not as your chief but as a Choctaw warrior, weighing this question beside you. As such I shall exercise my calm, deliberate judgment in behalf of those most dear to me and dependent on me, and I shall not suffer my reason to be swept away by this eloquent recital of alleged wrongs which I know naught of. I deplore this war, I earnestly hope it may be averted, but if it be forced upon us I shall take my stand with those who have stood by my people in the past and will be found fighting beside our good friends of St. Stephens and surrounding country. I have finished. I call on all Choctaws and Chickasaws indorsing my sentiments to cast their tomahawks on this side of the council fire with me.

[The majority of listeners did support Pushmataha. Tecumseh responded by calling Pushmataha a coward and Pushmataha made the following rebuttal.]

Halt, Tecumseh! Listen to me. You have come here, as you have often gone elsewhere, with a purpose to involve peaceful people in unnecessary trouble with their neighbors. Our people have had no undue friction with the whites. Why? Because we have had no leaders stirring up strife to serve their selfish, personal ambitions. You heard me say that our people are a peaceful people. They make their way, not by ravages upon their neighbors but by honest toil. In that regard they have nothing in common with you. I know your history well. You are a disturber. You have ever been a trouble maker. When you have found yourself unable to pick a quarrel with the white man, you have stirred up strife between different tribes of your own race. Not only that, you are a monarch and unyielding tyrant within your own domain; every Shawnee man, woman, and child must bow in humble submission to your imperious will. The Choctaws and Chickasaws have no monarchs. Their chieftains do not undertake the mastery of their people, but rather are they the people's servants, elected to serve the will of the majority. The majority has spoken on this question and it has spoken against your contention. Their decision has therefore become the law of the Choctaws and Chickasaws and Pushmataha will see that the will of the majority so recently expressed is rigidly carried out to the letter.

If, after this decision, any Choctaw should be so foolish as to follow your imprudent advice and enlist to fight against the Americans, thereby abandoning his own people and turning against the decision of his own council, Pushmataha will see that proper punishment is meted out to him, which is death. You have made your choice; you have elected to fight with the British. The Americans have been our friends and we shall stand by them. We will furnish you safe conduct to the boundaries of this nation as properly befits the dignity of your office. Farewell, Tecumseh. You will see Pushmataha no more until we meet on the fateful warpath.

VIEWPOINT 3

"It is a matter of surprise to me . . . that the Cherokees have advanced so far and so rapidly in civilization."

The Cherokee Are Creating a Civilized Society

Elias Boudinot (ca. 1802–1839)

Of all the eastern Indian tribes during the early nineteenth century, the Cherokee made the greatest effort to accommodate to white society. Faced with the loss of much of their land and the collapse of their economy based on hunting and the deerskin trade, the Cherokee determined to refashion their nation. With the assistance of missionaries and the federal government, the tribe developed an agricultural society that included many European elements, including plowed farms, mills, schools, and, beginning in 1827, a constitution modeled on the U.S. Constitution. Despite these efforts, many white settlers (especially in the state of Georgia) coveted the tribe's land and demanded that the Cherokee be removed.

Elias Boudinot, also known as Galagina, was a Cherokee born in Georgia and educated at a mission school in Cornwall, Connecticut (he took his English name from the Philadelphia philanthropist who sponsored his education). The following viewpoint is taken from an address delivered by Boudinot in a Presbyterian church on May 26, 1826, and published in Philadelphia the same year. In the address, Boudinot informs his audience of developments within the Cherokee nation and argues that his people are making significant progress in adopting European ways and in "civilizing" themselves. Among the achievements he cites are the creation of a system for writing the Cherokee language, the de-

From *An Address to the Whites*, by Elias Boudinot (Philadelphia: Geddes, 1826).

velopment and structure of Cherokee government, and the economic assets of the nation. He asks for philanthropic assistance in establishing a Cherokee seminary and a newspaper. Two years later, in 1828, Boudinot became the first editor of this newspaper, the *Cherokee Phoenix*.

By the 1830s pressure was mounting on the Cherokee to cede their lands and move west of the Mississippi River. An early opponent of removal, Boudinot later became part of a political faction within the Cherokee nation that viewed relocation to the west as an unavoidable necessity. He and others agreed to the Treaty of New Echota in 1835, ceding Cherokee lands. Along with the majority of the Cherokee nation, Boudinot relocated to Oklahoma, where he was killed in 1839—apparently in retaliation for his role in the removal of the Cherokee.

To those who are unacquainted with the manners, habits, and improvements of the Aborigines of this country, the term *Indian is* pregnant with ideas the most repelling and degrading. But such impressions, originating as they frequently do, from infant prejudices, although they hold too true when applied to some, do great injustice to many of this race of beings.

Some there are, perhaps even in this enlightened assembly, who at the bare sight of an Indian, or at the mention of the name, would throw back their imaginations to ancient times, to the ravages of savage warfare, to the yells pronounced over the mangled bodies of women and children, thus creating an opinion, inapplicable and highly injurious to those for whose temporal interest and eternal welfare, I come to plead.

What is an Indian? Is he not formed of the same materials with yourself? For "of one blood God created all the nations that dwell on the face of the earth." Though it be true that he is ignorant, that he is a heathen, that he is a savage; yet he is no more than all others have been under similar circumstances. Eighteen centuries ago what were the inhabitants of Great Britain?

You here behold an *Indian*, my kindred are *Indians*, and my fathers sleeping in the wilderness grave—they too were *Indians*. But I am not as my fathers were—broader means and nobler influences have fallen upon me. Yet I was not born as thousands are, in a stately dome and amid the congratulations of the great, for on a little hill, in a lonely cabin, overspread by the forest oak, I first drew my breath; and in a language unknown to learned and polished nations, I learnt to lisp my fond mother's name. In after

74

days, I have had greater advantages than most of my race; and I now stand before you delegated by my native country to seek her interest, to labour for her respectability, and by my public efforts to assist in raising her to an equal standing with other nations of the earth.

The time has arrived when speculations and conjectures as to the practicability of civilizing the Indians must forever cease. A period is fast approaching when the stale remark—"Do what you will, an Indian will still be an Indian", must be placed no more in speech. With whatever plausibility this popular objection may have heretofore been made, every candid mind must now be sensible that it can no longer be uttered, except by those who are uninformed with respect to us, who are strongly prejudiced against us, or who are filled with vindictive feelings towards us; for the present history of the Indians, particularly of that nation to which I belong, most incontrovertibly establishes the fallacy of this remark. I am aware of the difficulties which have ever existed to Indian civilization. I do not deny the almost insurmountable obstacles which we ourselves have thrown in the way of this improvement, nor do I say that difficulties no longer remain; but facts will permit me to declare that there are none which may not easily be overcome, by strong and continued exertions. It needs not abstract reasoning to prove this position. It needs not the display of language to prove to the minds of good men, that Indians are susceptible of attainments necessary to the formation of polished society. It needs not the power of argument on the nature of man, to silence forever the remark that "it is the purpose of the Almighty that the Indians should be exterminated." It needs only that the world should know what we have done in the few last years, to foresee what yet we may do with the assistance of our white brethren, and that of the common Parent of us all.

It is not necessary to present to you a detailed account of the various aboriginal tribes, who have been known to you only on the pages of history, and there but obscurely known. . . .

Nor is it my purpose to enter largely into the consideration of the remnants, of those who have fled with time and are no more—They stand as monuments of the Indian's fate. And should they ever become extinct, they must move off the earth, as did their fathers. My design is to offer a few disconnected facts relative to the present improved state, and to the ultimate prospects of that particular tribe called Cherokees to which I belong.

The Cherokee Nation

The Cherokee nation lies within the chartered limits of the states of Georgia, Tennessee, and Alabama. Its extent as defined by treaties is about 200 miles in length from East to West, and about 120 in breadth. This country which is supposed to contain about 10,000,000 of acres exhibits great varieties of surface, the most part being hilly and mountaneous, affording soil of no value. The vallies, however, are well watered and afford excellent land, in many parts particularly on the large streams, that of the first quality. The climate is temperate and healthy, indeed I would not be guilty of exaggeration were I to say, that the advantages which this country possesses to render it salubrious, are many and superior. Those lofty and barren mountains, defying the labour and ingenuity of man, and supposed by some as placed there only to exhibit omnipotence, contribute to the healthiness and beauty of the surrounding plains, and give to us that free air and pure water which distinguish our country. These advantages, calculated to make the inhabitants healthy, vigorous, and intelligent, cannot fail to cause this country to become interesting. And there can be no doubt that the Cherokee Nation, however obscure and trifling it may now appear, wil finally become, if not under its present occupants, one of the Garden spots of America. And here, let me be indulged in the fond wish, that she may thus become under those who now possess her; and ever be fostered, regulated and protected by the generous government of the United States.

The population of the Cherokee Nation increased from the year 1810 to that of 1824, 2000 exclusive of those who emigrated in 1818 and 19 to the west of the Mississippi—of those who reside on the Arkansas [River] the number is supposed to be about 5000.

The rise of these people in their movement towards civilization, may be traced as far back as the relinquishment of their towns; when game became incompetent to their support, by reason of the surrounding white population. They then betook themselves to the woods, commenced the opening of small clearings, and the raising of stock; still however following the chase. Game has since become so scarce that little dependence for subsistence can be placed upon it. They have gradually and I could almost say universally forsaken their ancient employment. In fact, there is not a single family in the nation, that can be said to subsist on the slender support which the wilderness would afford. The love and the practice of hunting are not now carried to a higher degree, than among all frontier people whether white or red. It cannot be doubted, however, that there are many who have commenced a life of agricultural labour from mere necessity, and if they could, would gladly resume their former course of living. But these are individual failings and ought to be passed over.

On the other hand it cannot be doubted that the nation is improving, rapidly improving in all those particulars which must finally constitute the inhabitants an industrious and intelligent people.

It is a matter of surprise to me, and must be to all those who are properly acquainted with the condition of the Aborigines of this country, that the Cherokees have advanced so far and so rapidly in civilization. But there are yet powerful obstacles, both within and without, to be surmounted in the march of improvement. The prejudices in regard to them in the general community are strong and lasting. The evil effects of their intercourse with their immediate white neighbours, who differ from them chiefly in name, are easily to be seen, and it is evident that from this intercourse proceed those demoralizing practices which in order to surmount, peculiar and unremitting efforts are necessary. In defiance, however, of these obstacles the Cherokees have improved and are still rapidly improving. To give you a further view of their condition, I will here repeat some of the articles of the two statistical tables taken at different periods.

In 1810 there were 19,500 cattle; 6,100 horses; 19,600 swine; 1,037 sheep; 467 looms; 1,600 spinning wheels; 50 waggons; 500 ploughs; 3 saw-mills; 13 grist-mills &c. At this time there are 22,000 cattle; 7,600 Horses; 46,000 swine; 2,500 sheep; 762 looms; 2,488 spinning wheels; 172 waggons; 2,945 ploughs; 10 saw-mills; 31 grist-mills; 62 Blacksmith-shops; 8 cotton machines; 18 schools; 18 ferries; and a number of public roads. In one district there were, last winter, upwards of 1000 volumes of good books; and 11 different periodical papers both religious and political, which were taken and read. On the public roads there are many decent Inns, and few houses for convenience, &c., would disgrace any country. Most of the schools are under the care and tuition of christian missionaries, of different denominations, who have been of great service to the nation, by inculcating moral and religious principles into the minds of the rising generation. In many places the word of God is regularly preached and explained, both by missionaries and natives; and there are numbers who have publicly professed their belief and interest in the merits of the great Saviour of the world. It is worthy of remark, that in no ignorant country have the missionaries undergone less trouble and difficulty, in spreading a knowledge of the Bible, than in this. Here, they have been welcomed and encouraged by the proper authorities of the nation, their persons have been protected, and in very few instances have some individual vagabonds threatened violence to them. Indeed it may be said with truth, that among no heathen people has the faithful minister of God experienced greater success, greater reward for his labour, than in this. He is surrounded by attentive hearers, the words which flow from his lips are not spent in vain. The Cherokees have had no established religion of their own, and perhaps to this circumstance we may attribute, in part, the facilities with which missionaries have pursued their ends. They cannot be called idolators; for they never worshipped Images. They believed in a Supreme Being, the Creator of all, the God of the white, the red, and the black man. They also believed in the existence of an evil spirit who resided, as they thought, in the setting sun, the future place of all who in their life time had done iniquitously. Their prayers were addressed alone to the Supreme Being, and which if written would fill a large volume, and display much sincerity, beauty and sublimity. When the ancient customs of the Cherokees were in their full force, no warrior thought himself secure, unless he had addressed his guardian angel; no hunter could hope for success, unless before the rising sun he had asked the assistance of his God, and on his return at eve he had offered his sacrifice to him.

Three Recent Developments

There are three things of late occurance, which must certainly place the Cherokee Nation in a fair light, and act as a powerful argument in favor of Indian improvement.

First. The invention of letters.
Second. The translation of the New Testament into Cherokee.
And third. The organization of a Government.

The Cherokee mode of writing lately invented by George Guest [Sequoyah], who could not read any language nor speak any other than his own, consists of eighty-six characters, principally syllabic, the combinations of which form all the words of the language. Their terms may be greatly simplified, yet they answer all the purposes of writing, and already many natives use them.

The translation of the New Testament, together with Guest's mode of writing, has swept away that barrier which has long existed, and opened a spacious channel for the instruction of adult Cherokees. Persons of all ages and classes may now read the precepts of the Almighty in their own language. Before it is long, there will scarcely be an individual in the nation who can say, "I know not God neither understand I what thou sayest," for all shall know him from the greatest to the least. The aged warrior over whom has rolled three score and ten years of savage life, will grace the temple of God with his hoary head; and the little child yet on the breast of its pious mother shall learn to lisp its Maker's name. . . .

The Government, though defective in many respects, is well suited to the condition of the inhabitants. As they rise in information and refinement, changes in it must follow, until they arrive at that state of advancement, when I trust they will be admitted into all the privileges of the American family.

The Cherokee Nation is divided into eight districts, in each of which are established courts of justice, where all disputed cases are decided by a Jury, under the direction of a circuit Judge, who has jurisdiction over two districts. Sheriffs and other public officers are appointed to execute the decisions of the courts, collect debts, and arrest thieves and other criminals. Appeals may be taken to the Superior Court, held annually at the seat of Government. The Legislative authority is vested in a General Court, which consists of the National Committee and Council. The National Committee consists of thirteen members, who are generally men of sound sense and fine talents. The National Council consists of thirty-two members, beside the speaker, who act as the representatives of the people. Every bill passing these two bodies, becomes the law of the land. Clerks are appointed to do the writings, and record the proceedings of the Council. The executive power is vested in two principal chiefs, who hold their office dur-

---

Our Nation Has Prospered

In an April 10, 1813, article for Niles Weekly Register, *To-Cha Lee and Chu Li-Oa, two Cherokee chiefs, plead for peace between the Cherokee people and the United States and describe the advancements being made in Cherokee society.*

By the rapid progress of settlements in the western part of the United States, our country is now nearly surrounded by our white brothers. . . . It is for the interest of all that harmony and good neighborhood should be preserved between us. . . .

In former years we were of *necessity* under the influence of your enemies. We spilled our blood in their cause; they were finally compelled by your arms to leave us; they made no stipulation for our security. When those years of distress had passed away, we found ourselves in the power of a generous nation; past transactions were consigned to oblivion; our boundaries were established by compact, and liberal provision was made for our future security and improvement, for which we placed ourselves under the protection of the United States. Under these provisions, our nation has prospered, our population has increased.—The knowledge and practice of agriculture and some of the useful arts, have kept pace with time. Our stocks of cattle and other domestic animals fill the forests, while the wild animals have disappeared. Our spinning wheels and looms now in use by the ingenious hands of our wives and our daughters, enable us to clothe ourselves principally in decent habits, from the production of materials . . . of our soil. In addition to these important acquisitions, many of our youth of both sexes have acquired such knowledge of letters and figures as to show to the most incredulous that our mental powers are not by nature inferior to yours—and we look forward to a period of time, when it may be said, this artist, this mathematician, this astronomer, is a Cherokee.

ing good behaviour, and sanction all the decisions of the legislative council. Many of the laws display some degree of civilization, and establish the respectability of the nation.

Polygamy is abolished. Female chastity and honor are protected
by law. The Sabbath is respected by the Council during session.
Mechanics are encouraged by law. The practice of putting aged
persons to death for witchcraft is abolished and murder has now
become a governmental crime.

From what I have said, you will form but a faint opinion of the
true state and prospects of the Cherokees. You will, however, be
convinced of three important truths.

First, that the means which have been employed for the chris-
tianization and civilization of this tribe, have been greatly
blessed. Second, that the increase of these means will meet with
final success. Third, that it has now become necessary, that efficient and more than ordinary means should be employed.

The Need for a Printing Press

Sensible of this last point, and wishing to do something for
themselves, the Cherokees have thought it advisable that there
should be established, a Printing Press and a Seminary of respectable character; and for these purposes your aid and patronage are now solicited. They wish the types, as expressed in their
resolution, to be composed of English letters and Cherokee characters. Those characters have now become extensively used in the
nation; their religious songs are written in them; there is an astonishing eagerness in people of all classes and ages to acquire a
knowledge of them; and the New Testament has been translated
into their language. All this impresses on them the immediate necessity of procuring types. The most informed and judicious of
our nation, believe that such a press would go further to remove
ignorance, and her offspring superstition and prejudice, than all
other means. The adult part of the nation will probably grovel on
in ignorance and die in ignorance, without any fair trial upon
them, unless the proposed means are carried into effect. The sim-
plicity of this method of writing, and the eagerness to obtain a
knowledge of it, are evinced by the astonishing rapidity with
which it is acquired, and by the numbers who do so. It is about
two years since its introduction, and already there are a great
many who can read it. In the neighbourhood in which I live, I do
not recollect a male Cherokee, between the ages of fifteen and
twenty five, who is ignorant of this mode of writing. But in con-
nexion with those for Cherokee characters, it is necessary to have
types for English letters. There are many [who] already speak and
read the English language, and can appreciate the advantages
which would result from the publication of their laws and trans-

actions in a well conducted newspaper. Such a paper, comprising a summary of religious and political events, &c. on the one hand; and on the other, exhibiting the feelings, disposition, improvements, and prospects of the Indians; their traditions, their true character, as it once was and as it now is; the ways and means most likely to throw the mantle of civilization over all tribes; and such other matter as will tend to diffuse proper and correct impressions in regard to their condition—such a paper could not fail to create much interest in the American community, favourable to the aborigines, and to have a powerful influence on the advancement of the Indians themselves. How can the patriot or the philanthropist devise efficient means, without full and correct information as to the subjects of his labour. And I am inclined to think, after all that has been said of the aborigines, after all that has been written in narratives, professedly to elucidate the leading traits of their character, that the public knows little of that character. To obtain a correct and complete knowledge of these people, there must exist a vehicle of Indian intelligence, altogether different from those which have heretofore been employed. Will not a paper published in an Indian country, under proper and judicious regulations, have the desired effect? I do not say that Indians will produce learned and elaborate dissertations in explanation and vindication of their own character; but they may exhibit specimens of their intellectual efforts, of their eloquence, of their moral, civil and physical advancement, which will do quite as much to remove prejudice and to give profitable information.

The Cherokees wish to establish their Seminary, upon a footing which will insure to it all the advantages, that belong to such institutions in the states. Need I spend one moment in arguments, in favour of such an institution; need I speak one word of the utility, of the necessity, of an institution of learning; need I do more than simply to ask the patronage of benevolent hearts, to obtain that patronage.

When before did a nation of Indians step forward and ask for the means of civilization? The Cherokee authorities have adopted the measures already stated, with a sincere desire to make their nation an intelligent and a virtuous people, and with a full hope that those who have already pointed out to them the road of happiness, will now assist them to pursue it. With that assistance, what are the prospects of the Cherokees? Are they not indeed glorious, compared to that deep darkness in which the nobler qualities of their souls have slept. Yes, methinks I can view my native country, rising from the ashes of her degradation, wearing her purified and beautiful garments, and taking her seat with the nations of the earth. I can behold her sons bursting the fetters of ignorance and unshackling her from the vices of heathenism. She is at this instant, risen like the first morning sun, which grows brighter and brighter, until it reaches its fulness of glory.

She will become not a great, but a faithful ally of the United States. In times of peace she will plead the common liberties of America. In times of war her intrepid sons will sacrifice their lives in your defence. And because she will be useful to you in coming time, she asks you to assist her in her present struggles. She asks not for greatness; she seeks not wealth; she pleads only for assistance to become respectable as a nation, to enlighten and ennoble her sons, and to ornament her daughters with modesty and virtue. She pleads for this assistance, too, because on her destiny hangs that of many nations. If she complete her civilization—then may we hope that all our nations will—then, indeed, may true patriots be encouraged in their efforts to make this world of the West, one continuous abode of enlightened, free, and happy people.

But if the Cherokee Nation fail in her struggle, if she die away, then all hopes are blasted, and falls the fabric of Indian civilization. Their fathers were born in darkness, and have fled in darkness; without your assistance so will their sons. You see, however, where the probability rests. Is there a soul whose narrowness will not permit the exercise of charity on such an occasion? Where is he that can withhold his mite from an object so noble? . . .

Two Alternatives

There are, with regard to the Cherokees and other tribes, two alternatives; they must either become civilized and happy, or sharing the fate of many kindred nations, become extinct. If the General Government continue its protection, and the American people assist them in their humble efforts, they will, they must rise. Yes, under such protection, and with such assistance, the Indian must rise like the Phoenix, after having wallowed for ages in ignorance and barbarity. But should this Government withdraw its care, and the American people their aid, then, to use the words of a writer, "they will go the way that so many tribes have gone before them; for the hordes that still linger about the shores of Huron, and the tributary streams of the Mississippi, will share the fate of those tribes that once forded it along the proud banks of the Hudson; of that gigantic race that are said to have existed on the borders of the Susquehanna; of those various nations that flourished about the Potomac and the Rhappahannoc, and that peopled the forests of the vast valley of Shenandoah. They will vanish like a vapour from the face of the earth, their very history will be lost in forgetfulness, and the places that now know them will know them no more."

There is, in Indian history, something very melancholy, and

which seems to establish a mournful precedent for the future events of the few sons of the forest, now scattered over this vast continent. We have seen every where the poor aborigines melt away before the white population. I merely speak of the fact, without at all referring to the cause. We have seen, I say, one family after another, one tribe after another, nation after nation, pass away; until only a few solitary creatures are left to tell the sad story of extinction.

Shall this precedent be followed? I ask you, shall red men live, or shall they be swept from the earth? With you and this public at large, the decision chiefly rests. Must they perish? Must they all, like the unfortunate Creeks, (victims of the unchristian policy of certain persons), go down in sorrow to their grave?

They hang upon your mercy as to a garment. Will you push them from you, or will you save them? Let humanity answer.

VIEWPOINT 4

"A large portion of the full blooded Cherokees still remain a poor degraded race of human beings."

The Cherokee Are Not Creating a Civilized Society

Wilson Lumpkin (1783–1870)

The development of the Cherokee nation in the early 1800s was on a direct collision course with the land claims and the ambitions of the state of Georgia. In an 1802 agreement, Georgia ceded to the United States western territory included in its original colonial charter in return for a U.S. pledge to purchase all Indian lands remaining within the state's new boundaries. A quarter century later, this pledge had run aground against the Cherokee's refusal to sell their lands in Georgia—a refusal the U.S. government respected as a sovereign right.

Many white Georgians chafed at what they viewed as unreasonable delays in acquiring Indian lands. Wilson Lumpkin was a leading spokesman for their cause. A U.S. commissioner among the Creek and Cherokee Indian tribes from 1818 to 1821, Lumpkin was one of the political leaders in Georgia who advocated the removal of all Indians from the state. In 1830 Lumpkin, then a Democratic representative in Congress and a member of the House Committee on Indian Affairs, was a major force behind the creation of federal legislation, the Indian Removal Act, that authorized the president "to exchange the public domain in the West for Indian lands in the East" and to "give aid and assistance in [Cherokee] emigration."

The following viewpoint is excerpted from Lumpkin's defense of the Indian Removal Act in the debates on the floor of the

From Wilson Lumpkin, speech before Congress, May 17, 1830.

House of Representatives. Lumpkin maintains that the United States has an obligation to the state of Georgia to remove its Indian population. In the course of his argument, he paints a far different picture of the Cherokee nation than that described by Elias Boudinot in the previous viewpoint. Arguing that the descriptions of the Cherokee's accomplishments found in some published accounts are not wholly true, Lumpkin insists that only an elite few of the tribe—most of whom are largely of white descent—can be considered socially advanced. Furthermore, he contends, those accomplishments the Cherokee nation has attained are dependent on federal government payments (made according to treaties for previously ceded land) and on white philanthropic efforts. Lumpkin also criticizes New England missionaries and their supporters for their efforts on behalf of the Cherokee nation. In particular, he mentions Jeremiah Evarts, secretary of the American Board of Foreign Missions, who under the pseudonym of "William Penn" had written a series of articles attacking the proposed removal of the Cherokee. Lumpkin concludes that both the state of Georgia and the Cherokee nation would be better off if the Cherokee were moved west of the Mississippi River.

The Indian Removal Act passed Congress and was signed into law by President Andrew Jackson in 1830. Lumpkin later served as governor of Georgia from 1831 to 1835, where he continued to work for the forcible removal of the Cherokee.

———————————

Amongst my earliest recollections are the walls of an old fort, which gave protection to the women and children from the tomahawk and scalping knife of the Indians. And let me inform you, that, while the Indians have receded thousands of miles before the civilized population, in other sections of the Union, the frontier of Georgia has comparatively remained stationary. My present residence is not more than one day's travel from the place of the old fort to which I alluded. It is but part of a day's travel from my residence to the line of the Cherokee country.

In entering upon this branch of my subject, I find it necessary to summon up all the powers of philosophy, to restrain feelings of indignation and contempt for those who are at this time straining every nerve and using every effort to perpetuate on the people whom I represent the evils which they have borne for so many years; and whatever has, or may be said to the contrary, I do verily believe that no other State of this Union would have submitted, with equal patriotism, to the many ills and wrongs which we have received at the hands of those who were bound by the strongest human obligations to aid in relieving us from Indian perplexities, give us justice, and assist in the advancement of our peace, happiness, and prosperity.

Georgia, sir, is one of the good old thirteen States; she entered the Union upon an equal footing with any of her sisters. She claims no superiority, but contends for equality. That sovereignty which she concedes to all the rest, and would at any time unite with them in defending from all encroachment, she will maintain for herself. Our social compact, upon which we stand as a State, gives you the metes and bounds of our sovereignty; and within the limits therein defined and pointed out, our State authorities claim entire and complete jurisdiction over soil and population, regardless of complexion.

The boundaries of Georgia have been defined, recognized, and admitted, by circumstances of a peculiar kind. Her litigations in relation to boundary and title to her soil may justly be considered as having been settled "according to law." Her boundaries are not only admitted by her sister States, but by this General Government; and every individual who administered any part of it, executive or legislative, must recollect that the faith of this Government has stood pledged for twenty-eight years past, to relieve Georgia from the embarrassment of Indian population. It is known to every member of this Congress, that this pledge was no gratuity to Georgia. No, sir, it was for and in consideration of the two entire States of Alabama and Mississippi. . . .

But, sir, upon this subject, this Government has been wanting in good faith to Georgia. It has, by its own acts and policy, forced the Indians to remain in Georgia, by the purchase of their lands in the adjoining States, and by holding out to the Indians strong inducements to remain where they are; by the expenditure of vast sums of money, spent in changing the habits of the savage for those of civilized life. All this was in itself right and proper; it has my hearty approbation; but it should not have been done at the expense of Georgia. The Government, long after it was bound to extinguish the title of the Indians to all the lands in Georgia, has actually forced the Cherokees from their lands in other States, settled them upon Georgia lands, and aided in furnishing the means to create the Cherokee aristocracy.

Sir, I blame not the Indians; I commiserate their case. I have considerable acquaintance with the Cherokees, and amongst them I have seen much to admire. To me, they are in many respects an interesting people. If the wicked influence of designing men, veiled in the garb of philanthropy and christian benevolence, should excite the Cherokees to a course that will end in their speedy destruction, I now call upon this Congress, and the whole American people, not to charge the Georgians with this sin; but let it be remembered that it is the fruit of cant and fanaticism, emanating from the land of steady habits, from the boasted progeny of the pilgrims and puritans. . . .

Questioning Opposing Publications

In the course of the last year, the numbers [articles] over the signature of "William Penn" [Jeremiah Evarts] appeared in the *National Intelligencer,* and, although said to be written by a very pious man, deeply merged in missionary efforts, they evidently have much more of the character of the politician and lawyer than that of an humble missionary. . . .

It is the statements found in [such] pamphlets and magazines, which are relied on as truth, that have induced so many worthy people at a distance to espouse the cause of Indian sovereignty, as assumed by the Cherokees. The general condition of the Cherokees, in these publications, is represented as being quite as comfortable and prosperous—yes, sir, and as enlightened, too, as the white population in most of the states. Compare the pictures drawn by these pamphlet writers and memorialists of the concert school, in which they have painted Georgia on the one side, and the Cherokee sovereignty on the other. From these publications, not only the stranger in a foreign land but the honest laboring people of New England, who stay at home, and would mind their own business if let alone by these canting fanatics, verily believe that the Georgians are the worst of all savages; that they can neither read nor write; that they are infidels, deists, and atheists; and they never hear a gospel sermon, except from a New England missionary. Upon the other hand, they are taught to believe that the Cherokee Indians are the most prosperous, enlightened, and religious nation of people on earth—except, indeed, the nation of New England. These . . . writers are not a people who work for nothing and find themselves. No, sir, I entertain no doubt but that they are well paid for all "their labors of love" in the cause of Cherokee sovereignty.

The Cherokees receive large annuities from this Government; they have a rich treasury, and their Northern allies understand giving a saving direction to their financial disbursements. These Northern intruders are numerous and influential among the Cherokees. One religious Board to the North [American Board of Foreign Missions] (of whom "William Penn" is chief secretary) furnishes the southern tribes of Indians with upwards of twenty stationary missionaries, besides superintendents, mechanics, &c., &c., chiefly composed of our northern friends. No doubt, sir, but [Cherokee] President [John] Ross himself, with all his official subordinates, has long since found it expedient to yield the chief control of the purse and the press (which you know are said to be the strength of nations) to his more skilful and eagle-eyed friends and allies. But for these annuities, we should not have been encumbered, throughout the session, with memorials from Maine to Steubenville, in Ohio. These self-interested reporters of the state and condition of the Cherokee Indians tell you they are already a civilized and christianized people.

Abounding in the necessary comforts of domestic and agricultural life, their civil, political, and religious advancement is ostentatiously compared with the whites in some of the States; and, for

---

A Wretched Race

From 1813 to 1831, Lewis Cass was the governor of the Michigan Territory as well as the superintendent of Indian affairs for the region; during his tenure he gained a reputation as an expert on Indians. In an 1830 article in the North American Review, *Cass questions the extent of the "civilization" of the Cherokee people.*

That individuals among the Cherokees have acquired property, and with it more enlarged views and juster notions of the value of our institutions, and the unprofitableness of their own, we have little doubt. And we have as little doubt, that this change of opinion and condition is confined, in a great measure, to some of the *half-breeds* and their immediate connexions. These are not sufficiently numerous to affect our general proposition. . . .

But, we believe, the great body of the people are in a state of helpless and hopeless poverty. With the same improvidence and habitual indolence, which mark the northern Indians, they have less game for subsistence, and less peltry for sale. We doubt whether there is, upon the face of the globe, a more wretched race than the Cherokees, as well as the other southern tribes, present. . . .

We are as unwilling to underrate, as we should be to overrate, the progress made by these Indians in civilization and improvement. We are well aware, that the constitution of the Cherokees, their press, and newspaper, and alphabet, their schools and police, have sent through all our borders the glad tidings, that the long night of aboriginal ignorance was ended, and that the day of knowledge had dawned. Would that it were so. . . . That a few principal men, who can secure favorable cotton lands, and cultivate them with slaves, will be comfortable and satisfied, we may well believe. And so long as the large annuities received from the United States, are applied to the support of a newspaper and to other objects, more important to the rich than the poor, erroneous impressions upon these subjects may prevail. But to form just conceptions of the spirit and objects of these efforts, we must look at their practical operation upon the community. It is here, if the facts which have been stated to us are correct, and of which we have no doubt, that they will be found wanting.

---

proof of their statements, they refer you to their hireling letter writers, and their magazines and newspapers; and the statements drawn from these sources are relied on by a certain portion of the community, in and out of this House, in preference to any testimony, whatever may be the merit of the source from which it emanates. Now, sir, I will tell you how far these statements are to be relied upon. I have carefully and repeatedly examined all these magazine and pamphlet publications. They contain a great deal of truth, but not the whole truth, and nothing else but the truth. These publications remind me of a long exploring tour which I made to the West, near twenty years ago. On my return home, my friends and neighbors called in, to hear the news from the western country. I described to them the rich and fertile lands of the Mississippi, its bountiful productions, &c.; and before I had got through with the good things, they said, "it is enough, let us all remove to the good country."

The Whole Truth

But when I told them of the evil things, and gave them the whole truth, they changed their hasty opinions, and concluded it would be best to remain in their beloved Georgia. Sir, the application of this story is easy—every gentleman can make it for himself. But I promised to inform you how far these magazine statements were entitled to credit; but, before I begin, I will refer you to my list of witnesses. They may be found amongst the Senators and Representatives of the present Congress, from the states bordering on the Cherokee country. I could multiply testimony to bear me out in all that I have or shall say on this subject; but, in law, we consider every word established by the corroborating testimony of two or three witnesses. I admit we do find in the Cherokee country many families enjoying all the common comforts of civil and domestic life, and possessing the necessary means to secure these enjoyments. Moreover, we find a number of schools and houses built for religious worship. Many of these comfortable families, too, are composed of natives born in the Cherokee country. But the principal part of these enjoyments are confined to the blood of the white man, either in whole or in part. But few, very few of the real Indians participate largely in these blessings. A large portion of the full blooded Cherokees still remain a poor degraded race of human beings. As to the proportion that are comfortable, or otherwise, I cannot speak from my own personal knowledge with any degree of certainty; but, from what I have seen, I can readily conclude that but a very small portion of the real Indians are in a state of improvement, whilst their lords and rulers are white men, and the descendants of white men, enjoying the fat of the land, and enjoying exclusively the

Government annuities, upon which they foster, feed, and clothe the most violent and dangerous enemies of our civil institutions.

While the smallest intrusion (as it is called) by the frontier citizens of Georgia on the lands occupied by the Cherokees, excites the fiery indignation of the fanatics, from one end of the chain of concert and coalition to the other, do we not find an annual increase of intruders, from these philanthropic ranks, flocking in upon the poor Cherokees, like the caterpillars and locusts of Egypt, leaving a barren waste behind them? Yes, sir, these are the intruders who devour the substance which of right belongs to the poor perishing part of the Cherokees. They divide the spoil with the Cherokee rulers, and leave the common Indians to struggle with want and misery, without hope of bettering their condition by any change but that of joining their brethren west of the Mississippi.

Defending Georgia

The inhumanity of Georgia, so much complained of, is nothing more nor less than the extension of her laws and jurisdiction over this mingled and misguided population who are found within her acknowledged limits.

And what, I would ask, is to be found in all this, that is so very alarming? Sir, I have endeavored to tear the mask from this subject, that the character and complexion of this opposition might be seen and known. The absolute rulers of the Cherokee country, like other men, love office, distinction, and power. They are enjoying great and peculiar benefits. They do not like the idea of becoming private citizens. It is with great reluctance they yield up their stewardship. They know they have not been faithful to the interest of the poor degraded Indians. They know the great mass of their people have been left to suffer in want and ignorance, whilst they have spent their substance in forming foreign alliances with an enthusiastic, selfish, and money-loving people. These men, when incorporated into the political family of Georgia, cannot calculate on becoming at once the [leaders] of the State. And if they join the western Cherokees [a group of eight hundred Cherokee had migrated to the Arkansas River valley in 1818], they cannot carry with them their present assumed sovereignty and rule. They will there find equals in many of their pioneer brethren. The Cadmus of the Cherokees, George Guess [Sequoyah], and many others, are already there. Yes, sir, these western Cherokees are in the full enjoyment of all the blessings of their emigrating enterprise, and there is but one opinion among them as to their relative comfort and prospect of future blessings. All the various emigrants to the West so far agree as to authorize the assurance that no inducement could be offered to them strong enough to bring them back again.

The Cherokees and Creeks are charmed with their country, and to the many things which attach to their comfort in it. The New England farmers who have emigrated to the fertile valleys of the West, would as soon consent to return to the barren sand and sterile rocks of their native land, as a western Cherokee or Creek would return to the sepulchre of his forefathers.

Pages may be filled with a sublimated cant of the day, and in wailing over the departure of the Cherokees from the bones of their forefathers. But if the heads of these pretended mourners were waters, and their eyes were a fountain of tears, and they were to spend days and years in weeping over the departure of the Cherokees from Georgia, yet they will go. The tide of emigration, with the Indians as well as the whites, directs its course westwardly.

VIEWPOINT 5

"We now propose to acquire the countries occupied by the red men . . . by a fair exchange, and . . . send them to a land where their existence may be prolonged and perhaps made perpetual."

Indians Should Be Removed to the West

Andrew Jackson (1767–1845)

In the late 1820s, the clash between the Cherokee nation and the state of Georgia came to a head over the issue of who held sovereign control over Cherokee land. In 1827 the Cherokee produced a governing constitution modeled after the U.S. Constitution and claimed national sovereignty over its territory. The Georgia legislature promptly passed laws nullifying the Cherokee declaration and extending state authority over Cherokee lands, actions that violated existing treaties between the Cherokee and the federal government. Both sides looked to Washington for support.

The state of Georgia was to find an ally in Andrew Jackson, elected president in 1828. In Jackson's previous career as a military general, he had gained national fame and popularity as an Indian fighter who had forced tribes to cede millions of acres of territory in Alabama, Georgia, and Florida. The following two-part viewpoint consists of excerpts from Jackson's first and second annual messages to Congress, given on December 8, 1829, and December 6, 1830, respectively. Jackson asserts that, despite past treaties, the national government has no authority to interfere with the state of Georgia in its dealings with the Indians. The

From Andrew Jackson, First Annual Message, December 8, 1829, and Second Annual Message, December 6, 1830, in *A Compilation of the Messages and Papers of the Presidents*, vols. 2–3 (Washington, DC: 1896–97).

only viable solution, he argues, is the removal of the Indians to lands west of the Mississippi River. Congress responded to Jackson's speeches by passing the Indian Removal Act in 1830, which authorized funds for the removal of all Indian tribes still east of the Mississippi.

I

The condition and ulterior destiny of the Indian tribes within the limits of some of our States have become objects of much interest and importance. It has long been the policy of Government to introduce among them the arts of civilization, in the hope of gradually reclaiming them from a wandering life. This policy has, however, been coupled with another wholly incompatible with its success. Professing a desire to civilize and settle them, we have at the same time lost no opportunity to purchase their lands and thrust them farther into the wilderness. By this means they have not only been kept in a wandering state, but been led to look upon us as unjust and indifferent to their fate. Thus, though lavish in its expenditures upon the subject, Government has constantly defeated its own policy, and the Indians in general, receding farther and farther to the west, have retained their savage habits. A portion, however, of the Southern tribes, having mingled much with the whites and made some progress in the arts of civilized life, have lately attempted to erect an independent government within the limits of Georgia and Alabama. These States, claiming to be the only sovereigns within their territories, extended their laws over the Indians, which induced the latter to call upon the United States for protection.

The Rights of States

Under these circumstances the question presented was whether the General Government had a right to sustain those people in their pretensions. The Constitution declares that "no new State shall be formed or erected within the jurisdiction of any other State" without the consent of its legislature. If the General Government is not permitted to tolerate the erection of a confederate State within the territory of one of the members of this Union against her consent, much less could it allow a foreign and independent government to establish itself there. Georgia became a member of the Confederacy which eventuated in our Federal Union as a sovereign State, always asserting her claim to certain limits, which, having been originally defined in her colonial charter and subsequently recognized in the treaty of peace, she has ever since continued to enjoy, except as they have been circumscribed by her own voluntary transfer of a portion of her territory to the United States in the articles of cession of 1802. Alabama was admitted into the Union on the same footing with the original States, with boundaries which were prescribed by Congress. There is no constitutional, conventional, or legal provision which allows them less power over the Indians within their borders than is possessed by Maine or New York. Would the people of Maine permit the Penobscot tribe to erect an independent government within their State? And unless they did would it not be the duty of the General Government to support them in resisting such a measure? Would the people of New York permit each remnant of the Six Nations [Iroquois] within her borders to declare itself an independent people under the protection of the United States? Could the Indians establish a separate republic on each of their reservations in Ohio? And if they were so disposed would it be the duty of this Government to protect them in the attempt? If the principle involved in the obvious answer to these questions be abandoned, it will follow that the objects of this Government are reversed, and that it has become a part of its duty to aid in destroying the States which it was established to protect.

Actuated by this view of the subject, I informed the Indians inhabiting parts of Georgia and Alabama that their attempt to establish an independent government would not be countenanced by the Executive of the United States, and advised them to emigrate beyond the Mississippi or submit to the laws of those States.

Our conduct toward these people is deeply interesting to our national character. Their present condition, contrasted with what they once were, makes a most powerful appeal to our sympathies. Our ancestors found them the uncontrolled possessors of these vast regions. By persuasion and force they have been made to retire from river to river and from mountain to mountain, until some of the tribes have become extinct and others have left but remnants to preserve for a while their once terrible names. Surrounded by the whites with their arts of civilization, which by destroying the resources of the savage doom him to weakness and decay, the fate of the Mohegan, the Narragansett, and the Delaware is fast overtaking the Choctaw, the Cherokee, and the Creek. That this fate surely awaits them if they remain within the limits of the States does not admit of a doubt. Humanity and national honor demand that every effort should be made to avert so great a calamity. It is too late to inquire whether it was just in the United States to include them and their territory within the bounds of new States, whose limits they could control. That step can not be retraced. A

State can not be dismembered by Congress or restricted in the exercise of her constitutional power. But the people of those States and of every State, actuated by feelings of justice and a regard for our national honor, submit to you the interesting question whether something can not be done, consistently with the rights of the States, to preserve this much-injured race.

A Proposed Solution

As a means of effecting this end I suggest for your consideration the propriety of setting apart an ample district west of the Mississippi, and without [outside] the limits of any State or Territory now formed, to be guaranteed to the Indian tribes as long as they shall occupy it, each tribe having a distinct control over the portion designated for its use. There they may be secured in the enjoyment of governments of their own choice, subject to no other control from the United States than such as may be necessary to preserve peace on the frontier and between the several tribes. There the benevolent may endeavor to teach them the arts of civilization, and, by promoting union and harmony among them, to raise up an interesting commonwealth, destined to perpetuate the race and to attest the humanity and justice of this Government.

This emigration should be voluntary, for it would be as cruel as unjust to compel the aborigines to abandon the graves of their fathers and seek a home in a distant land. But they should be distinctly informed that if they remain within the limits of the States they must be subject to their laws. In return for their obedience as individuals they will without doubt be protected in the enjoyment of those possessions which they have improved by their industry. But it seems to me visionary to suppose that in this state of things claims can be allowed on tracts of country on which they have neither dwelt nor made improvements, merely because they have seen them from the mountain or passed them in the chase. Submitting to the laws of the States, and receiving, like other citizens, protection in their persons and property, they will ere long become merged in the mass of our population.

II

It gives me pleasure to announce to Congress that the benevolent policy of the Government, steadily pursued for nearly thirty years, in relation to the removal of the Indians beyond the white settlements is approaching to a happy consummation. Two important tribes [the Choctaws and the Chickasaws] have accepted the provision made for their removal at the last session of Congress, and it is believed that their example will induce the remaining tribes also to seek the same obvious advantages.

The consequences of a speedy removal will be important to the United States, to individual States, and to the Indians themselves. The pecuniary advantages which it promises to the Government are the least of its recommendations. It puts an end to all possible danger of collision between the authorities of the General and State Governments on account of the Indians. It will place a dense and civilized population in large tracts of country now occupied by a few savage hunters. By opening the whole territory between Tennessee on the north and Louisiana on the south to the settlement of the whites it will incalculably strengthen the southwestern frontier and render the adjacent States strong enough to repel future invasions without remote aid. It will relieve the whole State of Mississippi and the western part of Alabama of Indian

Removal Is Our Only Hope

The removal issue created division within the Cherokee nation. Some leaders believed that the intransigence of Georgia and the failure of political and legal appeals signified that removal was unavoidable if the Cherokee wished to survive as a people. Elias Boudinot, a prominent Cherokee leader, expressed his views in an 1837 pamphlet excerpted here.

What is termed the "Cherokee question" may be considered in two points of view: the controversy with the States and the General Government, and the controversy among the Cherokees themselves. The first has been agitated in so many ways, and before so many tribunals, that it is needless, for any good purpose, to remark upon it at this place. The latter is founded upon the question of a remedy, to extricate the Cherokees from their difficulties, in consequence of their conflict with the States. Upon this point, less has been said or known before the public but it has not been the less interesting to the Cherokees. It is here where different views and different feelings have been excited.

"What is to be done?" was a natural inquiry, after we found that all our efforts to obtain redress from the General Government, *on the land of our fathers*, had been of no avail. The first rupture among ourselves was the moment we presumed to answer that question. To a portion of the Cherokee people it early became evident that the interest of their countrymen and the happiness of their posterity, depended upon an entire change of policy. Instead of contending uselessly against superior power, the only course left, was, to yield to circumstances over which they had no control. . . .

In another country, and under other circumstances, there is a *better* prospect. Removal . . . is the only remedy, the only *practicable* remedy. By it there *may be* finally a renovation; our people *may* rise from their very ashes, to become prosperous and happy, and a credit to our race.

occupancy, and enable those States to advance rapidly in population, wealth, and power. It will separate the Indians from immediate contact with settlements of whites; free them from the power of the States; enable them to pursue happiness in their own way and under their own rude institutions; will retard the progress of decay, which is lessening their numbers, and perhaps cause them gradually, under the protection of the Government and through the influence of good counsels, to cast off their savage habits and become an interesting, civilized, and Christian community. These consequences, some of them so certain and the rest so probable, make the complete execution of the plan sanctioned by Congress at their last session [the 1830 Indian Removal Act] an object of much solicitude.

Toward the aborigines of the country no one can indulge a more friendly feeling than myself, or would go further in attempting to reclaim them from their wandering habits and make them a happy, prosperous people. I have endeavored to impress upon them my own solemn convictions of the duties and powers of the General Government in relation to the State authorities. For the justice of the laws passed by the States within the scope of their reserved powers they are not responsible to this Government. As individuals we may entertain and express our opinions of their acts, but as a Government we have as little right to control them as we have to prescribe laws for other nations.

With a full understanding of the subject, the Choctaw and the Chickasaw tribes have with great unanimity determined to avail themselves of the liberal offers presented by the act of Congress, and have agreed to remove beyond the Mississippi River. Treaties have been made with them, which in due season will be submitted for consideration. In negotiating these treaties they were made to understand their true condition, and they have preferred maintaining their independence in the Western forests to submitting to the laws of the States in which they now reside. These treaties, being probably the last which will ever be made with them, are characterized by great liberality on the part of the Government. They give the Indians a liberal sum in consideration of their removal, and comfortable subsistence on their arrival at their new homes. If it be their real interest to maintain a separate existence, they will there be at liberty to do so without the inconveniences and vexations to which they would unavoidably have been subject in Alabama and Mississippi.

Humanity has often wept over the fate of the aborigines of this country, and Philanthropy has been long busily employed in devising means to avert it, but its progress has never for a moment been arrested, and one by one have many powerful tribes disappeared from the earth. To follow to the tomb the last of his race and to tread on the graves of extinct nations excite melancholy reflections. But true philanthropy reconciles the mind to these vicissitudes as it does to the extinction of one generation to make room for another. In the monuments and fortresses of an unknown people, spread over the extensive regions of the West, we behold the memorials of a once powerful race, which was exterminated or has disappeared to make room for the existing savage tribes. Nor is there anything in this which, upon a comprehensive view of the general interests of the human race, is to be regretted. Philanthropy could not wish to see this continent restored to the condition in which it was found by our forefathers. What good man would prefer a country covered with forests and ranged by a few thousand savages to our extensive Republic, studded with cities, towns, and prosperous farms, embellished with all the improvements which art can devise or industry execute, occupied by more than 12,000,000 happy people, and filled with all the blessings of liberty, civilization, and religion?

A Humane Policy

The present policy of the Government is but a continuation of the same progressive change by a milder process. The tribes which occupied the countries now constituting the Eastern States were annihilated or have melted away to make room for the whites. The waves of population and civilization are rolling to the westward, and we now propose to acquire the countries occupied by the red men of the South and West by a fair exchange, and, at the expense of the United States, to send them to a land where their existence may be prolonged and perhaps made perpetual. Doubtless it will be painful to leave the graves of their fathers; but what do they more than our ancestors did or than our children are now doing? To better their condition in an unknown land our forefathers left all that was dear in earthly objects. Our children by thousands yearly leave the land of their birth to seek new homes in distant regions. Does Humanity weep at these painful separations from everything, animate and inanimate, with which the young heart has become entwined? Far from it. It is rather a source of joy that our country affords scope where our young population may range unconstrained in body or in mind, developing the power and faculties of man in their highest perfection. These remove hundreds and almost thousands of miles at their own expense, purchase the lands they occupy, and support themselves at their new homes from the moment of their arrival. Can it be cruel in this Government when, by events which it can not control, the Indian is made discontented in his ancient home to purchase his lands, to give him a new and extensive territory, to pay the expense of his removal, and support him a year in his new abode? How many thousands of our own people would gladly embrace the opportunity of removing to the West on such conditions! If the offers made to the Indians were extended to them, they would be hailed with gratitude and joy.

And is it supposed that the wandering savage has a stronger attachment to his home than the settled, civilized Christian? Is it more afflicting to him to leave the graves of his fathers than it is to our brothers and children? Rightly considered, the policy of the General Government toward the red man is not only liberal, but generous. He is unwilling to submit to the laws of the States and mingle with their population. To save him from this alternative, or perhaps utter annihilation, the General Government kindly offers him a new home, and proposes to pay the whole expense of his removal and settlement.

In the consummation of a policy originating at an early period, and steadily pursued by every Administration within the present century—so just to the States and so generous to the Indians—the Executive feels it has a right to expect the cooperation of Congress and of all good and disinterested men. The States, moreover, have a right to demand it. It was substantially a part of the compact which made them members of our Confederacy. With Georgia there is an express contract; with the new States an implied one of equal obligation. Why, in authorizing Ohio, Indiana, Illinois, Missouri, Mississippi, and Alabama to form constitutions and become separate States, did Congress include within their limits extensive tracts of Indian lands, and, in some instances, powerful Indian tribes? Was it not understood by both parties that the power of the States was to be coextensive with their limits, and that with all convenient dispatch the General Government should extinguish the Indian title and remove every obstruction to the complete jurisdiction of the State governments over the soil? Probably not one of those States would have accepted a separate existence—certainly it would never have been granted by Congress—had it been understood that they were to be confined forever to those small portions of their nominal territory the Indian title to which had at the time been extinguished.

It is, therefore, a duty which this Government owes to the new States to extinguish as soon as possible the Indian title to all lands which Congress themselves have included within their limits. When this is done the duties of the General Government in relation to the States and the Indians within their limits are at an end. The Indians may leave the State or not, as they choose. The purchase of their lands does not alter in the least their personal relations with the State government. No act of the General Government has ever been deemed necessary to give the States jurisdiction over the persons of the Indians. That they possess by virtue of their sovereign power within their own limits in as full a manner before as after the purchase of the Indian lands; nor can this Government add to or diminish it.

May we not hope, therefore, that all good citizens, and none more zealously than those who think the Indians oppressed by subjection to the laws of the States, will unite in attempting to open the eyes of those children of the forest to their true condition, and by a speedy removal to relieve them from all the evils, real or imaginary, present or prospective, with which they may be supposed to be threatened.

VIEWPOINT 6

"We wish to remain on the land of our fathers. We have a perfect and original right to remain without interruption or molestation."

Indians Should Be Allowed to Remain in Their Homeland

Cherokee Nation

During the early 1800s, the Cherokee Indians successfully adopted and combined traits of Indian and white culture to create a prosperous agricultural society with plantations, gristmills, a newspaper, and a governing constitution. In 1828, however, the state government of Georgia passed laws ordering the seizure of Indian lands and declaring all Cherokee laws void. Faced with the growing threat of forced removal from their homes, the Cherokees sent a delegation to Washington in 1830 to plead their case before President Andrew Jackson and to Congress. Finding both the president and Congress unresponsive, they published an appeal to the American people, excerpted below, pleading for the right to stay in their homeland.

The Cherokee nation and their white supporters appealed Georgia's assertion of authority over their territory in two legal cases heard by the U.S. Supreme Court. In *Worcester v. Georgia*, the second of those cases, Chief Justice John Marshall ruled in 1832 that the state of Georgia had no authority over the Cherokee nation. However, this legal decision was ignored by Georgia and President Jackson and had little practical effect. Under continual pressure from Jackson and others, in 1835 a minority faction within the Cherokee nation signed the Treaty of New Echota, ceding the

From "Memorial of the Cherokee Nation," *Nile's Weekly Register*, August 21, 1830.

Georgia lands and providing for the removal of the Cherokees to lands west of the Mississippi. In 1838 seven thousand U.S. troops forced most of the remaining Cherokees in Georgia to leave for Indian Territory, in what is now Oklahoma. (A few hundred Cherokees managed to evade the soldiers, hiding in the Great Smoky Mountains.) Of the fourteen thousand members of the Cherokee nation who embarked on the "Trail of Tears," an estimated four thousand died on the way from cold, disease, and exhaustion.

Some months ago a delegation was appointed by the constituted authorities of the Cherokee nation to repair to the city of Washington, and in behalf of this nation, to lay before the government of the United States such representations as should seem most likely to secure to us, as a people, that protection, aid, and good neighborhood, which had been so often promised to us, and of which we stand in great need. Soon after their arrival in the city they presented to congress a petition from our national council, asking for the interposition of that body in our behalf, especially with reference to the laws of Georgia; which were suspended in a most terrifying manner over a large part of our population, and protesting in the most decided terms against the operation of these laws. In the course of the winter they presented petitions to congress, signed by more than four thousand of our citizens, including probably more than nineteen-twentieths, and for aught we can tell, ninety-nine hundredths, of the adult males of the nation . . . , pleading with the assembled representatives of the American people, that the solemn engagements between their fathers and our fathers may be preserved, as they have been till recently, in full force and continued operation; asking, in a word, for protection against threatened usurpation and for a faithful execution for a guaranty which is perfectly plain in its meaning, has been repeatedly and rigidly endorsed in our favour, and has received the sanction of the government of the United States for nearly forty years.

President Jackson's Unexpected Policies

More than a year ago we were officially given to understand by the secretary of war, that the president could not protect us against the laws of Georgia. This information was entirely unexpected; as it went upon the principle, that treaties made between the United States and the Cherokee nation have no power to withstand the legislation of separate states; and of course, that they have no efficacy whatever, but leave our people to the mercy of the neighboring whites, whose supposed interests would be promoted by our expulsion, or extermination. It would be impossible to describe the sorrow, which affected our minds on learning that the chief magistrate [president] of the United States had come to this conclusion, that all his illustrious predecessors had held intercourse with us on principles which could not be sustained; that they had made promises of vital importance to us, which could not be fulfilled—promises made hundreds of times in almost every conceivable manner,—often in the form of solemn treaties, sometimes in letters written by the chief magistrate with his own hand, very often in letters written by the secretary of war under his direction, sometimes orally by the president and the secretary to our chiefs, and frequently and always, both orally and in writing by the agent of the United States residing among us, whose most important business it was, to see the guaranty of the United States faithfully executed.

Soon after the war of the revolution, as we have learned from our fathers, the Cherokees looked upon the promises of the whites with great distrust and suspicion; but the frank and magnanimous conduct of General Washington did much to allay these feelings. The perseverance of successive presidents, and especially of Mr. Jefferson, in the same course of policy, and in the constant assurance that our country should remain inviolate, except so far as we voluntarily ceded it, nearly banished anxiety in regard to encroachments from the whites. To this result the aid which we received from the United States in the attempts of our people to become civilized, and the kind efforts of benevolent societies, have greatly contributed. Of late years, however, much solicitude was occasioned among our people by the claims of Georgia. This solicitude arose from the apprehension, that by extreme importunity, threats, and other undue influence, a treaty would be made, which should cede the territory, and thus compel the inhabitants to remove. But it never occurred to us for a moment, that without any new treaty, without any assent of our rulers and people, without even a pretended compact, and against our vehement and unanimous protestations, we should be delivered over to the discretion of those, who had declared by a legislative act, that they wanted the Cherokee lands and would have them.

Appealing to Congress

Finding that relief could not be obtained from the chief magistrate, and not doubting that our claim to protection was just, we made our application to congress. During four long months our delegation waited, at the doors of the national legislature of the United States, and the people at home, in the most painful suspense, to learn in what manner our application would be answered; and, now that congress has adjourned, on the very day before the date fixed by Georgia for the extension of her oppressive laws over the greater part of our country, the distressing intelligence has been received that we have received no answer at all; and no department of the government has assured us, that we are to receive the desired protection. But just at the close of the session, an act was passed, by which an half a million of dollars was appropriated towards effecting a removal of Indians; and we have great reason to fear that the influence of this act will be brought to bear most injuriously upon us. The passage of this act was certainly understood by the representatives of Georgia as abandoning us to the oppressive and cruel measures of the state, and as sanctioning the opinion that treaties with Indians do not restrain state legislation. We are informed by those, who are competent to judge, that the recent act does not admit of such construction; but that the passage of it, under the actual circumstances of the controversy, will be considered as sanctioning the pretensions of Georgia, there is too much reason to fear.

Thus have we realized, with heavy hearts, that our supplication has not been heard; that the protection heretofore experienced is now to be withheld; that the guaranty, in consequence of which our fathers laid aside their arms and ceded the best portions of their country, means nothing; and that we must either emigrate to an unknown region and leave the pleasant land to which we have the strongest attachment, or submit to the legislation of a state, which has already made our people outlaws, and enacted that any Cherokee, who shall endeavor to prevent the selling of his country, shall be imprisoned in the penitentiary of Georgia not less than four years. To our countrymen this has been melancholy intelligence, and with the most bitter disappointment has it been received.

But in the midst of our sorrows, we do not forget our obligations to our friends and benefactors. It was with sensations of inexpressible joy that we have learned that the voice of thousands, in many parts of the United States, has been raised in our behalf, and numerous memorials offered in our favor, in both houses of congress. To those numerous friends, who have thus sympathized with us in our low estate, we tender our grateful acknowledgements. In pleading our cause, they have pleaded the cause of the poor and defenceless throughout the world. Our special thanks are due, however, to those honorable men, who so ably and eloquently asserted our rights, in both branches of the national legislature. Their efforts will be appreciated wherever the merits of this question shall be known; and we cannot but think, that they have secured for themselves a permanent reputation among the disinterested advocates of humanity, equal rights, justice, and good faith. We even cherish the hope, that these efforts, seconded and followed by others of a similar character, will yet be available, so far as to mitigate our sufferings, if not to effect our entire deliverance.

Past Treaties

Before we close this address, permit us to state what we conceive to be our relations with the United States. After the peace of 1783, the Cherokees were an independent people; absolutely so, as much as any people on earth. They had been allies to Great Britain, and as a faithful ally took a part in the colonial war on her side. They had placed themselves under her protection, and had they, without cause, declared hostility against their protector, and had the colonies been subdued, what might not have been their fate? But her power on this continent was broken. She acknowledged the independence of the United States, and made peace. The Cherokees therefore stood alone; and, in these circumstances, continued the war. They were then under no obligations to the United States any more than to Great Britain, France or Spain. The United States never subjugated the Cherokees; on the contrary, our fathers remained in possession of their country, and with arms in their hands.

The people of the United States sought a peace; and, in 1785, the treaty of Hopewell was formed, by which the Cherokees came under the protection of the United States, and submitted to such limitations of sovereignty as are mentioned in that instrument. None of these limitations, however, affected, in the slightest degree, their rights of self-government and inviolate territory. The citizens of the United States had no right of passage through the Cherokee country till the year 1791, and then only in one direction, and by an express treaty stipulation. When the federal constitution was adopted, the treaty of Hopewell was confirmed, with all other treaties, as the supreme law of the land. In 1791, the treaty of Holston was made, by which the sovereignty of the Cherokees was qualified as follows: The Cherokees acknowledged themselves to be under the protection of the United States, and of no other sovereign.—They engaged that they would not hold any treaty with a foreign power, with any separate state of the union, or with individuals. They agreed that the United States should have the exclusive right of regulating their trade; that the citizens of the United States should have a right of way in one direction through the Cherokee country; and that if an Indian should do injury to a citizen of the United States he should be delivered up to be tried and punished. A cession of lands was also made to the United States. On the other hand, the United States paid a sum of money; offered protection; engaged to punish citizens of the United States who should do any injury to the Cherokees; abandoned white settlers on Cherokee lands to the discretion of the Cherokees; stipulated that white men should not hunt on these lands, nor even enter the country without a passport; and gave a solemn guaranty of all Cherokee lands not ceded. This treaty is the basis of all subsequent compacts; and in none of them are the relations of the parties at all changed.

After their legal struggles to retain their land failed, the Cherokee were evicted from their homeland by U.S. soldiers in 1838.

The Cherokees have always fulfilled their engagements. They have never reclaimed those portions of sovereignty which they surrendered by the treaties of Hopewell and Holston. These portions were surrendered for the purpose of obtaining the guaranty which was recommended to them as the great equivalent. Had they refused to comply with their engagements, there is no doubt the United States would have enforced a compliance. Is the duty of fulfilling engagements on the other side less binding than it would be, if the Cherokees had the power of enforcing their just claims?

The people of the United States will have the fairness to reflect, that all the treaties between them and the Cherokees were made, at the solicitation, and for the benefit, of the whites; that valuable considerations were given for every stipulation, on the part of the United States; that it is impossible to reinstate the parties in their former situation, that there are now hundreds of thousands of citizens of the United States residing upon lands ceded by the Cherokees in these very treaties; and that our people have trusted their country to the guaranty of the United States. If this guaranty fails them, in what can they trust, and where can they look for protection?

We Wish to Remain

We are aware, that some persons suppose it will be for our advantage to remove beyond the Mississippi. We think otherwise. Our people universally think otherwise. Thinking that it would be fatal to their interests, they have almost to a man sent their memorial to congress, deprecating the necessity of a removal. This question was distinctly before their minds when they signed their memorial. Not an adult person can be found, who has not an opinion on the subject, and if the people were to understand distinctly, that they could be protected against the laws of the neighboring states, there is probably not an adult person in the nation, who would think it best to remove; though possibly a few might emigrate individually. There are doubtless many, who would flee to an unknown country, however beset with dangers, privations and sufferings, rather than be sentenced to spend six years in a Georgia prison for advising one of their neighbors not to betray his country. And there are others who could not think of living as outlaws in their native land, exposed to numberless vexations, and excluded from being parties or witnesses in a court of justice. It is incredible that Georgia should ever have enacted the oppressive laws to which reference is here made, unless she had supposed that something extremely terrific in its character was necessary in order to make the Cherokees willing to remove. We are not willing to remove; and if we could be brought to this extremity, it would be not by argument, not because our judgment was satisfied, not because our condition will be improved; but only because we cannot endure to be deprived of our national and individual rights and subjected to a process of intolerable oppression.

We wish to remain on the land of our fathers. We have a perfect and original right to remain without interruption or molestation. The treaties with us, and laws of the United States made in pursuance of treaties, guaranty our residence and our privileges, and secure us against intruders. Our only request is, that these treaties may be fulfilled, and these laws executed.

But if we are compelled to leave our country, we see nothing but ruin before us. The country west of the Arkansas territory is unknown to us. From what we can learn of it, we have no prepossessions in its favor. All the inviting parts of it, as we believe, are preoccupied by various Indian nations, to which it has been assigned. They would regard us as intruders, and look upon us with an evil eye. The far greater part of that region is, beyond all controversy, badly supplied with wood and water; and no Indian tribe can live as agriculturists without these articles. All our neighbors, in case of our removal, though crowded into our near vicinity, would speak a language totally different from ours, and practice different customs. The original possessors of that region are now wandering savages lurking for prey in the neighborhood. They have always been at war, and would be easily tempted to turn their arms against peaceful emigrants. Were the country to which we are urged much better than it is represented to be, and were it free from the objections which we have made to it, still it is not the land of our birth, nor of our affections. It contains neither the scenes of our childhood, nor the graves of our fathers.

The Harms of Forced Removal

The removal of families to a new country, even under the most favorable auspices, and when the spirits are sustained by pleasing visions of the future, is attended with much depression of mind and sinking of heart. This is the case, when the removal is a matter of decided preference, and when the persons concerned are in early youth or vigorous manhood. Judge, then, what must be the circumstances of a removal, when a whole community, embracing persons of all classes and every description, from the infant to the man of extreme old age, the sick, the blind, the lame, the improvident, the reckless, the desperate, as well as the prudent, the considerate, the industrious, are compelled to remove by odious and intolerable vexations and persecutions, brought upon them in the forms of law, when all will agree only in this, that they have been cruelly robbed of their country, in violation of the most solemn compacts, which it is possible for communities to form with each other; and that, if they should make themselves comfortable in their new residence, they have nothing to expect hereafter but to be the victims of a future legalized robbery!

Such we deem, and are absolutely certain, will be the feelings of the whole Cherokee people, if they are forcibly compelled, by the laws of Georgia, to remove; and with these feelings, how is it possible that we should pursue our present course of improvement, or avoid sinking into utter despondency? We have been called a poor, ignorant, and degraded people. We certainly are not rich; nor have we ever boasted of our knowledge, or our moral or intellectual elevation. But there is not a man within our limits so ignorant as not to know that he has a right to live on the land of his fathers, in the possession of his immemorial privileges, and that this right has been acknowledged and guaranteed by the United

States; nor is there a man so degraded as not to feel a keen sense of injury, on being deprived of this right and driven into exile.

An Appeal to the American People

It is under a sense of the most pungent feelings that we make this, perhaps our last appeal to the good people of the United States. It cannot be that the community we are addressing, remarkable for its intelligence and religious sensibilities, and pre-eminent for its devotion to the rights of man, will lay aside this appeal, without considering that we stand in need of its sympathy and commiseration. We know that to the Christian and to the philanthropist the voice of our multiplied sorrows and fiery trials will not appear as an idle tale. In our own land, on our own soil, and in our own dwellings, which we reared for our wives and for our little ones, when there was peace on our mountains and in our valleys, we are encountering troubles which cannot but try our very souls. But shall we, on account of these troubles, forsake our beloved country? Shall we be compelled by a civilized and Christian people, with whom we have lived in perfect peace for the last forty years, and for whom we have willingly bled in war, to bid a final adieu to our homes, our farms, our streams and our beautiful forests? No. We are still firm. We intend still to cling, with our wonted affection, to the land which gave us birth, and which, every day of our lives, brings to us new and stronger ties of attachment. We appeal to the judge of all the earth, who will finally award us justice, and to the good sense of the American people, whether we are intruders upon the land of others. Our consciences bear us witness that we are the invaders of no man's rights—we have robbed no man of his territory—we have usurped no man's authority, nor have we deprived any one of his unalienable privileges. How then shall we indirectly confess the right of another people to our land by leaving it forever? On the soil which contains the ashes of our beloved men we wish to live—on this soil we wish to die.

We intreat those to whom the foregoing paragraphs are addressed, to remember the great law of love. "Do to others as ye would that others should do to you"—Let them remember that of all nations on the earth, they are under the greatest obligation to obey this law. We pray them to remember that, for the sake of principle, their forefathers were *compelled* to leave, therefore *driven* from the old world, and that the winds of persecution wafted them over the great waters and landed them on the shores of the new world, when the Indian was the sole lord and proprietor of these extensive domains—Let them remember in what way they were received by the savage of America, when power was in his hand, and his ferocity could not be restrained by any human arm. We urge them to bear in mind, that those who would now ask of them a cup of cold water, and a spot of earth, a portion of their own patrimonial possessions, on which to live and die in peace, are the descendants of those, whose origin, as inhabitants of North America, history and tradition are alike insufficient to reveal. Let them bring to remembrance all these facts, and they *cannot*, and we are sure, they *will* not fail to remember, and sympathize with us in these our trials and sufferings.

CHAPTER 3

American Indians and the Western Frontier

Chapter Preface

The last major staging area of Indian-white military conflict was the Great Plains, a vast, mostly treeless region that stretches from the Mississippi River to the Rocky Mountains and extends into Canada in the north and Mexico in the south. An estimated 360,000 Indians lived in the Great Plains in the middle of the nineteenth century. Some plains tribes, such as the Mandan, Kansas, and Pawnee, lived in log-framed, earth-covered lodges in river valley villages and cultivated corn, squash, and beans. Also living on the Great Plains were members of the "Five Civilized Tribes," who had relocated from the eastern United States and established an agricultural lifestyle. Other tribes created nomadic hunting societies, a development spurred by the introduction of the horse to the Great Plains by the Spanish in the early 1600s. Members of these tribes lived in tepees, frequently raided their agricultural neighbors, and hunted the giant herds of buffalo that roamed the prairies. Many of the tribes, including the Apache, Cheyenne, and Sioux, were relative newcomers to the region; some had moved there from the east after being displaced by whites and other Indians. It was these nomadic tribes that would provide the greatest military resistance to the United States.

At first U.S. government policy was to treat the Great Plains region, which most Americans considered too arid for farming, as territory reserved for Indians. In the 1840s, however, the United States gained significant new possessions on the Pacific coast from Mexico and Great Britain. California became a state in 1850 in the wake of a population boom due to gold discoveries, while Oregon became a state in 1859. Concerned about creating and maintaining communication and transportation links between the new states and the rest of the nation, many Americans began to think of the intervening region not as a general living space for Indians but as part of the internal geography of the United States. Historian Irwin Unger writes:

> Until the 1850s the federal government had tried to maintain a permanent Indian frontier beyond the Mississippi. But the opening of California and Oregon to settlers soon made a shambles of this plan, and the government replaced it with the "reservation" policy. In place of a solid wall of Indian communities blocking off white settlement and passage westward, the tribes would be concentrated in compact tracts. Here, suppos-

112

edly, they would be protected from white exploiters and taught the ways of agriculture and other "civilized" arts and practices.

This policy of "concentration" evolved through treaties negotiated with various tribes. The first important treaties, including one negotiated at Fort Laramie in Wyoming in 1851, established territorial and hunting boundaries for the different tribes and obtained agreements allowing settlers to travel freely through the area. In return, the Indians received annual payments of goods and services and promises that the lands defined in the treaties would remain in their possession. Most of these treaties were soon breached, however, as railroad construction disrupted buffalo herds and as miners, ranchers, and farmers sought Indian land. In turn, many Indians attempted to maintain their nomadic hunting lifestyle, refusing to sign or subsequently ignoring treaty agreements that confined them to reservations. (Some did this out of misunderstanding, believing that the reservations only referred to the location of their villages and did not define or restrict their hunting areas.)

Some Americans asserted that the confinement of Indians to reservations was not enough; extermination was the only answer to the "Indian problem." A U.S. soldier in the 1850s noted that Indians very easily "came to be thought of as game to be shot, or a vermin to be destroyed." Such attitudes led to incidents like the 1864 Sand Creek massacre in Colorado. The 1859 discovery of gold in Colorado had led to an influx of white settlers and miners, and the federal government therefore decided to remove the resident Cheyenne Indians to reservations. Some Cheyenne bands refused to move, leading to war in 1864. On November 29, 1864, Colorado state militia led by Colonel John M. Chivington attacked a Cheyenne encampment in Sand Creek in eastern Colorado, even though the Cheyenne leader Black Kettle had agreed to make peace with the United States. "Kill and scalp all, big and little," Chivington instructed his troops. "Nits make lice." The Colorado volunteers killed 150 people, mostly women and children. Many Americans were shocked when they received news of the attack. Both Congress and the U.S. military investigated the massacre and officially condemned Chivington's actions, relieving him of his command. However, he and his troops were praised as heroes by many white residents in Colorado.

Many historians credit Sand Creek for the escalation of hostilities between the Plains Indians and white Americans throughout the region; over the next several years Indians attacked ranches, stagecoaches, telegraph lines, and forts. Two years after Sand Creek, the American public was shocked again by news of massacre—only this time, the victims were Americans. On December 21, 1866, Sioux warriors in Wyoming near Fort Phil Kearny ambushed, killed, and mutilated Captain William J. Fetterman and all eighty soldiers under his command.

The increasing bloodshed on the Great Plains, exemplified by the Sand Creek and Fetterman massacres, rekindled debate in Congress over Indian policy. Some advocated an even harder military crackdown against the Indians. "We have come to this point in the history of the country that there is no place . . . to which you can remove the Indian," argued Maine senator Lot M. Morrill, "and the precise question is: Will you exterminate him or will you fix an abiding place for him?" Others in Congress contended that hostilities between whites and Indians were caused by "the aggressions of lawless white men" and could be prevented by treating Indians more fairly. In 1867 Congress decided to create a Peace Commission of appointed military and civilian officials to determine the reasons for Indian hostilities and to make peace arrangements with the tribes. After several months of investigation, the commission concluded that Indians on the Great Plains should be concentrated on small defined reservations, where they could be taught farming, English, and Christianity. Over the next few years, new treaties were negotiated in which Indian leaders agreed to move onto reservations. This renewed effort at treaty making failed to bring peace to the Plains, however, since both Indians and whites continued to ignore or defy most of the treaties.

Almost constant fighting between whites and Indians took place from the 1860s through the 1880s, with two hundred separate armed conflicts recorded between 1869 and 1874 alone. The Indians achieved some military successes—most famously in 1876, when the entire contingent of U.S. troops under General George Armstrong Custer was killed. However, the superior numbers and technology of the U.S. military—combined with campaigns that destroyed Indian villages and food supplies and the semiplanned extermination of the wild buffalo herds that provided the tribes' food, clothing, and shelter—eventually broke down Indian resistance. By 1890, the era of military conflict between whites and Indians on the Great Plains—and throughout the entire United States—was over.

VIEWPOINT 1

"We find no honor in waging such a war [against the Indians]; . . . we cannot see anything except a blot upon our character as a people and upon the honor . . . of the United States."

The Federal Government Should Pursue Peace with the Indians

James Henderson (1810–1885)

During the nineteenth century, Native Americans of the western United States were confronted with escalating numbers of white settlers, prospectors, ranchers, and railroad workers on their traditional territories and hunting grounds. The passage of the Homestead Act in 1862, which granted 160 acres of unoccupied public land to Americans who paid a small registration fee and agreed to cultivate it for five years, greatly increased the number of settlers who poured into the Great Plains. Many encroached on lands that had been promised to American Indian tribes in peace treaties signed with the U.S. government. A number of the Plains Indian tribes responded to the white intruders with warfare. For instance, Red Cloud, a leader of the Oglala Sioux, led attacks against a chain of forts that had been established to protect a road through Sioux territory by the Powder River (in what is now the state of Montana). His forces inflicted several defeats on U.S. troops, including the killing of an entire regiment at Fort Phil Kearney in 1866. The increasingly bloody conflict in the Plains provoked debate in Congress over what measures should be taken.

The following viewpoint is taken from a speech delivered on

From James Henderson, *Congressional Globe*, 40th Cong., 1st sess., July 16, 1867.

July 16, 1867, by James Henderson, an Oregon representative in Congress from 1865 to 1867. In his speech, Henderson, a member of the congressional Committee on Indian Affairs, introduces a committee proposal to create a peace commission of military and civilian officials that would be authorized to negotiate agreements with Indians and to induce the tribes to settle on prescribed reservations. He attacks the ongoing war against the Indians in the Great Plains as being a futile and costly endeavor, and he blames the violence on white Americans' infractions of past treaties and other misdeeds.

The legislation Henderson argued for on this day was passed, with amendments, by Congress in 1867. Over the next several years, under what became known as the "Peace Policy," the Indian Peace Commission and other government officials sought to reduce corruption in the U.S. government's dealings with Indians and to make peace agreements limiting Indians to reservations. Several important new treaties were signed, including the 1868 Fort Laramie Treaty, in which the United States made concessions to Red Cloud and withdrew from the disputed forts. However, the Peace Policy ultimately failed to live up to its name, both because of treaty violations by the U.S. government and because many tribes continued to resist relocation to reservations.

I will state that at a meeting of the Committee on Indian Affairs yesterday morning, a majority, four members, being present, the other three not being in the city, this bill, with the exception of the first section, naming the commissioners, was agreed upon as the result of their deliberations. It is known to us that an Indian war is now being waged. Hostilities are of daily occurrence upon the Plains. I have in my possession a report from General Wright, who started out to survey the [railroad] line of what is called the Smoky Hill route. He says that he will be compelled to abandon the survey. The fight at Fort Wallace the other day (on the 28th of June) occurred between the escort of his party and the Cheyenne Indians; a fight in which some fifty or sixty men were engaged on each side; a fair fight in the open Plains, in which our men got whipped. He says that the Indians are better mounted than our men; that it is idle to talk about making a survey through that section of country under present circumstances; that they are just as well armed as our men; that they have carbines and ammunitions equal to ours; that they fight with as much spirit as our men; that they are decidedly better mounted, as I have said; and a very great advantage they have is that they are better horsemen and their horses are better trained; and another great advantage which he suggests is that they use the bow and arrow, which our men cannot use, and in close conflict he says it is superior as a weapon for horsemen, far superior to the carbine.

Now we are attempting to construct across the Plains two railroads. With these facts before us it is useless to pretend that these railroads can be constructed. General [William T.] Sherman in his report says that fifty of these Indians can checkmate three thousand of our soldiers. It is unnecessary for me to go into the history of this Indian war—I have the notes of it before me—because there are but two tribes of any great extent that are engaged in hostilities against the United States; I mean the Sioux or Dakota Indians, as they are sometimes called, and the Cheyennes and Arapahoes united together.

It is useless for me to say who is in fault. I shall not pretend to enter into that discussion, for the reason that it will not facilitate the passage of this measure or any other measure to bring about peace. We know the fact that unless these hostilities are suppressed, and suddenly suppressed, a very large expenditure will be forced upon us. Our treasury is in no condition to meet it. We need to husband our resources, and if we can make peace with the Indians we had better do it. This war, if it lasts during the summer and fall, will cost us $100,000,000. I know that Senators will hear this statement with some degree of unbelief; but I state what I believe, and what will occur in point of fact in a very short time, and all Senators will be satisfied that what I say is correct. We are expending from $125,000 to $250,000, perhaps, daily in this war, and these expenditures will be rapidly increased from day to day, because our friends here from the [frontier] border now will offer an amendment to this bill—whether the Senate will adopt it or not I cannot say—providing for calling out a large number of volunteers for additional protection, such protection as they say the regular Army cannot give. They want border men called out, men who understand Indian character and understand best how to fight them. How many regiments will be called out? Perhaps four, five, six, seven, or eight regiments. If four regiments are called out, it will be but a short time until General Sherman will be compelled to call out others, and the State authorities will be compelled to offer to General Sherman or other commanders other volunteers in order to protect the frontiers. The war is but begun, and it will increase, and alarmingly increase, in its proportions of atrocity and also in its proportions of public debt. Now, it behooves the Congress of the United States in session to do something, if we possibly can, to put an end to it.

Now, what is the proposition before us? It is very plain and simple. I propose that a joint commission of military men, who have been engaged in this war, and who understand the condition of affairs, and certain eminent civilians, to whom I shall propose to add the Commissioner of Indian Affairs, be appointed; and that that commission shall undertake, if possible, to make peace. Here are the Cheyennes at war against us. Why? We made a treaty with the Cheyennes in 1851, after the discovery of the gold mines in California, in which they obligated themselves to let our emigrants pass over their lands. It will be remembered that the Cheyennes once owned all the mines of Colorado, even up to 1851. Under the treaty of 1825 we did not pretend to say that we had any rights there. Under the treaty of 1825 we said the Cheyennes and the Arapahoes owned that whole country, and with no right for a white man to pass across it at all. Did our emigrants to California ever meet with obstructions that amounted to anything from the Cheyennes and Arapahoes? Surely not. That thing lasted until 1861, when we made a treaty with these Indians, giving up the entire Territory of Colorado, all the rich mines of Colorado, and confining them to a very small reservation on the Arkansas river. In 1865 we asked them still further to go out of our way. Why? Because then we had concluded to build a railroad to California, and we insisted that they should go south of the Arkansas river, and we made a treaty with them which is now upon your statute-book. What was it? It proposed to give them a reservation, part of which was in Kansas, two thirds or three fourths of it in Kansas, and the rest of it belonged to other Indian tribes; but we said they should remain where they were on this small reservation on the north side of the Arkansas river until we secured the title to that country. When the treaty was under consideration a Senator from Kansas rose and moved an amendment. What was that? He said no part of the State of Kansas should be taken for this reservation except with the consent of the State of Kansas, and the President should find other quarters for these Indians. We have failed, so far, to procure the consent of the other Indian tribes owning the rest of the reservation, and it turns out that we have no home for the Cheyennes and Arapahoes at all, and now we propose to kill them. Why? Because they are standing in the way of a railroad to California. The Cheyennes and Arapahoes say, "Gentlemen, we have given you up the entire Territory of Colorado; we have given you up all our land there except a small reservation, and now you propose to build a railroad through it without our consent, and we tell you we intend to resist it." That is the whole case of the Cheyennes. General Sherman found them in the way, and they commenced their fight when we proposed to survey a line through there. General Sherman then said it was necessary to send them south of the Arkansas and to clean the line of these two roads; all the country between the Platte and the Arkansas, he said, must be cleaned of Indians, and if they remained there they must be looked upon as in hostility to the United States. We grumble and complain that the Cheyennes fight. I apprehend that if they were white men under these circumstances they would fight. I apprehend that if any of us here were in their situation we would fight. I am not justifying the Indians in their barbarity; but we, in the treaty, said they shall stay where they are until the President finds other quarters for them. He has been unable to do so: he has not got the consent of the State of Kansas to their being located in that State; and we have made no arrangements with the other Indian tribes who own a part of the reservation for purchasing out their title, and there is no place for these Indians to go.

The Sioux

Now, in regard to the Sioux Indians: in 1825 we made a treaty with them. That, I suppose, is superseded, and it is unnecessary for me now to refer to it. In 1851 the celebrated confederate treaty with all the Indian tribes there was made at Fort Laramie. The Sioux entered into that, the Cheyennes, the Assiniboines, the Crows, and others. I have a map before me to which I could refer gentlemen if I desired to do so, but it is unnecessary. That map includes all the territory arranged by the treaty at Fort Laramie up to Montana Territory, and including Montana Territory. They divided out the country; the Cheyennes took their share of it, taking Colorado Territory, running away down to the mouth of the South Platte and down to the Arkansas river; and the Sioux took the country lying north of Fort Laramie, and what is called the Powder river country, where we have now built the forts, Reno, Phil. Kearney, and C.F. Smith. Under that treaty we got along very well, and lived in peace with the Sioux Indians. That treaty was made by General D.D. Mitchell, of St. Louis, and the Indians respected it, and we had no trouble from that time on.

The treaty of Fort Laramie acknowledged on our part their ownership of the entire country with our right to pass to California. We did not reserve any right to pass to Montana then, because the mines of Montana had not been discovered; but the mines of California had been discovered, and we required of the Sioux Indians, the Ogallallas, and the Brulés that we should have the right to pass over their country by the South Pass on the way to California, and that our emigrants should be undisturbed. From 1851, the date of that treaty, up to 1861, I believe I may defy anybody to refer to an outrage committed by these hostile Sioux of Fort Laramie upon any of the emigrants of our country. I do not remember such an occurrence; but I do remember the fact that emigrants from the south of Missouri passed out from year to year in parties of two, three, four, and five, and, in fact, solitary and alone to California, and I never heard any fear of Indian depredations expressed by anybody.

In that treaty of 1851 we acknowledged the entire right of the Sioux to the country they claimed, with the exception of a right reserved to our citizens to pass to California. We claimed no right to go to Montana then, because nobody supposed a white man would want to go to Montana. No mines had been discovered there; the riches of that country had not been developed. We did not suppose we should ever want the Powder river country. We were to give the Sioux $50,000 per annum for fifty years for this right to pass through their country to California. When the treaty came to the Senate, the Senate amended it, reducing the time to ten years, but leaving the amount at $50,000 per annum, with a right in the President to continue the payment for five years longer if he should see fit. We commenced paying $50,000 a year in 1851, and kept it up to 1861. Mr. Lincoln extended the time for five years under the amendment to the treaty, and continued the payment up to 1866. Up to that time we had scarcely any difficulty. Perhaps there may have been murders, as there are murders almost daily in the various States of the Union. Murders and outrages are committed in various sections of the country. Perhaps there are some bad Indians as well as bad white men. They did commit some depredations, but there was nothing like general war in that section of the country. In 1866, then, under the amendment to the treaty of 1851, the time expired, and now what is our condition with the Sioux Indians? General [John] Pope at St. Louis issued an order in 1866, after the expiration of our treaty with these Indians. I do not mean to reflect on our military men, and I have the highest respect for General Pope; but I must call attention to this order. It was to establish three forts upon the Powder river route to Montana. Why? Because people wanted to go there and mine. He then went to work to establish the three forts called Fort Reno, Fort Phil. Kearney, and Fort C.F. Smith. He did that under military order, and there is our difficulty. . . .

I hold in my hand the letter of the agent of these Indians to the Department here, saying that if we undertook to establish these forts we must fight the Sioux; they were unwilling to submit to it. But after that order was issued, and after the difficulty came to pass, General Pope issues his order and goes to work to build the forts. . . . He acted of course from the very best intentions. His idea was to give facility to emigrants and miners to cross this territory. Of course the order was demanded by the people of the State of Missouri. I do not doubt it; and nine tenths of the people of my State in all probability sympathize with General Pope in it.

I perhaps stand almost alone. I know what the feeling is in the western States on this subject. . . .

[In] the treaty of 1851, . . . the Indians said we might pass west of the mountains there instead of east, but that by going to the eastern side of the mountains, passing over the valleys of the Powder river, we should interfere with the only game that they had left; that they had no other country upon which the buffalo could feed and subsist them there. If we would go to the west of the Big Horn mountains they would not object to our making a road up there, but they objected to the construction of a road and the building of forts on the eastern side of the mountains. They even said that they would not object to the building and garrisoning of the fort at Fort Reno, but further up than that they objected to our going, because there Powder river became a good large stream, and the bottoms upon it were large and the grass could grow. I understand that blue-grass grows there in large quantities. It is a good grazing country. They said that if we would turn off to the west and go to the west of the Big Horn mountains, through Fort Reno, we were welcome to march through their country there to that extent, but no further. That is some ninety miles north of the Platte river. Fort Phil. Kearney is, I understand, some two hundred miles north of the Platte river; and ninety miles further on is the Fort C.F. Smith on the route to Montana. . . .

General Sherman's Reaction

When this war came, and the massacre of Fort Phil. Kearney occurred, General Sherman, of course, was exasperated by this conduct; and he sent a telegram here which the Indians have full knowledge of now, which I will read. I have the greatest respect for General Sherman, but this was a sad mistake on his part. No greater mistake could possibly have been committed: We undertook to construct forts in that country in which we had no right. Gentlemen may say that the savage must give way to civilization. Surely so; but then we ought to make the savage give way to civilization in such a manner as that we shall show a decent respect for ourselves and something like a regard for our own honor. Civilization ought to be civil. We have treaty stipulations with them, in which we say that they are entitled to a particular country; but we discover a gold mine beyond there, and then we break that treaty stipulation by having a military order to erect forts upon it to protect the settlers. Now we know, as a matter of fact, that not a mortal has traveled over that route to Montana for the last twelve months except a soldier; and scarcely a soldier has traveled over it since the Fort Phil. Kearney massacre. I know of not a single soldier who has traversed the Powder river country from the time of that massacre in December last down to the present time. It will not be done; and let me tell you that if fifty of these Indians can checkmate three thousand of our best cavalry it will be a long time before there will be any travel over it.

When this war came, instead of going back to the root of the evil, and correcting our wrongs to the Indians, General Sherman, feeling of course as any other man would feel, stung and nettled by these reverses of our arms, and by the fact that so many good men had been killed, and perhaps not understanding our treaty stipulations—in fact I know he did not—because in another letter he calls General [U.S.] Grant's attention to that, and asks him to see the Interior Department and have the matter examined so as to know exactly what are our rights, and what the rights of the Indians, and when ascertained that he desired to stand by the rights of the Indians—but nettled, as I say, on the 28th of December last he sent this telegram here, which has been communicated to the Sioux, and which they understand quite well:

St. Louis,
December 28, 1866.

GENERAL: Just arrived in time to attend the funeral of my adjutant general, Sawyer. I have given general instructions to General Cooke about the Sioux. I do not yet understand how the massacre of Colonel Fetterman's party could have been so complete. We must act with vindictive earnestness against the Sioux, even to their extermination, men, women, and children. Nothing else will reach the root of this case.

W.T. SHERMAN,
Lieutenant General.

U.S. GRANT.

You will find that in this war of extermination twenty-five of our own men will fall for every man, woman, or child of the Sioux. Mark what I tell you. General Sherman himself is now satisfied of it. But suppose we do exterminate them all; suppose that stung to the quick by these reverses and by this attempt of a barbarous band of people to wage war against the United States with all their fiendish malignity we go to war and kill them all, what does it amount to? Is it any honor to the people of the United States? What amount of credit do we gain by it? Is there any glory in a war of that sort? None whatever.

Then, sir, what is the proposition of the committee? I come to it at once, for I do not desire to take up the time of the Senate. We find a war waging and we want to get rid of it. We find no honor in waging such a war; we cannot see any laurels to be won; we cannot see anything except a blot upon our character as a people and upon the honor and good faith of the United States and a large accumulation of our public debt. That is all I can see in it.

We might as well be honest, plain, blunt, and frank about this whole matter. We shall have thousands of our soldiers killed there, and all for glory. That is, an Indian has scalped somebody, and we must wage a perpetual war in order to avenge the wrong!

Mr. President, I am not here to justify the Indians. I am only here for the purpose of standing up to our own treaty obligations, and in my opinion when we do that we shall have less trouble with the Indians. We may have some trouble to be sure; but we shall have trouble with the negroes of the South, we shall have trouble with the white people of the South. Are not murders being committed in Texas? Certainly. Murders in North Carolina? Yes. Even in the fine old State of Massachusetts and in the very intelligent and great Empire State, New York, we find murders committed. Because a Sioux Indian commits a murder, because he steals a horse, (a light accomplishment that perhaps he has learned from the white man,) are you to wage war against an entire tribe? It will only inflict dishonor upon ourselves and accumulate our public debt.

Now, what is this proposition? It is to do something with these Indians; and what is that? To remove them off the line of these

Report of the Indian Peace Commission

The Indian Peace Commission established by Congress in 1867 released a report in 1868 in which the commission argued that peace could be preserved if white settlers and railroad employees would treat Indians more fairly.

The white and Indian must mingle together and jointly occupy the country, or one of them must abandon it. If they could have lived together, the Indian by this contact would soon have become civilized and war would have been impossible. . . . What prevented their living together? First. The antipathy of race. Second. The difference of customs and manners arising from their tribal or clannish organization. Third. The difference in language, which, in a great measure, barred intercourse and a proper understanding each of the other's motives and intentions.

Now by educating the children of these tribes in the English language these differences would have disappeared, and civilization would have followed at once. Nothing then would have been left but the antipathy of race, and that too is always softened in the beams of a higher civilization. . . .

To maintain peace with the Indian, let the frontier settler treat him with humanity, and railroad directors see to it that he is not shot down by employees in wanton cruelty. In short, if settlers and railroad men will treat Indians as they would treat whites under similar circumstances, we apprehend but little trouble will exist.

two railroads, the Platte road and the Smoky Hill road. We want to get them south of the Arkansas river and north of the Platte river, and bind them by treaty stipulations not to go upon the line of these roads. I do not propose even to close up the Powder river route, but to leave it open. The people of my State want it left open because it is the nearest and best route to Montana. I do not ask that it shall be closed, but I ask that a section of country be obtained for these Indians along the Missouri river, and that will enable us to furnish goods, annuities, &c., which we annually furnish to them under treaty stipulations, cheaper than in any other way. As it is now the Indians are scattered over an immense district of country. . . .

Protecting Routes of Travel

If we intend that the military shall operate against the Indians in time to come, let us put them in stated reservations, where forts can be built around them, so that so large a force will not be required to take care of them and watch them. Our proposition is to take the various Indians that are out in that section of country and bring them to a "district of country lying north of the State of Nebraska, west of the Missouri river, and east of the traveled routes to Montana Territory." That will leave the Powder river route entirely in our possession. I may be asked if I propose to select an immense district of country lying on the borders of the Little Missouri, the Yellowstone, the White Earth, and the Cheyenne rivers and leave it to the Indians for all time to come. I answer that I would do so for the present. We have got to do something with the Indians, and, the way the matter now stands, perhaps another thousand millions of debt will be added to our present heavy burden in that shape in order to exterminate them. They are now upon the lines of travel, and we have got to select some country to put them upon. . . .

If this thing is done, in the course of a few years we can get the entire body of Indians of the Northwest off from the lines of travel, the Pacific railway, the Powder river route, and various other routes of travel, and can confine them upon this district of country where they can be supplied more cheaply than in any other district of country that I know of with their goods; and if it be necessary hereafter to use the military, they will be confined within narrower bounds, where it will not require three thousand of our best cavalry to checkmate fifty wild Indians. . . .

[The proposed legislation] is an honest effort, as we conceive, on the part of the committee to get rid of this Indian war, a war that gives us no character at home or abroad; one that involves us in calamities and miseries; one that will cause the death of many of our soldiers; one which has already caused the desertion of numbers from the service, because it is the hardest service soldiers ever did, and which, in the end, must saddle us with large, increased debt. We are not particular about the shape of the bill at all. We only desire that some earnest effort be made on the part of civilians and of our military men who have been engaged in this war, and who understand perhaps by this time the Indian character, to do something toward that State of peace which existed from 1851 up to 1865.

"There is no such thing as peace except by war."

The Federal Government Must Wage War on the Indians

Samuel J. Crawford (1835–1913)

Samuel J. Crawford was governor of the state of Kansas from 1865 to 1868. During this time period, Kansas—which had just become a state in 1861—was experiencing rapid growth, including railroad construction and increased settlement. These developments resulted in heightened hostilities between settlers and the Indians of the region. The following viewpoint is taken from Crawford's June 29, 1867, letter to Edmund G. Ross, a Kansas senator. Asserting that the Indian tribes have "declared war," Crawford calls for the U.S. government to make a concerted military effort to defeat them. He criticizes the practice of paying Indians various goods (due to them under past treaties negotiated between the Indians and the federal government), arguing that the Indians use these supplies to aid them in their attacks against American citizens. The appointment of peace commissioners will not succeed in ending conflict in the Great Plains, Crawford contends, because the Indians will respond only to military force.

Dear Sir: Our Indian troubles are growing worse every day.

On Wednesday last a band of Kiowas attacked and captured a train between Harker and Larned, killing and scalping eleven of

From Samuel J. Crawford, *Congressional Globe*, 40th Cong., 1st sess., June 29, 1867.

the teamsters, (mostly Mexicans,) burning the wagons, and driving off the stock.

On Thursday they made another attack on the railroad men fifteen miles west of Harker, killing one engineer and mortally wounding an employé. This almost entirely stops the work on the road. . . .

It may be possible that during the present week we shall not suffer as we have during the past three or four months, since the same tribes which have been perpetrating these outrages are required to meet Colonel [Henry] Leavenworth, agent for the Comanches and Kiowas, and Major Wynkoop, agent for the Apaches, Arapahoes, and Cheyennes, at or near Salt Plains, in the southern part of this State, there to receive one hundred and sixty thousand pounds of annuity goods; which were shipped from Atchison last week, and will reach their destination and be distributed to the murderers within the next ten days. As soon as they receive these supplies from the Government they will, without the least shadow of doubt, return to their fields of operation, which are already stained from one end to the other with the blood of our own citizens, and which contain in Kansas alone the fresh graves of more than five hundred men, women, and children, victims of these "noble red men."

This state of affairs cannot be tolerated any longer. General [William T.] Sherman and other United States officers are willing to do all in their power to suppress further depredations, but they have not a sufficient force with which to operate.

They Have Declared War

The Indians, from Minnesota to Texas, have declared war. They have formed themselves into one powerful confederate band or army, and are moving with concert of action from one end of the line to the other.

Since the 1st day of July 1866, more than five hundred persons, to whom the Government of the United States guaranteed protection, have been killed, scalped, and their bodies most shamefully mutilated by the same Indians who are now receiving aid and comfort from the Government.

With the aid they are receiving this year they will be able to prosecute the war more vigorously than ever; while if their annuities were stopped, former treaties declared void, and a vigorous effort made, they could soon be reduced to a state of suffering and compelled to sue for peace.

Then if the Government would send them to the Indian territory south of Kansas, give each twenty acres of land, invest one twentieth part of the money that is now being foolishly expended for annuities in school-houses, farming implements, &c., for their use, and compel them to remain at home, we should have no further trouble.

But before this can be done, they will have to be reduced to actual want, and made to feel and fear the power of the Government.

They have a powerful army in the field, well organized, armed, and equipped.

They mean war, and the Government of the United States can meet them in no other way than by organizing an army and moving against them in force.

Congress might, with equal propriety and justice, have forwarded a train of supplies and munitions of war to the rebel army after the [Civil War] battle of Bull Run, and upon that demanded or expected their surrender, as to demand or expect the hostile Indians to stop the war by giving them annuities.

There is no such thing as peace except by war, and the sooner you convince Congress of this the better it will be for the country.

Those Who Want to Prevent War

It is to the pecuniary interests of Indian agents, traders, and contractors to prevent a war as long as possible, and, in my opinion, some of them representing wild tribes, rather than lose their position, would misrepresent the true state of affairs at whatever cost or sacrifice of life.

Most of them, if not all, represent their Indians as being at home quiet and peaceable, when in fact they know that every Indian belonging to their respective tribes (I mean those at war) is now and has been for months past murdering and scalping citizens whenever and wherever they could be found, either alone or in parties sufficiently small to be overpowered without the Indians incurring too much danger to themselves. Nine of them came into a small settlement a few days since on the frontier, west of Lake Sibley, murdered and scalped two men and one boy, and wounded another boy, who made his escape. They then took two women prisoners, upon one of whom each of the nine committed a fiendish outrage, and afterward, while she was lying in a helpless condition, plunged a tomahawk into her head and left her dead on the ground, and in this condition she was subsequently found by the citizens. The other woman they took with them as a prisoner, to suffer, if possible, even a worse fate.

I have represented the condition of affairs to the Secretary of War, who from some cause has taken no action.

I have appealed to Sherman, but he cannot engage in a war without troops or authority, so the whole subject rests with Congress, either to declare all former treaties with hostile tribes void by act of war on their part, declare war against them, and furnish

Sherman with a volunteer force sufficient to enable him to take the offensive, or send out peace commissioners, who will doubtless guaranty additional protection to the Indians, assure them that their conduct has been entirely satisfactory to the Government, and that their supply of annuity goods shall be largely increased in the future. I judge of the future by the past. If peace commissioners are sent out it is equivalent to saying to the Indians, "Go on with the war and we will pay you a premium for all you do:" or, in other words, "we will pay you a reward for the scalps you take." In the name of God and humanity, I do earnestly protest against such a policy.

National Archives

As head of the U.S. Army Division of the Missouri from 1869 to 1883, General Philip Sheridan was in charge of U.S. military campaigns against the American Indians. In 1869, while visiting Fort Cobb in Indian Territory, the former Civil War hero was approached by Tochoway, a Comanche chief, who introduced himself as a "good Indian." Sheridan's reply became famous: "The only good Indians I ever saw were dead."

I hope that the false impressions which exist in the minds of many persons East in regard to the character and disposition of the Indian will not prevent members of Congress from discharging their whole duty fearlessly.

The Duty of Government

If those who believe that the Indian embodies in his nature everything that is noble and great could see their friends butchered and mangled as we of the West have seen ours, the probability is they would change their opinions. But whether they do or not is a matter of indifference to me, and I trust it will also be to Congress, which in fact is responsible for these atrocities. I could within a short time complete the organization of a militia force, composed of experienced officers and soldiers, and move against the Indians in Western Kansas. But in doing this I would necessarily be compelled to violate the law (if treaties are valid) which I have no disposition to do if it can possibly be avoided; besides, it is the duty of the Government to protect her citizens. If Congress fails to make provision for protecting our citizens and those quietly traveling through the State then there is but one course for me to pursue.

I cannot and will not allow a band of irresponsible, uncivilized, bloody-thirsty fiends to invade the State, murder our citizens, stop the work on our most important railroads, and completely blockade the routes of travel to other States and Territories. This is asking a little too much, even though we have humanitarians in the country who may think it better to suffer a hundred or more of our people to be murdered and scalped than to sacrifice the life of one Indian.

I have submitted until forbearance has ceased to be a virtue.

If Congress will adopt prompt and decisive measures to bring this war to an end, or rather commence the war, I will render the Government all the assistance in my power. I will furnish troops, as many as may be desired. But if Congress fails to take action, I shall be compelled to declare all the Indians in Western Kansas invaders, outlaws, murderers, and highway robbers, and proceed against them with such force as may be necessary to bring them to justice or drive them from the State.

"Nature intended him for a savage state; every instinct, every impulse of his soul inclines him to it. . . . He cannot be himself and be civilized; he fades away and dies."

Indians Are Cruel and Unchangeable Savages

George Armstrong Custer (1839–1876)

George Armstrong Custer was a cavalry commander whose exploits in the Civil War—which were described in the *New York Times*, *Harper's Weekly*, and other publications—gained him a promotion to brevet brigadier general at age twenty-three. Although his rank reverted to captain following the Civil War (he later was promoted to lieutenant colonel), "General" Custer went on to become a nationally known Indian fighter. Ironically, Custer achieved his greatest fame for the Battle of Little Bighorn on June 25, 1876, in which he and all the soldiers under his command perished while fighting a large encampment of Sioux and Cheyenne Indians.

Prior to Little Bighorn, Custer wrote a series of articles for *Galaxy*, a popular magazine. The articles were later published in 1874 as the book *My Life on the Plains*, from which this viewpoint is excerpted. The character of Indians, Custer argues, has been romanticized by writers such as James Fenimore Cooper and by well-meaning reformers and philanthropists who believe that Indians can be "civilized." Efforts to civilize American Indians are doomed to failure, Custer maintains.

From George Armstrong Custer, *My Life on the Plains; or, Personal Experiences with Indians* (New York: Sheldon, 1874).

If the character given to the Indian by [James Fenimore] Cooper and other novelists, as well as by well-meaning but mistaken philanthropists of a later day, were the true one; if the Indian were the innocent, simple-minded being he is represented, more the creature of romance than reality, imbued only with a deep veneration for the works of nature, freed from the passions and vices which must accompany a savage nature; if, in other words, he possessed all the virtues which his admirers and works of fiction ascribe to him and were free from all the vices which those best qualified to judge assign to him, he would be just the character to complete the picture which is presented by the country embracing the Wichita Mountains. Cooper, to whose writings more than to those of any other author are the people speaking the English language indebted for a false and ill-judged estimate of the Indian character, might well have laid the scenes of his fictitious stories in this beautiful and romantic country.

The Character of the Indian

It is to be regretted that the character of the Indian as described in Cooper's interesting novels is not the true one. But as, in emerging from childhood into the years of a maturer age, we are often compelled to cast aside many of our earlier illusions and replace them by beliefs less inviting but more real, so we, as a people, with opportunities enlarged and facilities for obtaining knowledge increased, have been forced by a multiplicity of causes to study and endeavor to comprehend thoroughly the character of the red man. So intimately has he become associated with the government as ward of the nation, and so prominent a place among the questions of national policy does the much mooted "Indian question" occupy, that it behooves us no longer to study this problem from works of fiction, but to deal with it as it exists in reality. Stripped of the beautiful romance with which we have been so long willing to envelope him, transferred from the inviting pages of the novelist to the localities where we are compelled to meet with him, in his native village, on the war path, and when raiding upon our frontier settlements and lines of travel, the Indian forfeits his claim to the appellation of the "*noble* red man." We see him as he is, and, so far as all knowledge goes, as he ever has been, a *savage* in every sense of the word; not worse, perhaps, than his white brother would be similarly born and bred, but one whose cruel and ferocious nature far exceeds that of any wild beast of the desert. That this is true no one who had been brought into intimate contact with the wild tribes will deny. Perhaps there are some who, as members of peace commissions or as wandering agents of some benevolent society, may have visited these tribes or attended with them at councils held for some pacific purpose, and who, by passing through the villages of the Indian while *at peace*, may imagine their opportunities for judging of the Indian nature all that could be desired. But the Indian, while he can seldom be accused of indulging in a great variety of wardrobe, can be said to have character capable of adapting itself to almost every occasion. He has one character, perhaps his most serviceable one, which he preserves carefully, and only airs it when making his appeal to the government or its agents for arms, ammunition, and license to employ them. This character is invariably paraded, and often with telling effect, when the motive is a peaceful one. Prominent chiefs invited to visit Washington invariably don this character, and in their "talks" with the "Great Father" and other less prominent personages they successfully contrive to exhibit but this one phase. Seeing them under these or similar circumstances only, it is not surprising that by many the Indian is looked upon as a simple-minded "son of nature," desiring nothing beyond the privilege of roaming and hunting over the vast unsettled wilds of the West, inheriting and asserting but few native rights, and never trespassing upon the rights of others. This view is equally erroneous with that which regards the Indian as a creature possessing the human form but divested of all other attributes of humanity, and whose traits of character, habits, modes of life, disposition, and savage customs disqualify him from the exercise of all rights and privileges, even those pertaining to life itself.

Taking him as we find him, at peace or at war, at home or abroad, waiving all prejudices, and laying aside all partiality, we will discover in the Indian a subject for thoughtful study and investigation. In him we will find the representative of a race whose origin is, and promises to be, a subject forever wrapped in mystery; a race incapable of being judged by the rules or laws applicable to any other known race of men; one between which and civilization there seems to have existed from time immemorial a determined and unceasing warfare—a hostility so deep-seated and inbred with the Indian character that in the exceptional instances where the modes and habits of civilization have been reluctantly adopted, it has been at the sacrifice of power and influence as a tribe and the more serious loss of health, vigor, and courage as individuals. . . .

Why It Is Impossible to Civilize the Indian

Inseparable from the Indian character, wherever he is to be met with, is his remarkable taciturnity, his deep dissimulation, the perseverance with which he follows his plans of revenge or conquest, his concealment and apparent lack of curiosity, his stoical courage when in the power of his enemies, his cunning, his caution, and last, but not least, the wonderful power and subtlety of his senses. . . . In studying the Indian character, while shocked and disgusted by many of his traits and customs, I find much to be admired and still more of deep and unvarying interest. To me, Indian life, with its attendant ceremonies, mysteries, and forms, is a book of unceasing interest. Grant that some of its pages are frightful and, if possible, to be avoided, yet the attraction is none the weaker. Study him, fight him, civilize him if you can, he remains still the object of your curiosity, a type of man peculiar and undefined, subjecting himself to no known law of civilization, contending determinedly against all efforts to win him from his chosen mode of life. He stands in the group of nations solitary and reserved, seeking alliance with none, mistrusting and opposing the advances of all. Civilization may and should do much for him, but it can never civilize him. A few instances to the contrary may be quoted, but these are susceptible of explanation. No tribe enjoying its accustomed freedom has ever been induced to adopt

These People Must Die Out

Horace Greeley, editor of the New York Tribune, *was a noted social reformer who supported the abolition of slavery, universal suffrage, and other liberal causes. However, as is shown in this passage from his travel diary,* An Overland Journey, from New York to San Francisco in the Summer of 1859, *his opinion of American Indians was similar to Custer's.*

I have learned to appreciate better than hitherto, and to make more allowance for, the dislike, aversion, contempt, wherewith Indians are usually regarded by their white neighbors, and have been since the days of the Puritans. It needs but little familiarity with the actual, palpable aborigines to convince any one that the poetic Indian—the Indian of [James Fenimore] Cooper and [Henry Wadsworth] Longfellow—is only visible to the poet's eye. To the prosaic observer, the average Indian of the woods and prairies is a being who does little credit to human nature—a slave of appetite and sloth, never emancipated from the tyranny of one animal passion save by the more ravenous demands of another. As I passed over . . . the reservations of the Delawares, Potawatamies, etc., constituting the very best corn-lands on earth, and saw their owners sitting around the doors of their lodges at the height of the planting season and in as good, bright planting weather as sun and soil ever made, I could not help saying, "These people must die out—there is no help for them. God has given this earth to those who will subdue and cultivate it, and it is vain to struggle against His righteous decree."

a civilized mode of life or, as they express it, to follow the white man's road. At various times certain tribes have forsaken the pleasures of the chase and the excitement of the warpath for the more quiet life to be found on the "reservation." Was this course adopted voluntarily and from preference? Was it because the Indian chose the ways of his white brother rather than those in which he had been born and bred?

In no single instance has this been true. What then, it may be asked, have been the reasons which influenced certain tribes to abandon their predatory, nomadic life, and today to influence others to pursue a similar course? The answer is clear, and as undeniable as it is clear. The gradual and steady decrease in numbers, strength, and influence, occasioned by wars both with other tribes and with the white man, as well as losses brought about by diseases partly attributable to contact with civilization, have so lowered the standing and diminished the available fighting force of the tribe as to render it unable to cope with the more powerful neighboring tribes with any prospect of success. The stronger tribes always assume an overbearing and dominant manner toward their weaker neighbors, forcing them to join in costly and bloody wars or themselves to be considered enemies. When a tribe falls from the position of a leading one, it is at the mercy of every tribe that chooses to make war, being forced to take sides, and at the termination of the war is generally sacrificed to the interests of the more powerful. To avoid these sacrifices, to avail itself of the protection of civilization and its armed forces, to escape from the ruining influences of its more warlike and powerful neighbors, it reluctantly accepts the situation, gives up its accustomed haunts, its wild mode of life, and nestles down under the protecting arm of its former enemy, the white man, and tries, however feebly, to adopt his manner of life. In making this change, the Indian has to sacrifice all that is dear to his heart; he abandons the only mode of life in which he can be a warrior and win triumphs and honors worthy to be sought after; and in taking up the pursuits of the white man, he does that which he has always been taught from his earliest infancy to regard as degrading to his manhood—to labor, to work for his daily bread, an avocation suitable only for squaws.

To those who advocate the application of the laws of civilization to the Indian, it might be a profitable study to investigate the effect which such application produces upon the strength of the tribe as expressed in numbers. Looking at him as the fearless hunter, the matchless horseman and warrior of the Plains, where Nature placed him, and contrasting him with the reservation Indian, who is supposed to be reveling in the delightful comforts and luxuries of an enlightened condition, but who in reality is groveling in beggary, bereft of many of the qualities which in his wild state tended to render him noble, and heir to a combination of vices partly his own, partly bequeathed to him from the pale-face, one is forced, even against desire, to conclude that there in unending antagonism between the Indian nature and that with which his well-meaning white brother would endow him. Nature intended him for a savage state; every instinct, every impulse of his soul inclines him to it. The white race might fall into a barbarous state, and afterwards, subjected to the influence of civilization, be reclaimed and prosper. Not so the Indian. He cannot be himself and be civilized; he fades away and dies. Cultivation such as the white man would give him deprives him of his identity.

Education, strange as it may appear, seems to weaken rather than strengthen his intellect.

"There is not among these three hundred bands of Indians one which has not suffered cruelly at the hands either of the Government or of white settlers."

Indians Are Victims of American Injustice

Helen Hunt Jackson (1830–1885)

Helen Hunt Jackson, a writer and friend of the poet Emily Dickinson, was one of the leading critics of American Indian policy in the nineteenth century. She is remembered today for two books she wrote to publicize the plight of American Indians and to promote political reforms in their treatment. In 1881, Jackson published *A Century of Dishonor*, a general history that documented the mistreatment of American Indians by the U.S. government, and sent copies to each member of Congress. Her 1884 novel *Ramona* dramatized the condition of Indians in California and was partially based on information she gathered as a member of a commission that investigated the circumstances of these tribes. The following viewpoint is taken from the conclusion of *A Century of Dishonor*.

There are within the limits of the United States between two hundred and fifty and three hundred thousand Indians, exclusive of those in Alaska. The names of the different tribes and bands, as entered in the statistical tables of the Indian Office Reports, number nearly three hundred. One of the most careful estimates which has been made of their numbers and localities gives them

From Helen Hunt Jackson, *A Century of Dishonor: A Sketch of the United States Government's Dealings with Some of the Indian Tribes* (New York: Harper, 1881).

as follows: "In Minnesota and States east of the Mississippi, about 32,500; in Nebraska, Kansas, and the Indian Territory, 70,650; in the Territories of Dakota, Montana, Wyoming, and Idaho, 65,000; in Nevada and the Territories of Colorado, New Mexico, Utah, and Arizona, 84,000; and on the Pacific slope, 48,000."

Of these, 130,000 are self-supporting on their own reservations, "receiving nothing from the Government except interest on their own moneys, or annuities granted them in consideration of the cession of their lands to the United States." [Annual Report of Indian Commissioner for 1872]

This fact alone would seem sufficient to dispose forever of the accusation, so persistently brought against the Indian, that he will not work.

Of the remainder, 84,000 are partially supported by the Government—the interest money due them and their annuities, as provided by treaty, being inadequate to their subsistence on the reservations where they are confined. In many cases, however, these Indians furnish a large part of their support—the White River Utes, for instance, who are reported by the Indian Bureau as getting sixty-six per cent. of their living by "root-digging, hunting, and fishing;" the Squaxin band, in Washington Territory, as earning seventy-five per cent., and the Chippewas of Lake Superior as earning fifty per cent. in the same way. These facts also would seem to dispose of the accusation that the Indian will not work.

There are about 55,000 who never visit an agency, over whom the Government does not pretend to have either control or care. These 55,000 "subsist by hunting, fishing, on roots, nuts, berries, etc., and by begging and stealing;" and this also seems to dispose of the accusation that the Indian will not "work for a living." There remains a small portion, about 31,000, that are entirely subsisted by the Government.

Cruelty and Outrage

There is not among these three hundred bands of Indians one which has not suffered cruelly at the hands either of the Government or of white settlers. The poorer, the more insignificant, the more helpless the band, the more certain the cruelty and outrage to which they have been subjected. This is especially true of the bands on the Pacific slope. These Indians found themselves of a sudden surrounded by and caught up in the great influx of gold-seeking settlers, as helpless creatures on a shore are caught up in a tidal wave. There was not time for the Government to make treaties; not even time for communities to make laws. The tale of the wrongs, the oppressions, the murders of the Pacific-slope Indians in the last thirty years would be a volume by itself, and is too monstrous to be believed.

It makes little difference, however, where one opens the record of the history of the Indians; every page and every year has its dark stain. The story of one tribe is the story of all, varied only by differences of time and place; but neither time nor place makes any difference in the main facts. Colorado is as greedy and unjust in 1880 as was Georgia in 1830, and Ohio in 1795; and the United States Government breaks promises now as deftly as then, and with an added ingenuity from long practice.

One of its strongest supports in so doing is the wide-spread sentiment among the people of dislike to the Indian, of impatience with his presence as a "barrier to civilization," and distrust of it as a possible danger. The old tales of the frontier life, with its horrors of Indian warfare, have gradually, by two or three generations' telling, produced in the average mind something like an hereditary instinct of unquestioning and unreasoning aversion which it is almost impossible to dislodge or soften.

There are hundreds of pages of unimpeachable testimony on the side of the Indian; but it goes for nothing, is set down as sentimentalism or partisanship, tossed aside and forgotten.

Unread Reports

President after president has appointed commission after commission to inquire into and report upon Indian affairs, and to make suggestions as to the best methods of managing them. The reports are filled with eloquent statements of wrongs done to the Indians, of perfidies on the part of the Government; they counsel, as earnestly as words can, a trial of the simple and unperplexing expedients of telling truth, keeping promises, making fair bargains, dealing justly in all ways and all things. These reports are bound up with the Government's Annual Reports, and that is the end of them. It would probably be no exaggeration to say that not one American citizen out of ten thousand ever sees them or knows that they exist, and yet any one of them, circulated throughout the country, read by the right-thinking, right-feeling men and women of this land, would be of itself a "campaign document" that would initiate a revolution which would not subside until the Indians' wrongs were, so far as is now left possible, righted.

In 1869 President [U.S.] Grant appointed a commission of nine men, representing the influence and philanthropy of six leading States, to visit the different Indian reservations, and to "examine all matters appertaining to Indian affairs."

In the report of this commission are such paragraphs as the following: "To assert that 'the Indian will not work' is as true as it would be to say that the white man will not work.

"Why should the Indian be expected to plant corn, fence lands, build houses, or do anything but get food from day to day, when experience has taught him that the product of his labor will be seized by the white man to-morrow? The most industrious white man would become a drone under similar circumstances. Nevertheless, many of the Indians" (the commissioners might more forcibly have said 130,000 of the Indians) "are already at work, and furnish ample refutation of the assertion that 'the Indian will not work.' There is no escape from the inexorable logic of facts.

Killing Women and Children

Nine years after the publication of A Century of Dishonor, *in what would be the last significant military encounter between whites and American Indians, members of the U.S. Seventh Cavalry Division killed more than 150 Sioux men, women, and children at Wounded Knee, South Dakota. American Horse, an Indian who witnessed the massacre, described part of the scene in the* Fourteenth Annual Report of the Bureau of American Ethnology, *published in 1896.*

There was a woman with an infant in her arms who was killed as she almost touched the flag of truce, and the women and children of course were strewn all along the circular village until they were dispatched. Right near the flag of truce a mother was shot down with her infant; the child not knowing that its mother was dead was still nursing, and that especially was a very sad sight. The women as they were fleeing with their babes were killed together, shot right through, and the women who were heavy with child were also killed. All the Indians fled in these three directions, and after most all of them had been killed a cry was made that all those who were not killed or wounded should come forth and they would be safe. Little boys who were not wounded came out of their places of refuge, and as soon as they came in sight a number of soldiers surrounded them and butchered them there.

"The history of the Government connections with the Indians is a shameful record of broken treaties and unfulfilled promises. The history of the border white man's connection with the Indians is a sickening record of murder, outrage, robbery, and wrongs committed by the former, as the rule, and occasional savage outbreaks and unspeakably barbarous deeds of retaliation by the latter, as the exception.

"Taught by the Government that they had rights entitled to respect, when those rights have been assailed by the rapacity of the white man, the arm which should have been raised to protect them has ever been ready to sustain the aggressor.

"The testimony of some of the highest military officers of the United States is on record to the effect that, in our Indian wars, almost without exception, the first aggressions have been made by the white man; and the assertion is supported by every civilian of reputation who has studied the subject. In addition to the class of robbers and outlaws who find impunity in their nefarious pursuits on the frontiers, there is a large class of professedly reputable men who use every means in their power to bring on Indian wars for the sake of the profit to be realized from the presence of troops and the expenditure of Government funds in their midst. They proclaim death to the Indians at all times in words and publications, making no distinction between the innocent and the guilty. They irate the lowest class of men to the perpetration of the darkest deeds against their victims, and as judges and jurymen shield them from the justice due to their crimes. Every crime committed by a white man against an Indian is concealed or palliated. Every offence committed by an Indian against a white man is borne on the wings of the post or the telegraph to the remotest corner of the land, clothed with all the horrors which the reality or imagination can throw around it. Against such influences as these the people of the United States need to be warned."

No Easy Solution

To assume that it would be easy, or by any one sudden stroke of legislative policy possible, to undo the mischief and hurt of the long past, set the Indian policy of the country right for the future, and make the Indians at once safe and happy, is the blunder of a hasty and uninformed judgment. The notion which seems to be growing more prevalent, that simply to make all Indians at once citizens of the United States would be a sovereign and instantaneous panacea for all their ills and all the Government's perplexities, is a very inconsiderate one. To administer complete citizenship of a sudden, all round, to all Indians, barbarous and civilized alike, would be as grotesque a blunder as to dose them all round with any one medicine, irrespective of the symptoms and needs of their diseases. It would kill more than it would cure. Nevertheless, it is true, as was well stated by one of the superintendents of Indian Affairs in 1857, that, "so long as they are not citizens of the United States, their rights of property must remain insecure against invasion. The doors of the federal tribunals being barred against them while wards and dependents, they can only partially exercise the rights of free government, or give to those who make, execute, and construe the few laws they are allowed to enact, dignity sufficient to make them respectable. While they continue individually to gather the crumbs that fall from the table of the United States, idleness, improvidence, and indebtedness will be the rule, and industry, thrift, and freedom from debt the exception. The utter absence of individual title to particular lands deprives every one among them of the chief incentive to labor and exertion—the very mainspring on which the prosperity of a people depends."

All judicious plans and measures for their safety and salvation must embody provisions for their becoming citizens as fast as they are fit, and must protect them till then in every right and particular in which our laws protect other "persons" who are not citizens.

First Steps

There is a disposition in a certain class of minds to be impatient with any protestation against wrong which is unaccompanied or unprepared with a quick and exact scheme of remedy. This is illogical. When pioneers in a new country find a tract of poisonous and swampy wilderness to be reclaimed, they do not withhold their hands from fire and axe till they see clearly which way roads should run, where good water will spring, and what crops will best grow on the redeemed land. They first clear the swamp. So with this poisonous and baffling part of the domain of our national affairs—let us first "clear the swamp."

However great perplexity and difficulty there may be in the details of any and every plan possible for doing at this late day anything like justice to the Indian, however hard it may be for good statesmen and good men to agree upon the things that ought to be done, there certainly is, or ought to be, no perplexity whatever, no difficulty whatever, in agreeing upon certain things that ought not to be done, and which must cease to be done before the first steps can be taken toward righting the wrongs, curing the ills, and wiping out the disgrace to us of the present condition of our Indians.

Cheating, robbing, breaking promises—these three are clearly things which must cease to be done. One more thing, also, and that is the refusal of the protection of the law to the Indian's rights of property, "of life, liberty, and the pursuit of happiness."

When these four things have ceased to be done, time, statesmanship, philanthropy, and Christianity can slowly and surely do the rest. Till these four things have ceased to be done, statesmanship and philanthropy alike must work in vain, and even Christianity can reap but small harvest.

"The white man has no right to come here and take our country."

The White Takeover of Indian Land Was Unjust

Chief Joseph (ca. 1840–1904)

Chief Joseph was the son of a leader of the Nez Percé (a tribe of American Indians who lived in the Pacific Northwest in the area where Washington, Oregon, and Idaho meet) and grew up to become an important leader in his own right. An 1863 treaty, which neither Joseph nor his father signed or recognized, ceded most of their territory to the federal government. In 1877 U.S. troops attempted to force all the Nez Percé into the Lapwai Reservation created by the 1863 treaty. Joseph was one of several chiefs who led approximately seven hundred Nez Percé on a journey of four months and fifteen hundred miles in an attempt to escape to Canada. In the process, the band defeated and eluded U.S. troops sent to capture them.

The flight to Canada gained national attention and almost succeeded in its goal before Chief Joseph surrendered to General Nelson A. Miles on October 5, 1877. (Some Nez Percé did manage to reach Canada, but the majority did not.) In betrayal of Miles's promise that Joseph would be sent to the Lapwai Reservation in Idaho, he and his followers were instead transported to Indian Territory (now Oklahoma). In January 1879 Chief Joseph visited Washington, D.C., to meet with President Rutherford B. Hayes and plead for the return of his people to Lapwai. On January 14 he gave a speech to members of Congress; the speech was translated and published in the April 1879 issue of the *North American Review* and is excerpted here. Chief Joseph argues that the white takeover of Nez Percé land was achieved through dishonest

From Chief Joseph, "An Indian's Views of Indian Affairs," *North American Review*, April 1879.

means and that the treatment received by his people both before and after the 1877 war was marked by threats, lies, and broken promises. Although Joseph limits his remarks specifically to the experiences of the Nez Percé tribe, many other Indian tribes and leaders of this time period shared his feelings about the loss of their lands.

In 1885 some of the Nez Percé were permitted to return to Lapwai, while others, including Joseph, were sent to Colville Reservation in northeastern Washington. Joseph died in Colville in 1904.

My friends, I have been asked to show you my heart. I am glad to have a chance to do so. I want the white people to understand my people. Some of you think an Indian is like a wild animal. This is a great mistake. I will tell you all about our people, and then you can judge whether an Indian is a man or not. I believe much trouble and blood would be saved if we opened our hearts more. I will tell you in my way how the Indian sees things. The white man has more words to tell you how they look to him, but it does not require many words to speak the truth. What I have to say will come from my heart, and I will speak with a straight tongue. Ah-cum-kin-i-ma-me-hut (the Great Spirit) is looking at me, and will hear me.

My name is In-mut-too-yah-lat-lat (Thunder traveling over the Mountains). I am chief of the Wal-lam-wat-kin band of Chute-pa-lu, or Nez Percés (nose-pierced Indians). I was born in eastern Oregon, thirty-eight winters ago. My father was chief before me. When a young man, he was called Joseph by Mr. Spaulding, a missionary. He died a few years ago. There was no stain on his hands of the blood of a white man. He left a good name on the earth. He advised me well for my people.

Our fathers gave us many laws, which they had learned from their fathers. These laws were good. They told us to treat all men as they treated us; that we should never be the first to break a bargain; that it was a disgrace to tell a lie; that we should speak only the truth; that it was a shame for one man to take from another his wife, or his property without paying for it. We were taught to believe that the Great Spirit sees and hears everything, and that he never forgets; that hereafter he will give every man a spirit-home according to his deserts: if he has been a good man, he will have a good home; if he has been a bad man, he will have a bad home. This I believe, and all my people believe the same.

Encountering White Men

We did not know there were other people besides the Indian until about one hundred winters ago, when some men with white faces came to our country. They brought many things with them to trade for furs and skins. They brought tobacco, which was new to us. They brought guns with flint stones on them, which frightened our women and children. Our people could not talk with these white-faced men, but they used signs which all people understand. These men were Frenchmen, and they called our people "Nez Percés," because they wore rings in their noses for ornaments. Although very few of our people wear them now, we are still called by the same name. These French trappers said a great many things to our fathers, which have been planted in our hearts. Some were good for us, but some were bad. Our people were divided in opinion about these men. Some thought they taught more bad than good. An Indian respects a brave man, but he despises a coward. He loves a straight tongue, but he hates a forked tongue. The French trappers told us some truths and some lies.

The first white men of your people who came to our country were named Lewis and Clarke. They also brought many things that our people had never seen. They talked straight, and our people gave them a great feast, as a proof that their hearts were friendly. These men were very kind. They made presents to our chiefs and our people made presents to them. We had a great many horses, of which we gave them what they needed, and they gave us guns and tobacco in return. All the Nez Percés made friends with Lewis and Clarke, and agreed to let them pass through their country, and never to make war on white men. This promise the Nez Percés have never broken. No white man can accuse them of bad faith, and speak with a straight tongue. It has always been the pride of the Nez Percés that they were the friends of the white men. When my father was a young man there came to our country a white man (Rev. Mr. Spaulding) who talked spirit law. He won the affections of our people because he spoke good things to them. At first he did not say anything about white men wanting to settle on our lands. Nothing was said about that until about twenty winters ago, when a number of white people came into our country and built houses and made farms. At first our people made no complaint. They thought there was room enough for all to live in peace, and they were learning many things from the white men that seemed to be good. But we soon found that the white men were growing rich very fast, and were greedy to possess everything the Indian had. My father was the first to see through the schemes of the white men, and he warned his tribe to be careful about trading with them. He had suspicion of men who seemed so anxious to make money. I was a boy then, but I remember well my father's caution. He had sharper eyes than the rest of our people.

Next there came a white officer (Governor Stevens), who invited all the Nez Percés to a treaty council. After the council was opened he made known his heart. He said there were a great many white people in the country, and many more would come; that he wanted the land marked out so that the Indians and white men could be separated. If they were to live in peace it was necessary, he said, that the Indians should have a country set apart for them, and in that country they must stay. My father, who represented his band, refused to have anything to do with the council, because he wished to be a free man. He claimed that no man owned any part of the earth, and a man could not sell what he did not own.

Chief Joseph became famous throughout America in 1877 when he led his band of Nez Percé Indians on an arduous retreat toward Canada.

Mr. Spaulding took hold of my father's arm and said, "Come and sign the treaty." My father pushed him away, and said: "Why do you ask me to sign away my country? It is your business to talk to us about spirit matters, and not to talk to us about parting

146

with our land." Governor Stevens urged my father to sign his treaty, but he refused. "I will not sign your paper," he said; "you go where you please, so do I; you are not a child, I am no child; I can think for myself. No man can think for me. I have no other home than this. I will not give it up to any man. My people would have no home. Take away your paper. I will not touch it with my hand."

My father left the council. Some of the chiefs of the other bands of the Nez Percés signed the treaty, and then Governor Stevens gave them presents of blankets. My father cautioned his people to take no presents, for "after a while," he said, "they will claim that you have accepted pay for your country." Since that time four bands of the Nez Percés have received annuities from the United States. My father was invited to many councils, and they tried hard to make him sign the treaty, but he was firm as the rock, and would not sign away his home. His refusal caused a difference among the Nez Percés.

Eight years later (1863) was the next treaty council. A chief called Lawyer, because he was a great talker, took the lead in this council, and sold nearly all the Nez Percés country. My father was not there. He said to me: "When you go into council with the white man, always remember your country. Do not give it away. The white man will cheat you out of your home. I have taken no pay from the United States. I have never sold our land." In this treaty Lawyer acted without authority from our band. He had no right to sell the Wallowa (winding water) country. That had always belonged to my father's own people, and the other bands had never disputed our right to it. No other Indians ever claimed Wallowa.

In order to have all people understand how much land we owned, my father planted poles around it and said:

"Inside is the home of my people—the white man may take the land outside. Inside this boundary all our people were born. It circles around the graves of our fathers, and we will never give up these graves to any man."

The United States claimed they had bought all the Nez Percés country outside of Lapwai Reservation, from Lawyer and other chiefs, but we continued to live on this land in peace until eight years ago, when white men began to come inside the bounds my father had set. We warned them against this great wrong, but they would not leave our land, and some bad blood was raised. The white men represented that we were going upon the warpath. They reported many things that were false.

The United States Government again asked for a treaty council. My father had become blind and feeble. He could no longer speak for his people. It was then that I took my father's place as chief. In this council I made my first speech to white men. I said to the agent who held the council:

"I did not want to come to this council, but I came hoping that we could save blood. The white man has no right to come here and take our country. We have never accepted any presents from the Government. Neither Lawyer nor any other chief had authority to sell this land. It has always belonged to my people. It came unclouded to them from our fathers, and we will defend this land as long as a drop of Indian blood warms the hearts of our men."

The agent said he had orders, from the Great White Chief at Washington, for us to go upon the Lapwai Reservation, and that if we obeyed he would help us in many ways. "You *must* move to the agency," he said. I answered him: "I will not. I do not need your help; we have plenty, and we are contented and happy if the white man will let us alone. The reservation is too small for so many people with all their stock. You can keep your presents; we can go to your towns and pay for all we need; we have plenty of horses and cattle to sell, and we won't have any help from you; we are free now; we can go where we please. Our fathers were born here. Here they lived, here they died, here are their graves. We will never leave them." The agent went away, and we had peace for a little while.

A Man Must Love His Father's Grave

Soon after this my father sent for me. I saw he was dying. I took his hand in mine. He said: "My son, my body is returning to my mother earth, and my spirit is going very soon to see the Great Spirit Chief. When I am gone, think of your country. You are the chief of these people. They look to you to guide them. Always remember that your father never sold his country. You must stop your ears whenever you are asked to sign a treaty selling your home. A few years more, and white men will be all around you. They have their eyes on this land. My son, never forget my dying words. This country holds your father's body. Never sell the bones of your father and your mother." I pressed my father's hand and told him I would protect his grave with my life. My father smiled and passed away to the spirit-land.

I buried him in that beautiful valley of winding waters. I love that land more than all the rest of the world. A man who would not love his father's grave is worse than a wild animal.

For a short time we lived quietly. But this could not last. White men had found gold in the mountains around the land of winding water. They stole a great many horses from us, and we could not get them back because we were Indians. The white men told lies for each other. They drove off a great many of our cattle. Some white men branded our young cattle so they could claim them. We had no friend who would plead our cause before the law councils. It seemed to me that some of the white men in Wallowa were doing these things on purpose to get up a war. They knew that we were not strong enough to fight them. I labored hard to avoid trouble and bloodshed. We gave up some of our country to the white men, thinking that then we could have peace. We were mistaken. The white man would not let us alone. We could have avenged our wrongs many times, but we did not. Whenever the Government has asked us to help them against other Indians, we have never refused. When the white men were few and we were strong we could have killed them all off, but the Nez Percés wished to live at peace.

If we have not done so, we have not been to blame. I believe that the old treaty has never been correctly reported. If we ever owned the land we own it still, for we never sold it. In the treaty councils the commissioners have claimed that our country had been sold to the Government. Suppose a white man should come to me and say, "Joseph, I like your horses, and I want to buy them." I say to him, "No, my horses suit me, I will not sell them." Then he goes to my neighbor, and says to him: "Joseph has some good horses. I want to buy them, but he refuses to sell." My neighbor answers, "Pay me the money, and I will sell you Joseph's horses." The white man returns to me, and says, "Joseph, I have bought your horses, and you must let me have them." If we sold our lands to the Government, this is the way they were bought.

On account of the treaty made by the other bands of the Nez Percés, the white men claimed my lands. We were troubled greatly by white men crowding over the line. Some of these were good men, and we lived on peaceful terms with them, but they were not all good.

Nearly every year the agent came over from Lapwai and ordered us on to the reservation. We always replied that we were satisfied to live in Wallowa. We were careful to refuse the presents or annuities which he offered.

Through all the years since the white men came to Wallowa we have been threatened and taunted by them and the treaty Nez Percés. They have given us no rest. We have had a few good friends among white men, and they have always advised my people to bear these taunts without fighting. Our young men were quick-tempered, and I have had great trouble in keeping them from doing rash things. I have carried a heavy load on my back ever since I was a boy. I learned then that we were but few, while the white men were many, and that we could not hold our own with them. We were like deer. They were like grizzly bears. We had a small country. Their country was large. We were contented to let things remain as the Great Spirit Chief made them.

They were not; and would change the rivers and mountains if they did not suit them.

A New Threat

Year after year we have been threatened, but no war was made upon my people until General [Oliver] Howard came to our country two years ago and told us that he was the white war-chief of all that country. He said: "I have a great many soldiers at my back. I am going to bring them up here, and then I will talk to you again. I will not let white men laugh at me the next time I come. The country belongs to the Government, and I intend to make you go upon the reservation.". . .

General Howard informed me, in a haughty spirit, that he would give my people *thirty days* to go back home, collect all their stock, and move on to the reservation, saying, "If you are not here in that time, I shall consider that you want to fight, and will send my soldiers to drive you on.". . .

General Howard refused to allow me more than thirty days to move my people and their stock. I am sure that he began to prepare for war at once. . . .

No Way to Avoid War

We gathered all the stock we could find, and made an attempt to move. We left many of our horses and cattle in Wallowa, and we lost several hundred in crossing the river. All of my people succeeded in getting across in safety. Many of the Nez Percés came together in Rocky Cañon to hold a grand council. I went with all my people. This council lasted ten days. There was a great deal of war-talk, and a great deal of excitement. There was one young brave present whose father had been killed by a white man five years before. This man's blood was bad against white men, and he left the council calling for revenge.

Again I counseled peace, and I thought the danger was past. We had not complied with General Howard's order because we could not, but we intended to do so as soon as possible. I was leaving the council to kill beef for my family, when news came that the young man whose father had been killed had gone out with several other hot-blooded young braves and killed four white men. He rode up to the council and shouted: "Why do you sit here like women? The war has begun already." I was deeply grieved. All the lodges were moved except my brother's and my own. I saw clearly that the war was upon us when I learned that my young men had been secretly buying ammunition. I heard then that Too-hool-hool-suit, who had been imprisoned by General Howard, had succeeded in organizing a war-party. I knew that their acts would involve all my people. I saw that the war could not then be prevented. The time had passed. I counseled peace from the beginning. I knew that we were too weak to fight the United States. We had many grievances, but I knew that war would bring more. We had good white friends, who advised us against taking the war-path. . . .

There were bad men among my people who had quarreled with white men, and they talked of their wrongs until they roused all the bad hearts in the council. Still I could not believe that they would begin the war. I know that my young men did a great wrong, but I ask, Who was first to blame? They had been insulted a thousand times; their fathers and brothers had been killed; their mothers and wives had been disgraced; they had been driven to madness by whisky sold to them by white men; they had been told by General Howard that all their horses and cattle which they had been unable to drive out of Wallowa were to fall into the hands of white men; and, added to all this, they were homeless and desperate.

I would have given my own life if I could have undone the killing of white men by my people. I blame my young men and I blame the white men. I blame General Howard for not giving my people time to get their stock away from Wallowa. I do not acknowledge that he had the right to order me to leave Wallowa at any time. I deny that either my father or myself ever sold that land. It is still our land. It may never again be our home, but my father sleeps there, and I love it as I love my mother. I left there, hoping to avoid bloodshed.

If General Howard had given me plenty of time to gather up my stock, and treated Too-hool-hool-suit as a man should be treated, there *would have been no war*. . . .

I could see no other way to avoid a war. We moved over to White Bird Creek, sixteen miles away, and there encamped, intending to collect our stock before leaving; but the soldiers attacked us, and the first battle was fought. We numbered in that battle sixty men, and the soldiers a hundred. The fight lasted but a few minutes, when the soldiers retreated before us for twelve miles. They lost thirty-three killed, and had seven wounded. When an Indian fights, he only shoots to kill; but soldiers shoot at random. None of the soldiers were scalped. We do not believe in scalping, nor in killing wounded men. Soldiers do not kill many Indians unless they are wounded and left upon the battle-field. Then they kill Indians. . . .

Battles and Retreats

Finding that we were outnumbered, we retreated to Bitter Root Valley. Here another body of soldiers came upon us and demanded our surrender. We refused. They said, "You can not get by us." We answered, "We are going by you without fighting if you will let us, but we are going by you anyhow." We then made a treaty with these soldiers. We agreed not to molest any one, and they agreed that we might pass through the Bitter Root country in peace. We bought provisions and traded stock with white men there.

We understood that there was to be no more war. We intended to go peaceably to the buffalo country, and leave the question of returning to our country to be settled afterward.

With this understanding we traveled on for four days, and, thinking that the trouble was all over, we stopped and prepared tent-poles to take with us. We started again, and at the end of two days we saw three white men passing our camp. Thinking that peace had been made, we did not molest them. We could have killed or taken them prisoners, but we did not suspect them of being spies, which they were.

Chief Joseph's Surrender

Chief Joseph's surrender speech, made on October 5, 1877, became one of the most well known declarations of American Indian history.

I am tired of fighting. Our chiefs are killed. . . . The old men are all killed. . . . It is cold and we have no blankets. The little children are freezing to death. My people, some of them, have run away to the hills and have no blankets, no food; no one knows where they are, perhaps freezing to death. I want time to look for my children and see how many of them I can find. Maybe I shall find them among the dead. Hear me, my chiefs, I am tired; my heart is sick and sad. From where the sun now stands, I will fight no more forever.

That night the soldiers surrounded our camp. About daybreak one of my men went out to look after his horses. The soldiers saw him and shot him down like a coyote. I have since learned that these soldiers were not those we had left behind. They had come upon us from another direction. The new white war chief's name was Gibbon. He charged upon us while some of my people were still asleep. We had a hard fight. Some of my men crept around and attacked the soldiers from the rear. In this battle we lost nearly all our lodges, but we finally drove General Gibbon back.

Finding that he was not able to capture us, he sent to his camp a few miles away for his big guns (cannons), but my men had captured them and all the ammunition. We damaged the big guns all we could, and carried away the powder and lead. In the fight with General Gibbon we lost fifty women and children and thirty fighting men. We remained long enough to bury our dead. The

Nez Percés never make war on women and children; we could have killed a great many women and children while the war lasted, but we would feel ashamed to do so cowardly an act. . . .

We retreated as rapidly as we could toward the buffalo country. After six days General Howard came close to us, and we went out and attacked him, and captured nearly all his horses and mules (about two hundred and fifty head). We then marched on to the Yellowstone Basin.

On the way we captured one white man and two white women. We released them at the end of three days. They were treated kindly. The women were not insulted. Can the white soldiers tell me of one time when Indian women were taken prisoners, and held three days and then released without being insulted? Were the Nez Percés women who fell into the hands of General Howard's soldiers treated with as much respect? I deny that a Nez Percé was ever guilty of such a crime. . . .

Nine days' march brought us to the mouth of Clarke's Fork of the Yellowstone. We did not know what had become of General Howard, but we supposed that he had sent for more horses and mules. He did not come up, but another new war-chief (General Sturgis) attacked us. We held him in check while we moved all our women and children and stock out of danger, leaving a few men to cover our retreat.

Several days passed, and we heard nothing of General Howard, or Gibbon, or Sturgis. We had repulsed each in turn, and began to feel secure, when another army, under General [Nelson A.] Miles, struck us. This was the fourth army, each of which outnumbered our fighting force, that we had encountered within sixty days. . . .

We lost, the first day and night, eighteen men and three women. General Miles lost twenty-six killed and forty wounded. The following day General Miles sent a messenger into my camp under protection of a white flag. . . .

The Decision to Surrender

I could not bear to see my wounded men and women suffer any longer; we had lost enough already. General Miles had promised that we might return to our own country with what stock we had left. I thought we could start again. I believed General Miles, or *I never would have surrendered*. I have heard that he has been censured for making the promise to return us to Lapwai. He could not have made any other terms with me at that time. I would have held him in check until my friends came to my assistance, and then neither of the generals nor their soldiers would have ever left Bear Paw Mountain alive.

On the fifth day I went to General Miles and gave up my gun, and said, "From where the sun now stands I will fight no more."

My people needed rest—we wanted peace.

I was told we could go with General Miles to Tongue River and stay there until spring, when we would be sent back to our country. Finally it was decided that we were to be taken to Tongue River. We had nothing to say about it. After our arrival at Tongue River, General Miles received orders to take us to Bismarck [North Dakota]. The reason given was, that subsistence would be cheaper there.

General Miles was opposed to this order. He said: "You must not blame me. I have endeavored to keep my word, but the chief who is over me has given the order, and I must obey it or resign. That would do you no good. Some other officer would carry out the order."

I believe General Miles would have kept his word if he could have done so. I do not blame him for what we have suffered since the surrender. I do not know who is to blame. We gave up all our horses—over eleven hundred—and all our saddles—over one hundred—and we have not heard from them since. Somebody has got our horses.

General Miles turned my people over to another soldier, and we were taken to Bismarck. Captain Johnson, who now had charge of us, received an order to take us to Fort Leavenworth [Kansas]. At Leavenworth we were placed on a low river bottom with no water except river-water to drink and cook with. We had always lived in a healthy country, where the mountains were high and the water was cold and clear. Many of my people sickened and died, and we buried them in this strange land. I can not tell how much my heart suffered for my people while at Leavenworth. The Great Spirit Chief who rules above seemed to be looking some other way, and did not see what was being done to my people.

During the hot days (July, 1878) we received notice that we were to be moved farther away from our own country. We were not asked if we were willing to go. We were ordered to get into the railroad-cars. Three of my people died on the way to Baxter Springs. It was worse to die there than to die fighting in the mountains.

We were moved from Baxter Springs (Kansas) to the Indian Territory, and set down without our lodges. We had but little medicine, and we were nearly all sick. Seventy of my people have died since we moved there.

We have had a great many visitors who have talked many ways. Some of the chiefs (General Fish and Colonel Stickney) from Washington came to see us, and selected land for us to live upon. We have not moved to that land, for it is not a good place to live.

The Commissioner Chief (E.A. Hayt) came to see us. I told him, as I told every one, that I expected General Miles's word would be carried out. He said it "could not be done; that white men now lived in my country and all the land was taken up; that, if I returned to Wallowa, I could not live in peace; that law-papers were out against my young men who began the war, and that the Government could not protect my people." This talk fell like a heavy stone upon my heart. I saw that I could not gain anything by talking to him. Other law chiefs (Congressional Committee) came to see me and said they would help me to get a healthy country. I did not know who to believe. The white people have too many chiefs. They do not understand each other. They do not all talk alike. . . .

I Cannot Understand So Many Chiefs

At last I was granted permission to come to Washington and bring my friend Yellow Bull and our interpreter with me. I am glad we came. I have shaken hands with a great many friends, but there are some things I want to know which no one seems able to explain. I can not understand how the Government sends a man out to fight us . . . and then breaks his word. Such a Government has something wrong about it. I can not understand why so many chiefs are allowed to talk so many different ways, and promise so many different things. I have seen the Great Father Chief (the President), the next Great Chief (Secretary of the Interior), the Commissioner Chief (Hayt), the Law Chief (General [Benjamin F.] Butler), and many other law chiefs (Congressmen), and they all say they are my friends, and that I shall have justice, but while their mouths all talk right I do not understand why nothing is done for my people. I have heard talk and talk, but nothing is done. Good words do not last long unless they amount to something. Words do not pay for my dead people. They do not pay for my country, now overrun by white men. They do not protect my father's grave. They do not pay for all my horses and cattle. Good words will not give me back my children. Good words will not make good the promise of your War Chief General Miles. Good words will not give my people good health and stop them from dying. Good words will not get my people a home where they can live in peace and take care of themselves. I am tired of talk that comes to nothing. It makes my heart sick when I remember all the good words and all the broken promises. There has been too much talking by men who had no right to talk. Too many misrepresentations have been made, too many misunderstandings have come up between the white men about the Indians. If the white man wants to live in peace with the Indian he can live in peace. There need be no trouble. Treat all men alike. Give them all the same law. Give them all an even chance to live and grow. All men were made by the same Great Spirit Chief.

They are all brothers. The earth is the mother of all people, and all people should have equal rights upon it. You might as well expect the rivers to run backward as that any man who was born a free man should be contented when penned up and denied liberty to go where he pleases. If you tie a horse to a stake, do you expect he will grow fat? If you pen an Indian up on a small spot of earth, and compel him to stay there, he will not be contented, nor will he grow and prosper. I have asked some of the great white chiefs where they get their authority to say to the Indian that he shall stay in one place, while he sees white men going where they please. They can not tell me.

Treat Us Like All Other Men

I only ask of the Government to be treated as all other men are treated. If I can not go to my own home, let me have a home in some country where my people will not die so fast. I would like to go to Bitter Root Valley. There my people would be healthy; where they are now they are dying. Three have died since I left my camp to come to Washington.

When I think of our condition my heart is heavy. I see men of my race treated as outlaws and driven from country to country, or shot down like animals.

I know that my race must change. We can not hold our own with the white men as we are. We only ask an even chance to live as other men live. We ask to be recognized as men. We ask that the same law shall work alike on all men. If the Indian breaks the law, punish him by the law. If the white man breaks the law, punish him also.

Let me be a free man—free to travel, free to stop, free to work, free to trade where I choose, free to choose my own teachers, free to follow the religion of my fathers, free to think and talk and act for myself—and I will obey every law, or submit to the penalty.

Whenever the white man treats the Indian as they treat each other, then we will have no more wars. We shall all be alike— brothers of one father and one mother, with one sky above us and one country around us, and one government for all. Then the Great Spirit Chief who rules above will smile upon this land, and send rain to wash out the bloody spots made by brothers' hands from the face of the earth. For this time the Indian race are waiting and praying. I hope that no more groans of wounded men and women will ever go to the ear of the Great Spirit Chief above, and that all people may be one people.

In-mut-too-yah-lat-lat has spoken for his people.

"The settler and pioneer have at bottom had justice on their side; this great continent could not have been kept as nothing but a game preserve for squalid savages."

The White Takeover of Indian Land Was Inevitable

Theodore Roosevelt (1858–1919)

Theodore Roosevelt, president of the United States from 1901 to 1909, was also a prolific author and historian. Roosevelt lived and worked on a North Dakota cattle ranch from 1884 to 1886 and drew on these experiences in writing several books, including the multivolume study *The Winning of the West*. The following excerpts from the first volume of that work, published in 1889, include his views toward Indians, which were shared by many of the time. Roosevelt argues that the American expansion and takeover of Indian land, while often accompanied by cruel acts, was in the final assessment inevitable and just. Indians, being simple hunters and gatherers, never had real title to land they did not farm or develop, he asserts. Roosevelt also attacks "sentimental historians" for being overly critical of whites' treatment of Indians and for overlooking atrocities committed by Indians in the past.

Border warfare . . . was a war waged by savages against armed settlers, whose families followed them into the wilderness. Such a war is inevitably bloody and cruel; but the inhuman love of cru-

From Theodore Roosevelt, *The Winning of the West*, vol. 1 (New York: Knickerbocker Press, 1889).

elty for cruelty's sake, which marks the red Indian above all other savages, rendered these wars more terrible than any others. For the hideous, unnamable, unthinkable tortures practised by the red men on their captured foes, and on their foes' tender women and helpless children, were such as we read of in no other struggle, hardly even in the revolting pages that tell the deeds of the Holy Inquisition. It was inevitable—indeed it was in many instances proper—that such deeds should awake in the breasts of the whites the grimmest, wildest spirit of revenge and hatred.

The history of the border wars, both in the ways they were begun and in the ways they were waged, makes a long tale of injuries inflicted, suffered, and mercilessly revenged. It could not be otherwise when brutal, reckless, lawless borderers, despising all men not of their own color, were thrown in contact with savages who esteemed cruelty and treachery as the highest of virtues, and rapine and murder as the worthiest of pursuits. Moreover, it was sadly inevitable that the law-abiding borderer as well as the white ruffian, the peaceful Indian as well as the painted marauder, should be plunged into the struggle to suffer the punishment that should only have fallen on their evil-minded fellows.

An Unavoidable Struggle

Looking back, it is easy to say that much of the wrong-doing could have been prevented; but if we examine the facts to find out the truth, not to establish a theory, we are bound to admit that the struggle was really one that could not possibly have been avoided. The sentimental historians speak as if the blame had been all ours, and the wrong all done to our foes, and as if it would have been possible by any exercise of wisdom to reconcile claims that were in their very essence conflicting; but their utterances are as shallow as they are untruthful. Unless we were willing that the whole continent west of the Alleghanies should remain an unpeopled waste, the hunting-ground of savages, war was inevitable; and even had we been willing, and had we refrained from encroaching on the Indians' lands, the war would have come nevertheless, for then the Indians themselves would have encroached on ours. Undoubtedly we have wronged many tribes; but equally undoubtedly our first definite knowledge of many others has been derived from their unprovoked outrages upon our people. The Chippewas, Ottawas, and Pottawatamies furnished hundreds of young warriors to the parties that devastated our frontiers generations before we in any way encroached upon or wronged them.

Mere outrages could be atoned for or settled; the question which lay at the root of our difficulties was that of the occupation of the land itself, and to this there could be no solution save war.

The Indians had no ownership of the land in the way in which we understand the term. The tribes lived far apart; each had for its hunting-grounds all the territory from which it was not barred by rivals. Each looked with jealousy upon all interlopers, but each was prompt to act as an interloper when occasion offered. Every good hunting-ground was claimed by many nations. It was rare, indeed, that any tribe had an uncontested title to a large tract of land; where such title existed, it rested, not on actual occupancy and cultivation, but on the recent butchery of weaker rivals. For instance, there were a dozen tribes, all of whom hunted in Kentucky, and fought each other there, all of whom had equally good titles to the soil, and not one of whom acknowledged the right of any other; as a matter of fact they had therein no right, save the right of the strongest. The land no more belonged to them than it belonged to Boon [Daniel Boone] and the white hunters who first visited it.

On the borders there are perpetual complaints of the encroachments of whites upon Indian lands; and naturally the central government at Washington, and before it was at Washington, has usually been inclined to sympathize with the feeling that considers the whites the aggressors, for the government does not wish a war, does not itself feel any land hunger, hears of not a tenth of the Indian outrages, and knows by experience that the white borderers are not easy to rule. As a consequence, the official reports of the people who are not on the ground are apt to paint the Indian side in its most favorable light, and are often completely untrustworthy, this being particularly the case if the author of the report is an eastern man, utterly unacquainted with the actual condition of affairs on the frontier.

Indians Have No True Title to the Land

Such a man, though both honest and intelligent, when he hears that the whites have settled on Indian lands, cannot realize that the act has no resemblance whatever to the forcible occupation of land already cultivated. The white settler has merely moved into an uninhabited waste; he does not feel that he is committing a wrong, for he knows perfectly well that the land is really owned by no one. It is never even visited, except perhaps for a week or two every year, and then the visitors are likely at any moment to be driven off by a rival hunting-party of greater strength. The settler ousts no one from the land; if he did not chop down the trees, hew out the logs for a building, and clear the ground for tillage, no one else would do so. He drives out the game, however, and of course the Indians who live thereon sink their mutual animosities and turn against the intruder. The truth is, the Indians never had any real title to the soil; they had not half as good a claim to it, for instance, as the cattlemen now have to all eastern Montana, yet no one would assert that the cattlemen have a right to keep immigrants off their vast unfenced ranges. The settler and pioneer have at bottom had justice on their side; this great continent could not have been kept as nothing but a game preserve for squalid savages. Moreover, to the most oppressed Indian nations the whites often acted as a protection, or, at least, they deferred instead of hastening their fate. But for the interposition of the whites it is probable that the Iroquois would have exterminated every Algonquin tribe before the end of the eighteenth century; exactly as in recent time the Crows and Pawnees would have been destroyed by the Sioux, had it not been for the wars we have waged against the latter.

Again, the loose governmental system of the Indians made it as difficult to secure a permanent peace with them as it was to negotiate the purchase of the lands. The sachem, or hereditary peace chief, and the elective war chief, who wielded only the influence that he could secure by his personal prowess and his tact, were equally unable to control all of their tribesmen, and were powerless with their confederated nations. If peace was made with the Shawnees, the war was continued by the Miamis; if peace was made with the latter, nevertheless perhaps one small band was dissatisfied, and continued the contest on its own account; and even if all the recognized bands were dealt with, the parties of renegades or outlaws had to be considered; and in the last resort the full recognition accorded by the Indians to the right of private warfare, made it possible for any individual warrior who possessed any influence to go on raiding and murdering unchecked. Every tribe, every sub-tribe, every band of a dozen souls ruled over by a petty chief, almost every individual warrior of the least importance, had to be met and pacified. Even if peace were declared, the Indians could not exist long without breaking it. There was to them no temptation to trespass on the white man's ground for the purpose of settling; but every young brave was brought up to regard scalps taken and horses stolen, in war or peace, as the highest proofs and tokens of skill and courage, the sure means of attaining glory and honor, the admiration of men and the love of women. Where the young men thought thus, and the chiefs had so little real control, it was inevitable that there should be many unprovoked forays for scalps, slaves, and horses made upon the white borderers.

White Atrocities

As for the whites themselves, they too have many and grievous sins against their red neighbors for which to answer. They cannot be severely blamed for trespassing upon what was called the Indian's land; for let sentimentalists say what they will, the man who puts the soil to use must of right dispossess the man who does not, or the world will come to a standstill; but for many of their other deeds there can be no pardon. On the border each man was a law unto himself, and good and bad alike were left in perfect freedom to follow out to the uttermost limits their own desires; for the spirit of individualism so characteristic of American life reached its extreme of development in the backwoods. The whites who wished peace, the magistrates and leaders, had little more power over their evil and unruly fellows than the Indian sachems had over the turbulent young braves. Each man did what seemed best in his own eyes, almost without let or hindrance; unless, indeed, he trespassed upon the rights of his neighbors, who were ready enough to band together in their own defence, though slow to interfere in the affairs of others.

A Few Naked Barbarians

Lewis Cass, governor of Michigan Territory and superintendent of the territory's Indian affairs, wrote in an 1830 article in the North American Review *that Indians should not prevent America from expanding westward.*

What ignorance, or folly, or morbid jealousy of our national progress does it not argue, to expect that our civilized border would become stationary, and some of the fairest portions of the globe be abandoned to hopeless sterility. That a few naked wandering barbarians should stay the march of civilization and improvement, and hold in a state of perpetual unproductiveness, immense regions formed by Providence to support millions of human beings?

Thus the men of lawless, brutal spirit who are found in every community and who flock to places where the reign of order is lax, were able to follow the bent of their inclinations unchecked. They utterly despised the red man; they held it no crime whatever to cheat him in trading, to rob him of his peltries or horses, to murder him if the fit seized them. Criminals who generally preyed on their own neighbors, found it easier, and perhaps hardly as dangerous, to pursue their calling at the expense of the redskins, for the latter, when they discovered that they had been wronged, were quite as apt to vent their wrath on some outsider as on the original offender. If they injured a white, all the whites might make common cause against them; but if they injured a red man, though there were sure to be plenty of whites who disapproved of it, there were apt to be very few indeed whose disapproval took any active shape.

Each race stood by its own members, and each held all of the other race responsible for the misdeeds of a few uncontrollable spirits; and this clannishness among those of one color, and the refusal or the inability to discriminate between the good and the bad of the other color were the two most fruitful causes of border strife. When, even if he sought to prevent them, the innocent man was sure to suffer for the misdeeds of the guilty, unless both joined together for defence, the former had no alternative save to make common cause with the latter. Moreover, in a sparse backwoods settlement, where the presence of a strong, vigorous fighter was a source of safety to the whole community, it was impossible to expect that he would be punished with severity for offences which, in their hearts, his fellow townsmen could not help regarding as in some sort a revenge for the injuries they had themselves suffered. Every quiet, peaceable settler had either himself been grievously wronged, or had been an eye-witness to wrongs done to his friends; and while these were vivid in his mind, the corresponding wrongs done the Indians were never brought home to him at all. If his son was scalped or his cattle driven off, he could not be expected to remember that perhaps the Indians who did the deed had themselves been cheated by a white trader, or had lost a relative at the hands of some border ruffian, or felt aggrieved because a hundred miles off some settler had built a cabin on lands they considered their own. When he joined with other exasperated and injured men to make a retaliatory inroad, his vengeance might or might not fall on the heads of the real offenders; and, in any case, he was often not in the frame of mind to put a stop to the outrages sure to be committed by the brutal spirits among his allies—though these brutal spirits were probably in a small minority.

Terrible Provocations

The excesses so often committed by the whites, when, after many checks and failures, they at last grasped victory, are causes for shame and regret; yet it is only fair to keep in mind the terrible provocations they had endured. Mercy, pity, magnanimity to the fallen, could not be expected from the frontiersmen gathered together to war against an Indian tribe. Almost every man of such a band had bitter personal wrongs to avenge. He was not taking part in a war against a civilized foe; he was fighting in a contest where women and children suffered the fate of the strong men, and instead of enthusiasm for his country's flag and a general national animosity towards its enemies, he was actuated by a furious flame of hot anger, and was goaded on by memories of which merely to think was madness. His friends had been treacherously slain while on messages of peace; his house had been burned, his cattle driven off, and all he had in the world destroyed before he knew that war existed and when he felt quite guiltless of all offence; his sweetheart or wife had been carried off, ravished, and was at the moment the slave and concubine of some dirty and brutal Indian warrior; his son, the stay of his house, had been burned at the stake with torments too horrible to mention; his sister, when ransomed and returned to him, had told of the weary journey through the woods, when she carried around her neck as a horrible necklace the bloody scalps of her husband and children; seared into his eyeballs, into his very brain, he bore ever with him, waking or sleeping, the sight of the skinned, mutilated, hideous body of the baby who had just grown old enough to recognize him and to crow and laugh when taken in his arms. Such incidents as these were not exceptional; one or more, and often all of them, were the invariable attendants of every one of the countless Indian inroads that took place during the long generations of forest warfare. It was small wonder that men who had thus lost every thing should sometimes be fairly crazed by their wrongs. Again and again on the frontier we hear of some such unfortunate who has devoted all the remainder of his wretched life to the one object of taking vengeance on the whole race of the men who had darkened his days forever. Too often the squaws and pappooses fell victims of the vengeance that should have come only on the warriors; for the whites regarded their foes as beasts rather than men, and knew that the squaws were more cruel than others in torturing the prisoner, and that the very children took their full part therein, being held up by their fathers to tomahawk the dying victims at the stake.

Thus it is that there are so many dark and bloody pages in the book of border warfare, that grim and iron-bound volume, wherein we read how our forefathers won the wide lands that we inherit. It contains many a tale of fierce heroism and adventurous ambition, of the daring and resolute courage of men and the patient endurance of women; it shows us a stern race of freemen who toiled hard, endured greatly, and fronted adversity bravely, who prized strength and courage and good faith, whose wives were chaste, who were generous and loyal to their friends. But it shows us also how they spurned at restraint and fretted under it, how they would brook no wrong to themselves, and yet too often inflicted wrong on others; their feats of terrible prowess are interspersed with deeds of the foulest and most wanton aggression, the darkest treachery, the most revolting cruelty; and though we meet with plenty of the rough, strong, coarse virtues, we see but little of such qualities as mercy for the fallen, the weak, and the helpless, or pity for a gallant and vanquished foe.

CHAPTER 4

Native Traditions Versus Assimilation: The Conflict over Culture

Chapter Preface

At the same time that the Indian Wars were winding down in the late nineteenth century, a growing number of Americans began to voice the opinion that the U.S. government had badly mistreated the Indians. Many of these critics were inspired by the 1881 publication of *A Century of Dishonor* by Helen Hunt Jackson. Jackson's book outlined the federal government's poor record in honoring treaty obligations. She and other reformers concluded that the American Indians were doomed to extinction unless they adopted the ways of the dominant white society. Survival would require the Indians to replace hunting and gathering with agriculture, communal land possession with individual land ownership, and traditional Indian beliefs, clothing, and lifestyles with white customs and practices, reformers believed. Largely through the efforts of Jackson, former abolitionist Wendell Phillips, Massachusetts senator Henry L. Dawes, and other people who considered themselves "friends of the Indian," assimilationist goals dominated federal Indian policy until the 1930s.

The passage of the Dawes Act (or General Allotment Act) by Congress in 1887 ensured that assimilation would remain the focus of U.S. Indian policy for years to come. Under that law, tribal lands were divided up into property units of 40 to 160 acres and allotted to individual Indian families. The federal government was authorized to sell remaining tribal land and use the money for Indian schools. Reformers hoped that the land dispersals would encourage the Indians to give up tribal allegiances and to become independent farmers and ranchers like their white neighbors. Indian schools funded by the Dawes Act and other government funds furthered the cause of assimilation by separating students from their families, requiring them to cut their hair, and forbidding Indian languages, clothing, dancing, and religious ceremonies. In the words of President Theodore Roosevelt, the Dawes Act and subsequent legislation sought "to break up the tribal mass" and thus eradicate Native American tribes as distinct cultural entities.

Reactions of Native Americans to the policies of assimilation were mixed. Some, such as Sitting Bull, steadfastly refused to abandon traditional ways of life. A few Indians adapted and prospered, successfully making the transition to becoming independent farmers or ranchers while retaining some elements of Indian culture. Goodbird, a North Dakota resident and member of the Hidatsa tribe, told a visiting anthropologist in 1906 that "my family and I own four thousand acres of land. . . . I own cattle and horses. I can read English, and my children are in school. . . . I am not afraid." Many Indians, however, found their land allotments under the Dawes Act insufficient for farming or had difficulties in abandoning traditional ways. Caught between two cultures, a significant number succumbed to drink, idleness, and crime.

Congress took the added step of granting citizenship to all Native Americans in 1924. By this time, however, the assimilationist goal was increasingly coming under attack by both Indians and white reformers. Native Americans such as Luther Standing Bear wrote and lectured on the necessity of teaching and preserving traditional Indian values, such as respect for the land. A new generation of white reformers led by anthropologist John Collier challenged the view that Indians should be compelled to abandon tribal unity and cultural traditions. Their criticisms eventually influenced a shift in government policy away from assimilation in the 1930s.

The viewpoints in this chapter examine some of the arguments made in the late nineteenth and early twentieth centuries over U.S. Indian policy and its focus on assimilation.

VIEWPOINT 1

"Necessary for the absorption of the Indians in the great body of American citizenship . . . [is] their individualization in the possession of property."

Indian Tribal Land Should Be Divided and Distributed to Individuals

Carl Schurz (1829–1906)

Carl Schurz served as secretary of the interior under President Rutherford B. Hayes from 1877 to 1881. During his tenure, the German-born liberal political reformer, journalist, and former senator from Missouri sought to reduce corruption in the Bureau of Indian Affairs and to improve the federal government's treatment of American Indians. In the following viewpoint, excerpted from an 1881 article written shortly after he left office, Schurz expresses some of his views on the state of American Indians and on government policy. Arguing that the only choices facing Indians are "extermination or civilization," he calls for reforms that would help Indians assimilate within American society.

One of the changes Schurz suggests in his article was endorsed by many reformers of the time: the breaking up of communally held tribal lands into individual and family lots (the legal term for such division was "allotment in severalty"). Such division, these reformers believed, would encourage the rise of Indian-owned farms, break down tribal authority, and ultimately aid in assimilating Native Americans into "civilized" life. Schurz maintains that such reforms would not only help American Indians adapt to their changing circumstances, but would also reduce

From Carl Schurz, "Present Aspects of the Indian Problem," *North American Review,* July 1881.

conflict between Indians and whites over land and help facilitate the "development of the country." The proposed division of tribal lands Schurz advocates in this article became law in 1887 with the passage of the General Allotment Act, known more commonly as the Dawes Act.

I am profoundly convinced that a stubborn maintenance of the system of large Indian reservations must eventually result in the destruction of the red men, however faithfully the Government may endeavor to protect their rights. It is only a question of time. . . . What we can and should do is, in general terms, to fit the Indians, as much as possible, for the habits and occupations of civilized life, by work and education; to individualize them in the possession and appreciation of property, by allotting to them lands in severalty, giving them a fee simple title individually to the parcels of land they cultivate, inalienable for a certain period, and to obtain their consent to a disposition of that part of their lands which they cannot use, for a fair compensation, in such a manner that they no longer stand in the way of the development of the country as an obstacle, but form part of it and are benefited by it.

The circumstances surrounding them place before the Indians this stern alternative: extermination or civilization. The thought of exterminating a race, once the only occupant of the soil upon which so many millions of our own people have grown prosperous and happy, must be revolting to every American who is not devoid of all sentiments of justice and humanity. To civilize them, which was once only a benevolent fancy, has now become an absolute necessity, if we mean to save them.

Can Indians be civilized? This question is answered in the negative only by those who do not want to civilize them. My experience in the management of Indian affairs, which enabled me to witness the progress made even among the wildest tribes, confirms me in the belief that it is not only possible but easy to introduce civilized habits and occupations among Indians, if only the proper means are employed. We are frequently told that Indians will not work. True, it is difficult to make them work as long as they can live upon hunting. But they will work when their living depends upon it, or when sufficient inducements are offered to them. Of this there is an abundance of proof. To be sure, as to Indian civilization, we must not expect too rapid progress or the attainment of too lofty a standard. We can certainly not transform them at once into great statesmen, or philosophers, or manufacturers, or merchants; but we can make them small farmers and herders. Some of them show even remarkable aptitude for mercantile pursuits on a small scale. I see no reason why the degree of civilization attained by the Indians in the States of New York, Indiana, Michigan, and some tribes in the Indian Territory, should not be attained in the course of time by all. I have no doubt that they can be sufficiently civilized to support themselves, to maintain relations of good neighborship with the people surrounding them, and altogether to cease being a disturbing element in society. The accomplishment of this end, however, will require much considerate care and wise guidance. That care and guidance is necessarily the task of the Government which, as to the Indians at least, must exercise paternal functions until they are sufficiently advanced to take care of themselves. . . .

To fit the Indians for their ultimate absorption in the great body of American citizenship, three things are suggested by common sense as well as philanthropy.

1. That they be taught to work by making work profitable and attractive to them.

2. That they be educated, especially the youth of both sexes.

3. That they be individualized in the possession of property by settlement in severalty with a fee simple title, after which the lands they do not use may be disposed of for general settlement and enterprise without danger and with profit to the Indians.

This may seem a large programme, strangely in contrast with the old wild life of the Indians, but they are now more disposed than ever before to accept it. Even those of them who have so far been in a great measure living upon the chase, are becoming aware that the game is fast disappearing, and will no longer be sufficient to furnish them a sustenance. In a few years the buffalo will be exterminated, and smaller game is gradually growing scarce except in the more inaccessible mountain regions. The necessity of procuring food in some other way is thus before their eyes. The requests of Indians addressed to the Government for instruction in agriculture, for agricultural implements, and for stock cattle, are in consequence now more frequent and pressing than ever before. A more general desire for the education of their children springs from the same source, and many express a wish for the allotment of farm tracts among them, with "the white man's paper," meaning a good, strong title like that held by white men. This progressive movement is, of course, different in degree with different tribes, but it is going on more or less everywhere. The failure of [Sioux leader] Sitting Bull's attempt to maintain himself and a large number of followers on our northern frontier in the old wild ways of Indian life will undoubtedly strengthen the tendency among the wild Indians of the North-west to recognize the situation and to act accordingly. The general state of feeling among the red men is therefore now exceedingly favorable to the civilizing process. . . .

The Allotment of Land Will Advance the Race

The Indian Rights Association, founded in Philadelphia in 1882, was one of several groups that lobbied for reforms in U.S. government policy toward American Indians. The following passage is taken from an 1884 pamphlet produced by the group that promotes the allotment of tribal lands to individual Indians in order to make them self-sufficient.

For many years past those who have given earnest thought to the best method of placing the Indian on a right footing among us, and patient effort to accomplish this result, have united in the belief that the allotment of land to individual Indians by a secure title would prove one of the most powerful agencies in the advancement of the race.

It has been often pointed out that we have by our policy taken from the Indian the ordinary and essential stimulus to labor. While under our system of pauperizing Indians by the issuing of rations we deprive them of the ordinary necessity for self-support, by our refusal to protect them in the possession of their land and by our incessant removals we take away the common motives for cultivating it. The great mass of men work from the imperative necessity for self-support, and from the knowledge that the law will protect them in the possession of their rightful earnings. We have so alienated the Indian from all natural and general conditions, we have placed him in such an artificial and unjust position, that he has neither the necessity for self-support nor any proper protection in the result of his labor. It is a matter of surprise to all who fairly consider all the elements in the case, not that the result is no better, but that it is not far worse.

To give the Indian, then, a secure title to land, so that he may have the assurance of reaping what he has sown, is the plainest justice and good policy.

As the third thing necessary for the absorption of the Indians in the great body of American citizenship, I mentioned their individualization in the possession of property by their settlement in severalty upon small farm tracts with a fee simple title. When the Indians are so settled, and have become individual property-owners, holding their farms by the same title under the law by which white men hold theirs, they will feel more readily inclined to part with such of their lands as they cannot themselves cultivate, and from which they can derive profit only if they sell them, either in lots or in bulk, for a fair equivalent in money or in annuities. This done, the Indians will occupy no more ground than so many white people; the large reservations will gradually be opened to general settlement and enterprise, and the Indians, with their possessions, will cease to stand in the way of the "development of the country." The difficulty which has provoked so many encroachments and conflicts will then no longer exist. When the Indians are individual owners of real property, and as individuals enjoy the protection of the laws, their tribal cohesion will necessarily relax, and gradually disappear. They will have advanced an immense step in the direction of the "white man's way."

Is this plan practicable? In this respect we are not entirely without experience. Allotments of farm tracts to Indians and their settlement in severalty have already been attempted under special laws or treaties with a few tribes; in some instances, with success; in others, the Indians, when they had acquired individual title to their land, and before they had learned to appreciate its value, were induced to dispose of it, or were tricked out of it by unscrupulous white men, who took advantage of their ignorance. They were thus impoverished again, and some of them fell back upon the Government for support. This should be guarded against, as much as it can be, by a legal provision making the title to their farm tracts inalienable for a certain period, say twenty-five years, during which the Indians will have sufficient opportunity to acquire more provident habits, to become somewhat acquainted with the ways of the world, and to learn to take care of themselves. In some cases where the allotment of lands in severalty and the granting of patents conveying a fee simple title to Indians was provided for in Indian treaties, the Interior Department under the last administration saw fit to put off the full execution of this provision for the reason that the law did not permit the insertion in the patent of the inalienability clause, that without such a clause the Indians would be exposed to the kind of spoliation above mentioned, and that it was hoped Congress would speedily supply that deficiency by the passage of the general "Severalty bill," then under discussion. Indeed, without such a clause in the land-patents, it cannot be denied that the conveyance of individual fee simple title to Indians would be a hazardous experiment, except in the case of those most advanced in civilization. . . .

Protecting Indians from White Encroachment

Complications may arise at any time where the pressure of advancing enterprise upon Indian reservations is very great, and sustained by a numerous and rapidly increasing population, but especially where valuable mineral deposits have been discovered or their discovery is in prospect. There is nothing more dangerous to an Indian reservation than a rich mine. But the repeated invasions of the Indian Territory, as well as many other similar occurrences, have shown clearly enough that the attraction of good agricultural lands is apt to have the same effect, especially when great railroad enterprises are pushing in the same direction. It required, on the part of the Government, the greatest vigilance and energy to frustrate the attempted invasions of the Indian Territory, year after year. But as the endeavors of the Government have not always in similar cases had the same success in the past, they may not always be equally successful in the future, and there is now scarcely a single Indian reservation in the country that will not soon be exposed to the same chances. It is, therefore, of the utmost importance to the Indians, as well as to the country generally, that a policy be adopted which will secure to them and their descendants the safe possession of such tracts of land as they can cultivate, and a fair compensation for the rest; and that such a policy be proceeded with before the protection of their present large possessions by the Government becomes too precarious, that is to say, before conflicts are precipitated upon them which the Government is not always able to prevent, and by which they may be in danger of losing their lands, their compensation, and even their lives, at the same time. It would undoubtedly be better if they could be carefully prepared for such a change of condition, so that they might clearly appreciate all its requirements and the consequences which are to follow. But those intrusted with the management of Indian affairs must not forget that, with regard to some Indian tribes and reservations at least, the matter is pressing; that the Government cannot control circumstances but is rather apt to be controlled by them, and that it must not only devise the necessary preparations for the change in the condition of the Indians with forecast and wisdom, but must push them with the greatest possible expedition and energy if untoward accidents are to be avoided.

A Necessary Law

It is, therefore, very much to be regretted that the bill authorizing and enabling the Interior Department to settle the Indians in severalty wherever practicable, to give them patents, conveying a fee simple title to their allotments, inalienable for a certain period, and to dispose of the reservation lands not so allotted with the consent of the Indians and for their benefit, so that they may be opened for general settlement and enterprise, did not become a law at the last session of Congress, or, rather, that such a law was not enacted years ago. The debate in the Senate on the Severalty bill, last winter [1880], turned on the imperfections of its details. No doubt, such imperfections existed. It would, indeed, be very difficult, if not impossible, to draw up a bill of this kind so perfect in all its details that further experience gathered from its practical application might not suggest some desirable amendment. But the essential thing is that opportunity be given to the branch of the Government managing Indian affairs to gather such further experience from the actual experiment, and that opportunity will be given only by the enactment of a law containing the principal features of the plan, and allowing the Executive sufficient latitude in applying it, according to circumstances, wherever the Indians may be prepared for it, or wherever, even without such preparation, the exigencies of the case may demand prompt action. The Executive will then be able understandingly to recommend amendments in the details of the law, as practical experience may point out their necessity. Certainly, not another session of Congress should he permitted to pass without comprehensive legislation on this important subject.

I am aware that I have not discussed here all points of importance connected with the Indian problem, such, for instance, as the necessity of extending the jurisdiction of the courts over Indian reservations, bringing the red men under the protection as well as the restraints of the law; and the question how the service should be organized to secure to the Indians intelligent, honest, and humane management, etc. It has been my purpose merely to set forth those important points which, in the practical management of Indian affairs, should be steadily kept in view. I will recapitulate them:

(1) The greatest danger hanging over the Indian race arises from the fact that, with their large and valuable territorial possessions which are lying waste, they stand in the way of what is commonly called "the development of the country."

(2) A rational Indian policy will make it its principal object to avert that danger from the red men, by doing what will be most beneficial to them, as well as to the whole people: namely, by harmonizing the habits, occupations, and interests of the Indians with that "development of the country."

(3) To accomplish this object, it is of pressing necessity to set the Indians to work, to educate their youth of both sexes, to make them small proprietors of land, with the right of individual ownership under the protection of the law, and to induce them to make that part of their lands which they do not need for cultivation, profitable to themselves in the only possible way, by selling it at a just rate of compensation, thus opening it to general settlement and enterprise.

Two Classes of Opponents

The policy here outlined is apt to be looked upon with disfavor by two classes of people: on the one hand, those who think that "the only good Indian is a dead Indian," and who denounce every recognition of the Indian's rights and every desire to promote his advancement in civilization, as sickly sentimentality; and on the other hand, that class of philanthropists who, in their treatment of the Indian question, pay no regard to surrounding circumstances and suspect every policy contemplating a reduction of the Indian reservations of being a scheme of spoliation and robbery, gotten up by speculators and "land-grabbers." With the first class it seems useless to reason. As to the second, they do not themselves believe, if they are sensible, that twenty-five years hence millions of acres of valuable land will, in any part of the country, still be kept apart as Indian hunting-grounds. The question is, whether the Indians are to be exposed to the danger of hostile collisions, and of being robbed of their lands in consequence, or whether they are to be induced by proper and fair means to sell that which, as long as they keep it, is of no advantage to anybody, but which, as soon as they part with it for a just compensation, will be of great advantage to themselves and their white neighbors alike. No true friend of the Indian will hesitate to choose the latter line of policy as one in entire accord with substantial justice, humanity, the civilization and welfare of the red men, and the general interests of the country.

VIEWPOINT 2

"The main purpose of this bill is not to help the Indian . . . so much as it is to provide a method for getting at the valuable Indian lands."

Indian Tribal Land Should Not Be Divided and Distributed to Individuals

Minority Members of the House Committee on Indian Affairs

During the 1870s and 1880s, there was growing support for the passage of federal legislation that would institute the allotment of Indian reservation land in severalty—that is, the division of communally owned tribal lands into individually owned lots. Many missionary and philanthropic organizations endorsed such land reform because they believed it would encourage Native Americans to become self-sufficient farmers and would weaken their tribal identities, thus hastening their assimilation into American life. The proposed legislation also gained backing from many western representatives in Congress who supported provisions that would open up to public sale the "surplus" Indian land that remained following individual allotment.

In 1880 the Committee on Indian Affairs of the House of Representatives proposed that Congress pass a land severalty measure. However, a minority of the committee dissented and filed a minority report, from which the following viewpoint is taken. The document, one of the few congressional expressions of opposition to the idea of allotment in severalty, includes several arguments against the idea. The authors of the report argue that past experiments with distributing tribal lands to individual Indian families

From the U.S. House of Representatives Minority Report, no. 1576, 46th Cong., 2nd sess., serial 1938, pp. 7–10, 1880.

have failed in their goals of encouraging assimilation and self-sufficiency. They maintain that such distribution will not produce positive results for most Indians, who have little conception of private property. In addition, the minority members of the committee charge that the true purpose of such legislation is to further deprive Indians of their land.

Congress failed to pass allotment legislation in 1880. However, similar proposals continued to be introduced, and in 1887 land reform was enacted with the passage of the General Allotment Act (or Dawes Act). The federal government promoted the policy of individual land ownership until 1934. By that time, through a variety of means, the amount of land possessed by American Indians had fallen from 138 million acres to 52 million acres.

The undersigned, members of the Committee on Indian Affairs of the House of Representatives, are unable to agree with the majority of the committee in reporting favorably upon this bill, for these, among other, reasons, viz:

I. The bill is confessedly in the nature of an experiment. It is formed solely upon a theory, and it has no practical basis to stand upon. For many years it has been the hobby of speculative philanthropists that the true plan to civilize the Indian was to assign him lands in severalty, and thereby make a farmer and self-sustaining citizen of him; and so far back as 1862 Congress established the policy that—

> Whenever any Indian, being a member of any band or tribe with whom the government has or shall have entered into treaty stipulations, being desirous to adopt the habits of civilized life, has had a portion of the lands belonging to his tribe allotted to him in severalty, in pursuance of such treaty stipulations, the agent and superintendent of such tribe shall take such measures, not inconsistent with law, as may be necessary to protect such Indian in the quiet enjoyment of the lands so allotted to him.

This law stands to-day on the statute book as the recognized policy of this government of the United States in its dealings with the Indians. It does not make allotments of lands in severalty obligatory, but recognizing the plea of those who contend for the beneficent effects sure to flow from the allotment policy, it has opened the door to its establishment, allowing any Indian, in any tribe, desiring to try that policy, a full opportunity to do so under the protection of the government. That law has been upon the statute book for nearly eighteen years, and how many Indians have availed themselves of its provisions? Manifestly, very few; and yet we are told, with great pertinacity, that the Indians are strongly in favor of that policy, and will adopt it if they get a chance. It is surpassing strange, if this be true, that so few have availed themselves of the privileges opened to them by the act of 1862.

Being an experiment merely, it would seem to be the dictate of wisdom to make the trial of putting it into practice on a small basis, say with any one tribe that offers a good opportunity for trying it fairly. The Chippewa bands on Lake Superior, for instance, are alleged to be willing to enter upon the experiment. They have good agricultural lands, are partially civilized and educated, and are sufficiently removed from barbarism to give ground for hope that the experiment may succeed. There could be no very strong reason against trying the experiment merely as an experiment with them. But this bill, without any previous satisfactory test of the policy, proposes to enact a merely speculative theory into a law, and to apply the law to all the Indians, except a few civilized tribes, and to bring them all under its operation without reference to their present condition. It includes the blanket Indians with those who wear the clothing of civilized life; the wild Apaches and Navajos with the nearly civilized Chippewas; and it applies the same rule to all without regard to the wide differences in their condition. It seeks to make a farmer out of the roving and predatory Ute by the same process as would be applied to the nearly civilized Omahas and Poncas. It needs no argument to prove that these Indian tribes vary widely from each other in their civilized attainments, but this bill ignores all these variances as if they did not exist, and erects a Procrustean bed, upon which it would place every Indian, stretching out those who are too short, and cutting off the heads or feet of those who are too long.

It is true that the bill leaves a great deal as to the time of putting the bill in operation to the discretion of the Secretary of the Interior; but we submit that the interests of these tribes are of too great a magnitude to be left to the discretion of any one man, even though he be a Secretary of the Interior. We know of nothing in the constitution of that department that qualifies it peculiarly for such a great trust. Secretaries of the Interior change as frequently as the occurrence of a Mexican or South American revolution; and Congress, we think, is a safer depository for such trusts than any one man, no matter what place he may hold. Let us deal with these people intelligently and wisely, and not at haphazard.

We have said that this bill has no practical basis and is a mere legislative speculation; but it may be added that the experiment it proposes *has* been partially tried, and has always resulted in failure. In the hurry of drawing up reports we cannot be ex-

177

The Allotment of Land Will Impoverish the Indians

In 1881, leaders of the "Five Civilized Tribes" in Indian Territory were sufficiently concerned about congressional debate over land reform legislation to send a formal letter of protest in which they objected to the concept of dividing tribal land into individual lots. The Five Civilized Tribes were excluded from the 1887 Dawes Act, but in 1898 Congress extended allotment to them and abolished their constitutional governments.

To the Congress of the United States:

As representatives of the leading nations of the Indian Territory we desire to call your attention to several measures pending before you, the purpose of which is to change the condition and compromise the safety of the Indian people. We refer to the bills for sectionizing and allotting in severalty the lands of the Indians. We have understood that such bills were not intended to apply to the Indian Territory, as there is no provision for white settlement in that country, and the treaties define that this allotment in severalty can only be done on the request of the Indian nations.

We therefore appeal to you not to violate your pledges to us in treaties. Doing this . . . would lead to local disturbance and produce great mischief.

Our people have not asked for or authorized this, for the reason that they believe it could do no good and would only result in mischief in their present condition. Our own laws regulate a system of land tenure suited to our condition and much safer than that which is proposed to be established for it. Improvements can be and are frequently sold, but the land itself is not a chattel. Its occupancy and

pected to be very specific in our citations, but we may cite the case of the Catawbas, who had lands assigned them in severalty, and who were protected by the inalienability of their homesteads for twenty-five years, just as this bill proposes; and the result was a failure—a flat, miserable failure. The Catawbas gradually withered away under the policy, until there is not one of them left to attest the fact that they ever existed, and their lands fell a prey to the whites who surrounded them and steadily encroached upon them. . . .

II. The plan of this bill is not, in our judgment, the way to civilize the Indian. However much we may differ with the humanitarians who are riding this hobby, we are certain that they will agree with us in the proposition that it does not make a farmer out of an Indian to give him a quarter-section of land. There are hundreds of thousands of white men, rich with the experiences of centuries of Anglo-Saxon civilization, who cannot be transformed into cultivators of the land by any such gift. Their habits unfit them for it; and possession are indispensable to holding it, and its abandonment for two years makes it revert to the public domain. In this way every one of our citizens is sure of a home.

The change to individual title would throw the whole of our domain in a few years into the hands of a few persons. In your treaties with us you have agreed that this shall not be done without our consent; we have not asked for it, and we call on you not to violate your pledges with us.

There are other reasons involving prosperity and safety, why the limitations of sectionizing should not be thrust over us. A large portion of our country, and at least two-thirds of the Indian Territory, are only suitable for grazing purposes. No man can afford to live by stock-raising and herding who is restricted to one hundred and sixty or even three hundred and twenty acres, especially on lands away from water. The herds must be sufficiently large to justify the care of them. The pasture country of the United States is fast being reduced. It is necessary for your prosperity, as well as our own, that what little is left of it should not be destroyed by vicious and ill-adapted systems of legislation. We would instance a single case outside of the Indian Territory. The Navajos, in New Mexico, do not number much more than one-fourth of the Cherokee Nation. Their reserve is as large as the reserved lands of the Cherokee Nation. Not more than one acre in twenty is suitable for cultivation. They live by pastoral pursuits. They are stated to have 800,000 sheep, 300,000 head of cattle, and 40,000 horses; by this business they live, comfortable, exporting wool and livestock. By sectionizing or reducing them to one hundred and sixty acres, you would pauperize and ruin a people who are now holding to your productive industries.

how much more do the habits of the Indian, begotten of hundreds of years of wild life, unfit *him* for entering at once and peremptorily upon a life for which he has no fitness? It requires inclination, knowledge of agriculture, and training in farming life to make a successful farmer out of even white men, many of whom have failed at the trial of it, even with an inclination for it. How, then, is it expected to transform all sorts of Indians, with no fitness or inclination for farming, into successful agriculturists? Surely an act of Congress, however potent in itself, with the addition of the discretion of a Secretary of the Interior, no matter how much of a *doctrinnaire* he may be, are not sufficient to work such a miracle.

The Tribal System

The whole training of an Indian from his birth, the whole history of the Indian race, and the entire array of Indian tradition, running back for at least four hundred years, all combine to predispose the Indian against this scheme for his improvement, devised by those who judge him exclusively from *their* standpoint instead of from *his*. From the time of the discovery of America, and for centuries probably before that, the North American Indian has been a communist. Not in the offensive sense of modern communism, but in the sense of holding property in common. The tribal system has kept bands and tribes together as families, each member of which was dependent on the other. The very idea of property in the soil was unknown to the Indian mind. In all the Indian languages there is no word answering to the Latin *habeo*—have or possess. They had words to denote holding, as "I have a hatchet"; but the idea of the separate possession of property by individuals is as foreign to the Indian mind as communism is to us.

This communistic idea has grown into their very being, and is an integral part of the Indian character. From our point of view this is all wrong; but it is folly to think of uprooting it, strengthened by the traditions of centuries, through the agency of a mere act of Congress, or by the establishment of a theoretical policy. The history of the world shows that it is no easy matter to change old methods of thought or force the adoption of new methods of action. The inborn conservatism of human nature tends always more strongly to the preservation of old ideas than to the establishment of new ones. The world progresses steadily, but always slowly. There are singularities in the Anglo-Saxon character and peculiarities in Anglo-Saxon belief which run back over a thousand years, and which all the enlightenment of progressive centuries has been unable to overcome. There are, even in our own land system, peculiarities which are the remnants of feudal forms and practices, and which still inhere in our methods simply from the force of habit and the conservatism of forms. And if this is true of ourselves, with a written history running back well-nigh two thousand years, why should we be so vain as to expect that the Indian can throw off in a moment, at the bidding of Congress or the Secretary of the Interior, the shackles which have bound his thoughts and action from time immemorial? In this, as in all other cases, it is the dictate of statesmanship to make haste slowly.

We are free to admit that the two civilizations, so different throughout, cannot well co-exist, or flourish together. One must, in time, give way to the other, and the weak must in the end be supplanted by the strong. But it cannot be violently wrenched out of place and cast aside. Nations cannot be made to change their habits and methods and modes of thought in a day. To bring the Indian to look at things from our standpoint is a work requiring time, patience, and the skill as well as the benign spirit of Christian statesmanship. Let us first demonstrate, on a small scale, the practibility of the plans we propose; and when we have done that, if we can do it, a persevering patience will be needed to make the policy general.

III. The theory that the Indian is a man and a citizen, able to take care of himself, possessed of the attributes of manhood in their broadest sense, and fully responsible to all the laws of our civilized life—a man like other men, and therefore to be treated exactly as other men—is embodied in the first part of this bill, which provides for giving every Indian a farm, and leaving him then to take care of himself, because, as is assumed by the framers of the bill, he *is* able to take care of himself; but having thus launched the Indian upon his future course of life, the bill turns round upon itself and, assuming that the Indian *is not* and *will not be* able to take care of himself, at once proceeds to hedge him around with provisions intended to prevent him from exercising any of the rights of a land-owner except that of working and living on his allotment. He cannot sell, mortgage, lease, or in any way alienate his land; and although he is to be under and amenable to the laws, he is to be free from taxation for all purposes. He is to be treated as a man in giving him land and exacting from him the duty of maintaining himself upon and off of it, and all this upon the plea that he is simply a man, who is to be treated as other men are; and then, as soon as we do this, we proceed to treat him as a child, an infant, a ward in chancery, who is unable to take care of himself and therefore needs the protecting care of government. If he *is* able to take care of himself, all this precaution is unnecessary; if he is *not* able to take care of himself, all this effort to make him try to do it is illogical. If the Indian is a ward under the paternal care of government, he might as well hold his lands in common as in severalty. He cannot be made to feel the pride which a man feels in the ownership of property while he is made to feel that he does not possess one single attribute of separate ownership in the soil. . . .

The Real Purpose of This Bill

The main purpose of this bill is not to help the Indian, or solve the Indian problem, or provide a method for getting out of our Indian troubles, so much as it is to provide a method for getting at the valuable Indian lands and opening them up to white settlement. The main object of the bill is in the last sections of it, not in the first. The sting of this animal is in its tail. When the Indian has got his allotments, the rest of his land is to be put up to the highest bidder, and he is to be surrounded in his allotments with a wall of fire, a cordon of white settlements, which will gradually but surely hem him in, circumscribe him, and eventually crowd him out. True, the proceeds of the sale are to be invested for the Indians; but when the Indian is smothered out, as he will be under the operations of this bill, the investment will revert to the national Treasury, and the Indian, in the long run, will be none the better for it; for nothing can be surer than the eventual extermination of the Indian under the operation of this bill.

The real aim of this bill is to get at the Indian lands and open them up to settlement. The provisions for the apparent benefit of the Indian are but the pretext to get at his lands and occupy them. With that accomplished, we have securely paved the way for the extermination of the Indian races upon this part of the continent. If this were done in the name of Greed, it would be bad enough; but to do it in the name of Humanity, and under the cloak of an ardent desire to promote the Indian's welfare by making him like ourselves, whether he will or not, is infinitely worse. Of all the attempts to encroach upon the Indian, this attempt to manufacture him into a white man by act of Congress and the grace of the Secretary of the Interior is the baldest, the boldest, and the most unjustifiable.

Whatever civilization has been reached by the Indian tribes has been attained under the tribal system, and not under the system proposed by this bill. The Cherokees, Choctaws, Chickasaws, Creeks, and Seminoles, all five of them barbarous tribes within the short limit of our history as a people, have all been brought to a creditable state of advancement under the tribal system. The same may be said of the Sioux and Chippewas, and many smaller tribes. Gradually, under that system, they are working out their own deliverance, which will come in their own good time if we but leave them alone and perform our part of the many contracts we have made with them. But that we have never yet done, and it seems from this bill we will never yet do. We want their lands, and we are bound to have them. Let those take a part in despoiling them who will; for ourselves, we believe the entire policy of this bill to be wrong, ill-timed, and unstatesmanlike; and we put ourselves on record against it as about all that is now left us to do, except to vote against the bill on its final passage.

VIEWPOINT 3

"The Indian youth . . . should be imbued with a genuine patriotism, and made to feel that the United States, and not some paltry reservation, is their home."

Indian Education Should Emphasize American Culture

Thomas J. Morgan (1839–1902)

Thomas J. Morgan was appointed commissioner of Indian affairs by President Benjamin Harrison in 1889. Previously a Civil War officer, Baptist minister, and Rhode Island education official, Morgan was a strong believer in the potential of education to inculcate in American Indian children the cultural values of white Protestant America.

The following viewpoint is taken from a statement of general principles that was included both in Morgan's 1889 annual report to the secretary of the interior and in his presentation at a conference of Indian policy reformers that met at Lake Mohonk, New York, that same year. In his statement, Morgan argues for the creation of a national school system that would provide universal education for American Indian children. Such a program, he maintains, would prepare these children "for American citizenship and assimilation into the national life."

From Thomas J. Morgan, "Supplemental Report on Indian Education," House Executive Document no. 1, part 5, vol. 2, 51st Cong., 1st sess., serial 2725, 1889.

The American Indians, not including the so-called Indians of Alaska, are supposed to number about 250,000, and to have a school population (six to sixteen years) of perhaps 50,000. If we exclude the five civilized tribes which provide for the education of their own children and the New York Indians, who are provided for by that State, the number of Indians of school age to be educated by the Government does not exceed 36,000, of whom 15,000 were enrolled in schools last year [1888], leaving but 21,000 to be provided with school privileges.

These people are separated into numerous tribes, and differ very widely in their language, religion, native characteristics, and modes of life. Some are very ignorant and degraded, living an indolent and brutish sort of life, while others have attained to a high degree of civilization, scarcely inferior to that of their white neighbors. Any generalizations regarding these people must, therefore, be considered as applicable to any particular tribe with such modifications as its peculiar place in the scale of civilization warrants. It is certainly true, however, that as a mass the Indians are far below the whites of this country in their general intelligence and mode of living. They enjoy very few of the comforts, and almost none of the luxuries, which are the pride and boast of their more fortunate neighbors.

Converting Indians into American Citizens

When we speak of the education of the Indians, we mean that comprehensive system of training and instruction which will convert them into American citizens, put within their reach the blessings which the rest of us enjoy, and enable them to compete successfully with the white man on his own ground and with his own methods. Education is to be the medium through which the rising generation of Indians are to be brought into fraternal and harmonious relationship with their white fellow-citizens, and with them enjoy the sweets of refined homes, the delight of social intercourse, the emoluments of commerce and trade, the advantages of travel, together with the pleasures that come from literature, science, and philosophy, and the solace and stimulus afforded by a true religion.

That such a great revolution for these people is possible is becoming more and more evident to those who have watched with an intelligent interest the work which, notwithstanding all its hindrances and discouragements, has been accomplished for them during the last few years. It is no longer doubtful that, under a wise system of education, carefully administered, the condition of this whole people can be radically improved in a single generation.

Under the peculiar relations which the Indians sustain to the Government of the United States, the responsibility for their education rests primarily and almost wholly upon the nation. This grave responsibility, which has now been practically assumed by the Government, must be borne by it alone. It can not safely or honorably either shirk it or delegate it to any other party. The task is not by any means an herculean one. The entire Indian school population is less than that of Rhode Island. The Government of the United States, now one of the richest on the face of the earth, with an overflowing Treasury, has at its command unlimited means, and can undertake and complete the work without feeling it to be in any degree a burden. Although very imperfect its details, and needing to be modified and improved in many particulars, the present system of schools is capable, under wise direction, of accomplishing all that can be desired.

Necessary Steps

In order that the Government shall be able to secure the best results in the education of the Indians, certain things are desirable, indeed, I might say necessary, viz:

First. Ample provision should be made at an early day for the accommodation of the entire mass of Indian school children and youth. To resist successfully and overcome the tremendous downward pressure of inherited prejudice and the stubborn conservatism of centuries, nothing less than universal education should be attempted.

Second. Whatever steps are necessary should be taken to place these children under proper educational influences. If, under any circumstances, compulsory education is justifiable, it certainly is in this case. Education, in the broad sense in which it is here used, is the Indians' only salvation. With it they will become honorable, useful, happy citizens of a great republic, sharing on equal terms in all its blessings. Without it they are doomed either to destruction or to hopeless degradation.

Third. The work of Indian education should be completely systematized. The camp schools, agency boarding schools, and the great industrial schools should be related to each other so as to form a connected and complete whole. So far as possible there should be a uniform course of study, similar methods of instruction, the same textbooks, and a carefully organized and well-understood system of industrial training.

Fourth. The system should be conformed, so far as practicable, to the common-school system now universally adopted in all the States. It should be non-partisan, non-sectarian. The teachers and employes should be appointed only after the most rigid scrutiny into their qualifications for their work. They should have a stable tenure of office, being removed only for cause. They should receive for their service wages corresponding to those paid for similar service in the public schools. They should be carefully inspected and supervised by a sufficient number of properly qualified superintendents.

Fifth. While, for the present, special stress should be laid upon that kind of industrial training which will fit the Indians to earn an honest living in the various occupations which may be open to them, ample provision should also be made for that general literary culture which the experience of the white race has shown to be the very essence of education. Especial attention should be directed toward giving them a ready command of the English language. To this end, only English should be allowed to be spoken, and only English-speaking teachers should be employed in schools supported wholly or in part by the Government.

Sixth. The scheme should make ample provision for the higher education of the few who are endowed with special capacity or ambition, and are destined to leadership. There is an imperative necessity for this, if the Indians are to be assimilated into the national life.

Against Reservations and Tribes

Seventh. That which is fundamental in all this is the recognition of the complete manhood of the Indians, their individuality, their right to be recognized as citizens of the United States, with the same rights and privileges which we accord to any other class or people. They should be free to make for themselves homes wherever they will. The reservation system is an anachronism which has no place in our modern civilization. The Indian youth should be instructed in their rights, privileges, and duties as American citizens; should be taught to love the American flag; should be imbued with a genuine patriotism, and made to feel that the United States, and not some paltry reservation, is their home. Those charged with their education should constantly strive to awaken in them a sense of independence, self-reliance, and self-respect.

Eighth. Those educated in the large industrial boarding-schools should not be returned to the camps against their will, but should be not only allowed, but encouraged to choose their own vocations, and contend for the prizes of life wherever the opportunities are most favorable. Education should seek the disintegration of the tribes, and not their segregation. They should be educated, not as Indians, but as Americans. In short, the public school should do for them what it is so successfully doing for all the other races in this country, assimilate them.

Ninth. The work of education should begin with them while they are young and susceptible, and should continue until habits of industry and love of learning have taken the place of indolence and indifference. One of the chief defects which have heretofore characterized the efforts made for their education has been the failure to carry them far enough, so that they might compete suc-

Kill the Indian, Save the Man

Richard Henry Pratt, a former captain in the U.S. Army, founded the Carlisle Indian School in Pennsylvania and was its superintendent from 1879 to 1904. The Indian students were given industrial training and were immersed in white culture and society; during the summers they worked in surrounding communities. Both Pratt and the institution he founded received much acclaim for their work. In the following passages from an 1892 address in Denver, Colorado, Pratt expresses his views on the goals of educating American Indians.

A great general has said that the only good Indian is a dead one, and that high sanction of his destruction has been an enormous factor in promoting Indian massacres. In a sense, I agree with the sentiment, but only in this: that all the Indian there is in the race should be dead. Kill the Indian in him, and save the man. . . .

It is a great mistake to think that the Indian is born an inevitable savage. He is born a blank, like all the rest of us. Left in the surroundings of savagery, he grows to possess a savage language, superstition, and life. We, left in the surroundings of civilization, grow to possess a civilized language, life, and purpose. Transfer the infant white to the savage surroundings, he will grow to possess a savage language, superstition, and habit. Transfer the savage-born infant to the surroundings of civilization, and he will grow to possess a civilized language and habit. These results have been established over and over again beyond all question; and it is also well established that those advanced in life, even to maturity, of either class, lose already acquired qualities belonging to the side of their birth, and gradually take on those of the side to which they have been transferred. . . .

The school at Carlisle is an attempt on the part of the government to do this. Carlisle has always planted treason to the tribe and loyalty to the nation at large. It has preached against colonizing Indians, and in favor of individualizing them. It has demanded for them the same multiplicity of chances which all others in the country enjoy. Carlisle fills young Indians with the spirit of loyalty to the stars and stripes, and then moves them out into our communities to show by their conduct and ability that the Indian is no different from the white or the colored, that he has the inalienable right to liberty and opportunity that the white and the negro have. Carlisle does not dictate to him what line of life he should fill, so it is an honest one. It says to him that, if he gets his living by the sweat of his brow, and demonstrates to the nation that he is a man, he does more good for his race than hundreds of his fellows who cling to their tribal communistic surroundings.

cessfully with the white youth, who have enjoyed the far greater advantages of our own system of education. Higher education is even more essential to them than it is for white children.

Tenth. Special pains should be taken to bring together in the large boarding-schools members of as many different tribes as possible, in order to destroy the tribal antagonism and to generate in them a feeling of common brotherhood and mutual respect. Wherever practicable, they should be admitted on terms of equality into the public schools, where, by daily contact with white children, they may learn to respect them and become respected in turn. Indeed, it is reasonable to expect that at no distant day, when the Indians shall have all taken up their lands in severalty and have become American citizens, there will cease to be any necessity for Indian schools maintained by the Government. The Indians, where it is impracticable for them to unite with their white neighbors, will maintain their own schools.

Eleventh. Co-education of the sexes is the surest and perhaps only way in which the Indian women can be lifted out of that position of servility and degradation which most of them now occupy, on to a plane where their husbands and the men generally will treat them with the same gallantry and respect which is accorded to their more favored white sisters.

Twelfth. The happy results already achieved at Carlisle, Hampton, and elsewhere by the so-called "outing system," which consists in placing Indian pupils in white families where they are taught the ordinary routine of housekeeping, farming, etc., and are brought into intimate relationship with the highest type of American rural life, suggests the wisdom of a large extension of the system. By this means they acquire habits of industry, a practical acquaintance with civilized life, a sense of independence, enthusiasm for home, and the practical ability to earn their own living. This system has in it the "promise and the potency" of their complete emancipation.

Thirteenth. Of course, it is to be understood that, in addition to all of the work here outlined as belonging to the Government for the education and civilization of the Indians, there will be requisite the influence of the home, the Sabbath-school, the church, and religious institutions of learning. There will be urgent need of consecrated missionary work and liberal expenditure of money on the part of individuals and religious organizations in behalf of these people. Christian schools and colleges have already been established for them by missionary zeal, and others will doubtless follow. But just as the work of the public schools is supplemented in the States by Christian agencies, so will the work of Indian education by the Government be supplemented by the same agencies. There need be no conflict and no unseemly rivalry. The Indians, like any other class of citizens, will be free to patronize those schools which they believe to be best adapted to their purpose. . . .

Economic Costs and Benefits

[T]he estimated amount which will be required annually for the maintenance of a Government system of education for all Indians will amount to $3,102,500. Of course, in addition to this, an expenditure will have to be made each year to repair and otherwise keep in good order the various school buildings and furnishings.

In this connection, it is well to note that the sum paid for education by the city of Boston amounts to $1,700,000; by the State of New York more than $16,000,000 annually; while the cost of the maintenance of the public-school system of the States and Territories of this country as a whole, according to the report of the Commissioner of Education, is more than $115,000,000. The United States pays for the maintenance of a little army of about 25,000 men nearly $25,000,000 annually; the appropriation for the fiscal year ended June 30, 1889, aggregated $24,575,700.

In estimating the cost of maintaining an adequate school system for the Indians two great economical facts should steadily be borne in mind. The first is that by this system of public education the Indian will, at no distant day, be prepared not only for self-support, but also to take his place as a productive element in our social economy. The pupils at the Carlisle Indian Training School earned last year [1888] by their labors among the Pennsylvania farmers more than $10,000, and this year [1889] more than $12,000. From facts like these it can easily be demonstrated that, simply as a matter of investment, the nation can afford to pay the amount required for Indian education, with a view of having it speedily returned to the aggregate of national wealth by the increased productive capacity of the youth who are to be educated.

The second great economical fact is that the lands known as Indian reservations now set apart by the Government for Indian occupancy aggregate nearly 190,000 square miles. This land, for the most part, is uncultivated and unproductive. When the Indians shall have been properly educated they will utilize a sufficient quantity of those lands for their own support and will release the remainder that it may be restored to the public domain to become the foundation for innumerable happy homes; and thus will be added to the national wealth immense tracts of farming land and vast mineral resources which will repay the nation more than one hundred fold for the amount which it is proposed shall be expended in Indian education. . . .

It will be seen that there is nothing radically new, nothing experimental nor theoretical, and that the present plans of the Indian Office contemplate only the putting into more systematic and organic form, and pressing with more vigor the work in which the Government has been earnestly engaged for the past thirteen years, with a view of carrying forward as rapidly as possible to its final consummation that scheme of public education which during these years has been gradually unfolding itself.

That the time is fully ripe for this advanced movement must be evident to every intelligent observer of the trend of events connected with the condition of the Indians. Practically all the land in this vast region known as the United States, from ocean to ocean again, has now been organized into States or Territories. The Indian populations are surrounded everywhere by white populations, and are destined inevitably, at no distant day, either to be overpowered or to be assimilated into the national life. The most feasible, and indeed it seems not too strong to say the only, means by which they can be prepared for American citizenship and assimilation into the national life is through the agency of some such scheme of public education as that which has been outlined, and upon which the Government, through the Indian Office, is busily at work. The welfare of the Indians, the peace and prosperity of the white people, and the honor of the nation are all at stake, and ought to constrain every lover of justice, every patriot, and every philanthropist, to join in promoting any worthy plan that will reach the desired end.

This great nation, strong, wealthy, aggressive, can signalize its spirit of fairness, justice, and philanthropy in no better way, perhaps, than by making ample provision for the complete education and absorption into the national life of those who for more than one hundred years have been among us but not of us. Where in human history has there been a brighter example of the humane and just spirit which ought to characterize the actions of a Christian nation superior in numbers, intelligence, riches, and power, in dealing with those whom it might easily crush, but whom it is far nobler to adopt as a part of its great family?

"The pressure that has been brought to bear upon the native people . . . in the attempt to force conformity of custom and habit has caused a reaction more destructive than war."

Indian Education Should Not Destroy Indian Culture

Luther Standing Bear (ca. 1868–1939)

Luther Standing Bear, a Lakota Sioux, was born on the Rosebud Reservation in South Dakota. In 1879 he became one of the first students to attend the Carlisle Indian School in Pennsylvania. A boarding school headed by a former U.S. Army captain and the most renowned institution of its kind, Carlisle saw its mission as the transformation of its students from "primitive" Indians into fully acculturated Americans. Following his stay at Carlisle, Standing Bear worked as a teacher, a clerk, a minister, a rancher, an interpreter for Buffalo Bill's Wild West Show, and an actor in motion pictures. Late in life he achieved some success as a writer.

The following viewpoint is excerpted from two chapters of his 1933 autobiography *Land of the Spotted Eagle*. Standing Bear describes how the teachers at Carlisle attempted to remove from him and his fellow students any traces of their native language and culture. He also takes issue with white society's characterization of Indian culture as "uncivilized" and "savage," arguing that Native Americans should be rightfully proud of their heritage.

Young Indians should be taught to honor, not disregard, their traditional culture, Standing Bear maintains. Indian students should be "doubly educated," he proposes, so that they can learn to succeed in modern American society while still retaining their cultural heritage.

I grew up leading the traditional life of my people, learning the crafts of hunter, scout, and warrior from father, kindness to the old and feeble from mother, respect for wisdom and council from our wise men, and was trained by grandfather and older boys in the devotional rites to the Great Mystery. This was the scheme of existence as followed by my forefathers for many centuries, and more centuries might have come and gone in much the same way had it not been for a strange people who came from a far land to change and reshape our world.

An Alien World

At the age of eleven years, ancestral life for me and my people was most abruptly ended without regard for our wishes, comforts, or rights in the matter. At once I was thrust into an alien world, into an environment as different from the one into which I had been born as it is possible to imagine, to remake myself, if I could, into the likeness of the invader.

By 1879, my people were no longer free, but were subjects confined on reservations under the rule of agents. One day there came to the agency a party of white people from the East. Their presence aroused considerable excitement when it became known that these people were school teachers who wanted some Indian boys and girls to take away with them to train as were white boys and girls.

Now, father was a 'blanket Indian,' but he was wise. He listened to the white strangers, their offers and promises that if they took his son they would care well for him, teach him how to read and write, and how to wear white man's clothes. But to father all this was just 'sweet talk,' and I know that it was with great misgivings that he left the decision to me and asked if I cared to go with these people. I, of course, shared with the rest of my tribe a distrust of the white people, so I know that for all my dear father's anxiety he was proud to hear me say 'Yes.' That meant that I was brave.

I could think of no reason why white people wanted Indian boys and girls except to kill them, and not having the remotest idea of what a school was, I thought we were going East to die. But so well had courage and bravery been trained into us that it became a part of our unconscious thinking and acting, and personal life was nothing when it came time to do something for the tribe. Even in our play and games we voluntarily put ourselves to various tests in the effort to grow brave and fearless, for it was most discrediting to be called *can'l wanka,* or a coward. Accordingly there were few cowards, most Lakota men preferring to die in the performance of some act of bravery than to die of old age. Thus, in giving myself up to go East I was proving to my father that he was honored with a brave son. In my decision to go, I gave up many things dear to the heart of a little Indian boy, and one of the things over which my child mind grieved was the thought of saying good-bye to my pony. I rode him as far as I could on the journey, which was to the Missouri River, where we took the boat. There we parted from our parents, and it was a heart-breaking scene, women and children weeping. Some of the children changed their minds and were unable to go on the boat, but for many who did go it was a final parting.

On our way to school we saw many white people, more than we ever dreamed existed, and the manner in which they acted when they saw us quite indicated their opinion of us. It was only about three years after the Custer battle, and the general opinion was that the Plains people merely infested the earth as nuisances, and our being there simply evidenced misjudgment on the part of Wakan Tanka [the Creator in the Lakota religion]. Whenever our train stopped at the railway stations, it was met by great numbers of white people who came to gaze upon the little Indian 'savages.' The shy little ones sat quietly at the car windows looking at the people who swarmed on the platform. Some of the children wrapped themselves in their blankets, covering all but their eyes. At one place we were taken off the train and marched a distance down the street to a restaurant. We walked down the street between two rows of uniformed men whom we called soldiers, though I suppose they were policemen. This must have been done to protect us, for it was surely known that we boys and girls could do no harm. Back of the rows of uniformed men stood the white people craning their necks, talking, laughing, and making a great noise. They yelled and tried to mimic us by giving what they thought were war-whoops. We did not like this, and some of the children were naturally very much frightened. I remember how I tried to crowd into the protecting midst of the jostling boys and girls. But we were all trying to be brave, yet going to what we thought would end in death at the hands of the white people whom we knew had no love for us. Back on the train the older boys sang brave songs in an effort to keep up their spirits and ours too. In my mind I often recall that scene—eighty-odd blanketed boys and girls marching down the street surrounded by a jeering, unsympathetic people whose only emotions were those of hate and fear; the conquerors looking upon the conquered. And no more understanding us than if we had suddenly been dropped from the moon.

The Transforming Process

At last at Carlisle the transforming, the 'civilizing' process began. It began with clothes. Never, no matter what our philosophy or spiritual quality, could we be civilized while wearing the moccasin and blanket. The task before us was not only that of accepting new ideas and adopting new manners, but actual physical changes and discomfort has to be borne uncomplainingly until the body adjusted itself to new tastes and habits. Our accustomed dress was taken and replaced with clothing that felt cumbersome and awkward. Against trousers and handkerchiefs we had a distinct feeling—they were unsanitary and the trousers kept us from breathing well. High collars, stiff-bosomed shirts, and suspenders fully three inches in width were uncomfortable, while leather boots caused actual suffering. We longed to go barefoot, but were told that the dew on the grass would give us colds. That was a new warning for us, for our mothers had never told us to beware of colds, and I remember as a child coming into the tipi with moccasins full of snow. Unconcernedly I would take them off my feet, pour out the snow, and put them on my feet again without any thought of sickness, for in that time colds, catarrh, bronchitis, and *la grippe* were unknown. But we were soon to know them. Then, red flannel undergarments were given us for winter wear, and for me, at least, discomfort grew into actual torture. I used to endure it as long as possible, then run upstairs and quickly take off the flannel garments and hide them. When inspection time came, I ran and put them on again, for I knew that if I were found disobeying the orders of the school I should be punished. My niece once asked me what it was that I disliked the most during those first bewildering days, and I said, 'red flannel.' Not knowing what I meant, she laughed, but I still remember those horrid, sticky garments which we had to wear next to the skin, and I still squirm and itch when I think of them. Of course, our hair was cut, and then there was much disapproval. But that was part of the transformation process and in some mysterious way long hair stood in the path of our development. For all the grumbling among the bigger boys, we soon had our heads shaven. How strange I felt! Involuntarily, time and time again, my hands went to my head, and that night it was a long time before I went to sleep. If we did not learn much at first, it will not be wondered at,

I think. Everything was queer, and it took a few months to get adjusted to the new surroundings.

Almost immediately our names were changed to those in common use in the English language. Instead of translating our names into English and calling Zinkcaziwin, Yellow Bird, and Wanbli K'leska, Spotted Eagle, which in itself would have been educational, we were just John, Henry, or Maggie, as the case might be. I was told to take a pointer and select a name for myself from the list written on the blackboard. I did, and since one was just as good as another, and as I could not distinguish any difference in them, I placed the pointer on the name Luther. I then learned to call myself by that name and got used to hearing others call me by it, too. By that time we had been forbidden to speak our mother tongue, which is the rule in all boarding-schools. This rule is uncalled for, and today is not only robbing the Indian, but America of a rich heritage. The language of a people is part of their history. Today we should be perpetuating history instead of destroying it, and this can only be effectively done by allowing and encouraging the young to keep it alive. A language, unused, embalmed, and reposing only in a book, is a dead language. Only the people themselves, and never the scholars, can nourish it into life.

Of all the changes we were forced to make, that of diet was doubtless the most injurious, for it was immediate and drastic. White bread we had for the first meal and there after, as well as coffee and sugar. Had we been allowed our own simple diet of meat, either boiled with soup or dried, and fruit, with perhaps a few vegetables, we should have thrived. But the change in clothing, housing, food, and confinement combined with lonesomeness was too much, and in three years nearly one half of the children from the Plains were dead and through with all earthly schools. In the graveyard at Carlisle most of the graves are those of little ones.

A Father's Visit

I am now going to confess that I had been at Carlisle a full year before I decided to learn all I could of the white man's ways, and then the inspiration was furnished by my father, the man who has been the greatest influence in all my life. When I had been in school a year, father made his first trip to see me. After I had received permission to speak to him, he told me that on his journey he had seen that the land was full of 'Long Knives.' 'They greatly outnumber us and are here to stay,' he said, and advised me, 'Son, learn all you can of the white man's ways and try to be like him.' From that day on I tried. Those few words of my father I remember as if we talked but yesterday, and in the maturity of my mind I have thought of what he said. He did not say that he thought the white man's ways better than our own; neither did he say that I could be like a white man. He said, 'Son, try to be like a white man.' So, in two more years I had been 'made over.' I was Luther Standing Bear wearing the blue uniform of the school, shorn of my hair, and trying hard to walk naturally and easily in stiff-soled cowhide boots. I was now 'civilized' enough to go to work in John Wanamaker's fine store in Philadelphia.

Tom Torleno, a Navajo, was, like Luther Standing Bear, a student at the Carlisle Indian School in the 1880s. The two pictures illustrate how Torleno was transformed in accordance with the assimilative ideology of Carlisle and other Indian schools.

I returned from the East at about the age of sixteen, after five years' contact with the white people, to resume life upon the reservation. But I returned, to spend some thirty years before again leaving, just as I had gone—a Lakota.

Outwardly I lived the life of the white man, yet all the while I kept in direct contact with tribal life. While I had learned all that I could of the white man's culture, I never forgot that of my people. I kept the language, tribal manners and usages, sang the songs and danced the dances. I still listened to and respected the advice of the older people of the tribe. I did not come home so 'progressive' that I could not speak the language of my father and mother. I did not learn the vices of chewing tobacco, smoking, drinking, and swearing, and for all this I am grateful. I have never, in fact, 'progressed' that far.

A Sad Sight

But I soon began to see the sad sight, so common today, of returned students who could not speak their native tongue, or,
worse yet, some who pretended they could no longer converse in
the mother tongue. They had become ashamed and this led them
into deception and trickery. The boys came home wearing stiff paper collars, tight patent-leather boots, and derby hats on heads
that were meant to be clothed in the long hair of the Lakota brave.
The girls came home wearing muslin dresses and long ribbon
sashes in bright hues which were very pretty. But they were trying
to squeeze their feet into heeled shoes of factory make and their
waists into binding apparatuses that were not garments—at least
they served no purpose of a garment, but bordered on some me-
chanical device. However, the wearing of them was part of the
'civilization' received from those who were doing the same thing.
So we went to school to copy, to imitate; not to exchange languages and ideas, and not to develop the best traits that had come
out of uncountable experiences of hundreds and thousands of
years living upon this continent. Our annals, all happenings of human import, were stored in our song and dance rituals, our history differing in that it was not stored in books, but in the living
memory. So, while the white people had much to teach us, we had
much to teach them, and what a school could have been established upon that idea! However, this was not the attitude of the
day, though the teachers were sympathetic and kind, and some
came to be my lifelong friends. But in the main, Indian qualities
were undivined and Indian virtues not conceded. And I can well
remember when Indians in those days were stoned upon the
streets as were the dogs that roamed them. We were 'savages,' and
all who had not come under the influence of the missionary were
'heathen,' and Wakan Tanka, who had since the beginning
watched over the Lakota and his land, was denied by these men of
God. Should we not have been justified in thinking them heathen?
And so the 'civilizing' process went on, killing us as it went. . . .

The White Man and America

The white man does not understand the Indian for the reason
that he does not understand America. He is too far removed from
its formative processes. The roots of the tree of his life have not
yet grasped the rock and soil. The white man is still troubled with
primitive fears; he still has in his consciousness the perils of this
frontier continent, some of its fastnesses not yet having yielded to
his questing footsteps and inquiring eyes. He shudders still with
the memory of the loss of his forefathers upon its scorching
deserts and forbidding mountain-tops. The man from Europe is

still a foreigner and an alien. And he still hates the man who questioned his path across the continent.

But in the Indian the spirit of the land is still vested; it will be until other men are able to divine and meet its rhythm. Men must be born and reborn to belong. Their bodies must be formed of the dust of their forefathers' bones.

The attempted transformation of the Indian by the white man and the chaos that has resulted are but the fruits of the white man's disobedience of a fundamental and spiritual law. The pressure that has been brought to bear upon the native people, since the cessation of armed conflict, in the attempt to force conformity of custom and habit has caused a reaction more destructive than war, and the injury has not only affected the Indian, but has extended to the white population as well. Tyranny, stupidity, and lack of vision have brought about the situation now alluded to as the 'Indian Problem.'

There is, I insist, no Indian problem as created by the Indian himself. Every problem that exists today in regard to the native population is due to the white man's cast of mind, which is unable, at least reluctant, to seek understanding and achieve adjustment in a new and a significant environment into which it has so recently come. . . .

Calling Indians Savages

After subjugation, after dispossession, there was cast the last abuse upon the people who so entirely resented their wrongs and punishments, and that was the stamping and the labeling of them as savages. To make this label stick has been the task of the white race and the greatest salve that it has been able to apply to its sore and troubled conscience now hardened through the habitual practice of injustice.

But all the years of calling the Indian a savage has never made him one; all the denial of his virtues has never taken them from him; and the very resistance he has made to save the things inalienably his has been his saving strength— that which will stand him in need when justice does make its belated appearance and he undertakes rehabilitation.

All sorts of feeble excuses are heard for the continued subjection of the Indian. One of the most common is that he is not yet ready to accept the society of the white man— that he is not yet ready to mingle as a social entity.

This, I maintain, is beside the question. The matter is not one of making-over the external Indian into the likeness of the white race—a process detrimental to both races. Who can say that the white man's way is better for the Indian? Where resides the human judgment with the competence to weigh and value Indian ideals and spiritual concepts; or substitute for them other values?

Then, has the white man's social order been so harmonious and ideal as to merit the respect of the Indian, and for that matter the thinking class of the white race? Is it wise to urge upon the Indian a foreign social form? Let none but the Indian answer!

Rather, let the white brother face about and cast his mental eye upon a new angle of vision. Let him look upon the Indian world as a human world; then let him see to it that human rights be accorded to the Indians. And this for the purpose of retaining for his own order of society a measure of humanity.

Teach Indians Old and New Ways

I say . . . that Indians should teach Indians; that Indians should serve Indians, especially on reservations where the older people remain. There is a definite need of the old for the care and sympathy of the young and they are today perishing for the joys that naturally belong to old Indian people. Old Indians are very close to their progeny. It was their delightful duty to care for and instruct the very young, while in turn they looked forward to being cared for by sons and daughters. These were the privileges and blessings of old age.

Many of the grievances of the old Indian, and his disagreements with the young, find root in the far-removed boarding-school which sometimes takes the little ones at a very tender age. More than one tragedy has resulted when a young boy or girl has returned home again almost an utter stranger. I have seen these happenings with my own eyes and I know they can cause naught but suffering. The old Indian cannot, even if he wished, reconcile himself to an institution that alienates his young. And there is something evil in a system that brings about an unnatural reaction to life; when it makes young hearts callous and unheedful of the needs and joys of the old. . . .

To the end that young Indians will be able to appreciate both their traditional life and modern life they should be doubly educated. Without forsaking reverence for their ancestral teachings, they can be trained to take up modern duties that relate to tribal and reservation life. And there is no problem of reservation importance but can be solved by the joint efforts of the old and the young Indians. . . .

With school facilities already fairly well established and the capability of the Indian unquestioned, every reservation could well be supplied with Indian doctors, nurses, engineers, road- and bridge-builders, draughtsmen, architects, dentists, lawyers, teachers, and instructors in tribal lore, legends, orations, song, dance, and ceremonial ritual. The Indian, by the very sense of duty, should become his own historian, giving his account of the race—

fairer and fewer accounts of the wars and more of statecraft, legends, languages, oratory, and philosophical conceptions. No longer should the Indian be dehumanized in order to make material for lurid and cheap fiction to embellish street-stands. Rather, a fair and correct history of the native American should be incorporated in the curriculum of the public school.

Caucasian youth is fed, and rightly so, on the feats and exploits of their old-world heroes, their revolutionary forefathers, their adventurous pioneer trail-blazers, and in our Southwest through pageants, fiestas, and holidays the days of the Spanish *conquistador* is kept alive.

But Indian youth! They, too, have fine pages in their past history; they, too, have patriots and heroes. And it is not fair to rob Indian youth of their history, the stories of their patriots, which, if impartially written, would fill them with pride and dignity. Therefore, give back to Indian youth all, everything in their heritage that belongs to them and augment it with the best in the modern schools. I repeat, doubly educate the Indian boy and girl.

What a contrast this would make in comparison with the present unhealthy, demoralized place the reservation is today, where the old are poorly fed, shabbily clothed, divested of pride and incentive; and where the young are unfitted for tribal life and untrained for the world of white man's affairs except to hold an occasional job!

Why not a school of Indian thought, built on the Indian pattern and conducted by Indian instructors? Why not a school of tribal art?

Why should not America be cognizant of itself; aware of its identity? In short, why should not America be preserved?

There were ideals and practices in the life of my ancestors that have not been improved upon by the present-day civilization; there were in our culture elements of benefit; and there were influences that would broaden any life. But that almost an entire public needs to be enlightened as to this fact need not be discouraging. For many centuries the human mind labored under the delusion that the world was flat; and thousands of men have believed that the heavens were supported by the strength of an Atlas. The human mind is not yet free from fallacious reasoning; it is not yet an open mind and its deepest recesses are not yet swept free of errors.

But it is now time for a destructive order to be reversed, and it is well to inform other races that the aboriginal culture of America was not devoid of beauty. Furthermore, in denying the Indian his ancestral rights and heritages the white race is but robbing itself. But America can be revived, rejuvenated, by recognizing a native school of thought. The Indian can save America. . . .

Regarding the 'civilization' that has been thrust upon me since the days of reservation, it has not added one whit to my sense of justice; to my reverence for the rights of life; to my love for truth, honesty, and generosity; nor to my faith in Wakan Tanka—God of the Lakotas. For after all the great religions have been preached and expounded, or have been revealed by brilliant scholars, or have been written in books and embellished in fine language with finer covers, man—all man—is still confronted with the Great Mystery.

So if today I had a young mind to direct, to start on the journey of life, and I was faced with the duty of choosing between the natural way of my forefathers and that of the white man's present way of civilization, I would, for its welfare, unhesitatingly set that child's feet in the path of my forefathers. I would raise him to be an Indian!

Chapter 5

Twentieth-Century Debates on American Indian Issues

Chapter Preface

The twentieth century has witnessed several major shifts in federal Indian policy as well as the growth of Indian political and cultural activism. Recurring debates have focused on greater powers of self-government for American Indians and on the federal government's treaty obligations.

In 1928 the Institute for Government Research (now called the Brookings Institution) was commissioned by the secretary of the interior to examine the social and economic status of American Indians. The resulting report, named the Meriam Report for Lewis Meriam, the director of the survey, concluded that most American Indians faced disastrous conditions of poverty, housing, health, and education. The study found that two-thirds of all American Indians earned less than $100 a year and that only 2 percent of Indian families had annual incomes of more than $500. Infant mortality and death rates were high, and the work of the Bureau of Indian Affairs in administrating health, education, and social programs for the Indian tribes was often of poor quality. The policy of land allotment and forced assimilation, the report argued, had "resulted in much loss of land and an enormous increase in the details of administration without a compensating advance in the economic ability of the Indians."

The Meriam Report received much publicity and helped to stimulate public opinion in favor of reform that ultimately resulted in several major changes in federal Indian policy. Most of these changes occurred under the leadership of John Collier, commissioner of Indian affairs from 1933 to 1945. Among the major legislative reforms that Collier instigated were the creation of a board to promote Indian arts and crafts, the cessation of bureau efforts to ban Indian religious practices, and the Johnson-O'Malley Act promoting federal and state cooperation in providing for the public health and education of Native Americans.

The centerpiece of Collier's reforms was the Indian Reorganization Act (IRA), passed in 1934. That law reversed two key assumptions that had governed U.S. Indian policy since the 1887 Dawes Act: the assumption that dividing up tribal lands and allotting them to individuals would help make Indians self-sufficient, and the assumption that Indian tribes would and should disappear as political bodies. The IRA provided legal mechanisms for chartering and reorganizing tribal governments, enabled tribes to regain control of unallotted lands, and established a revolving credit fund for economic development. Historians W. Richard West Jr. and Kevin Gover write that under the IRA,

> tribal government structures were recognized as the appropriate means for effecting federal policies towards Indians. The right of Indian people to maintain distinct political communities was recognized by Congress for the first time in over half a century. The assumption that tribes would disappear no longer was the basis for federal Indian policy.

The IRA was criticized both for going too far and not going far enough in authorizing tribal self-government for American Indians. Some opponents decried the reversal of the longstanding federal goal of assimilating Indians within white society. They claimed that the plan treated Indian reservations as "living museums" and Indian people as an exotic minority to be set apart from modern American life. Criticism also came from those who argued that the law gave too much power to Collier and other government officials and did not give Indians true autonomy. West and Gover write that

> many tribes had IRA constitutions foisted upon them against the wishes of a clear majority of tribal members. Most Indians remained suspicious and reluctant to be involved in any government scheme to help them.

Some Indian tribes welcomed the changes, however, and during the 1930s living conditions and political autonomy for Indians did improve on many reservations.

American Indian policy underwent further shifts during and immediately after World War II—changes that were in part a backlash to Collier's reforms. These changes, aimed at ending Native Americans' autonomous status and integrating them into American society, fell under the general heading of "termination." Among the policies pursued by the federal government during this period were programs to encourage Indians to relocate from reservations to cities and the transfer of criminal justice, education, and health programs from federal and tribal authorities to state and local governments. In addition, between 1954 and 1962 more than one hundred tribal groups were terminated, losing the federal status that entitled them to receive government payments and services and to maintain tribal governments.

The policy of termination was never fully implemented, however, partly because of Indian protest. In addition to opposition expressed by individual tribal councils, a major source of resistance was the National Congress of American Indians, the nation's first major intertribal organization. The NCAI, founded in 1944, and later Indian groups were distinguished from older organizations by their membership. Organizations such as the Indian Rights Association were composed of whites interested in Indian affairs, while the newer groups consisted mainly of Native Americans. The National Indian Youth Council, begun in 1961, and the militant American Indian Movement, formed in 1968, were among the most prominent organizations that sought to gain civil and treaty rights for Native Americans in the 1960s and 1970s. Some activists sued states they claimed had violated past treaties by taking Indian land and by restricting Indian hunting and fishing rights. Others staged dramatic demonstrations—such as the 1969 seizure of Alcatraz Island in San Francisco—to draw attention to the plight of Indians. Such actions as these influenced a shift in federal policy from "termination" to "self-determination" and resulted in government reforms that gave American Indians greater autonomy in managing their own affairs.

The extent to which Indians should have sovereign authority over their own communities has been and remains a central question surrounding U.S. Indian policy. This chapter presents a sampling of views on Indian affairs and federal Indian policy from the New Deal to the 1970s.

VIEWPOINT 1

"This movement to de-individualize *the Indian grows out of the theory that the red man's original status was communistic, and that his welfare will best be served by a return to that condition. The facts do not support either assumption."*

New Deal Reforms Will Harm American Indians

Flora Warren Seymour (1888–1948)

In 1932, in the midst of the Great Depression, Franklin D. Roosevelt was elected president of the United States on his promise of a "New Deal." Among the components of Roosevelt's New Deal were major reforms in government policy toward American Indians.

Roosevelt's appointee as commissioner of Indian affairs, John Collier, sought a reversal of the government policy, dating back to the 1887 Dawes Act, of dividing up Indian land among individuals and diminishing the authority and vitality of Indian tribal organizations. In particular, Collier pushed for passage of the Indian Reorganization Act, also known as the Wheeler-Howard Act. This legislation was designed to end the practice of partitioning or selling Indian land, to provide for the election of tribal councils to govern the tribes and represent them in dealings with state and federal governments, and to create a loan fund for Indian business enterprises. In early 1934 Collier held several conferences with Indian leaders, seeking to gain their support for the legislation.

However, Collier's ideas also met with opposition. Many of those concerned with Indian policy still supported the goals of cultural assimilation and viewed the proposed changes as regres-

From Flora Warren Seymour, "Trying It on the Indian," *New Outlook*, May 1934.

sive. Among Collier's detractors was Flora Warren Seymour, a lawyer and author who had worked for six years for the federal Bureau of Indian Affairs (BIA). Seymour was a former member of the Board of Indian Commissioners, an appointed and unpaid panel of religious and public leaders established in 1869 to oversee the BIA; the board had been disbanded in early 1934.

The following viewpoint is taken from a May 1934 article in which Seymour criticizes the proposed Wheeler-Howard legislation. She argues that many American Indians are, for good reason, suspicious of this latest attempt to reform Indian policy. Among her concerns about the bill are the expenses it would create for the American taxpayer and its underlying assumption that a communal society is the best and only way for Indians to live.

After some debate and modifications by Congress, the Indian Reorganization Act became law on June 18, 1934. Soon after the act's passage, many Indian tribes held elections and created tribal constitutions and governments under the provisions of the law, although some other tribes—including the Navajo, the nation's largest—initially refused to participate in such measures.

In tribal meetings on reservations over the country today the American Indian has taken his own particular New Deal under consideration. The cards were explained to his various representatives at a recent Congress of Plains Indians, held at Rapid City, South Dakota. They were called together, at government expense, to be sold, and in turn to sell their fellow tribesmen, a unique program of regimentation, which in several basic features is the most extreme gesture yet made by the administration in this country toward a Communistic experiment. The majority did not appear to be unduly impressed. They said they would talk it over, and went their various ways. They are keeping their promise to the white man. The meetings are now going on around reservation campfires. On some of the Sioux reservations bitter dissension between different factions has already broken out, and still more trouble may be expected. The red men opponents to regimentation and the proposal to establish Indian communal camps are calling a spade a spade, and a Democrat, a Communist. The whole program has been referred to by one of their speakers, this one a woman, as a plan devised by Chief Facing-Both-Ways.

The members of a once proud and independent race are exercising their customary diplomacy in dealing with the white man's latest proposal for their salvation. This feature and their stoic reticence make it dangerous to predict a happy outcome for the entire undertaking. The Indian is aware that he is standing at an important fork of the road.

At the close of the congress held at Rapid City, a prominent Sioux was invited to visit in another jurisdiction than his own.

"No," he said, "I feel that I must go back now to my own people. I am going to campaign for—or against—this bill." Surely this was a sufficiently diplomatic statement of his purpose.

If Commissioner of Indian Affairs John Collier, who with a staff of eight or nine officials of the Indian Bureau and the Interior Department, spent four days in urging upon the assembled Indians the importance and desirability of a speedy passage of the Howard-Wheeler bill, did not know at the outset that the Sioux and their kindred tribes are versed in the ways of diplomacy, he was well aware of their ability before the congress was over. Not in the least influenced by the fact that they were gathered to the meeting at government expense and paid a *per diem* during their stay, these delegates listened intently, although impassively, through the long hours of exposition and argument, heard answers to some of the many questions they were permitted to present—in writing only—kept within their hearts the speeches they were not granted opportunity to make, and went away having given the emissaries of the Great White Father no greater assurance of agreement than the promise to present the subject to their respective tribes for further discussion.

A Complete Change

It is indeed a serious matter which is being presented to the Indians of the United States for discussion. A bill, introduced in the House on February 12 [1934] and in the Senate on the day following, designs a complete change in Indian life and Indian land tenure in America. Years ago General R.H. Pratt, whom no man ever excelled in devotion to the interests of the Indian, urged his conviction on the subject:

"To civilize the Indian, put him in the midst of civilization. To keep him civilized, keep him there."

Today, the avowed intent of the official guardians of our red brother is to remove him from the ways of the white man and to remove the white man from proximity to the Indian. Almost complete and quite perpetual segregation is contemplated by the provisions of this bill.

First, the Indians of any given tribe are to organize themselves into a community, to which a charter shall be issued by the Secretary of the Interior. As the Secretary deems the Indians capable, they are to be entrusted with the management of their own affairs. They will make their own laws and enforce them. They are to take over by degrees the work now being done by Civil Service employees of the Indian Bureau in the field, but while such employees remain, the Indian community will have the right to demand dismissal or transfer to another jurisdiction should any one of these chance to become *persona non grata*.

Second, provision is to be made by the government for the education of Indians in all the services and functions the community may take over, including preparation in law, medicine, accountancy, pedagogy, social service, forestry, scientific agriculture and civil engineering. At the same time the lower schools, maintained especially for Indians, are to specialize in the inculcation of Indian arts crafts, skills and traditions. There remains a question as to whether schools of professional standing will accept courses in beadwork and scalp dancing as meeting entrance requirements, but this may be—and is—passed over for the time.

The great purpose of this community organization, aside from the return to Indian ways, rests in the third section of the bill, which provides for the taking over by the chartered community of the title to the lands within the borders of the reservation. Though the charter need be ratified by no more than three fifths of the Indians voting at the election—regardless of their ratio to the number of possible qualified voters—yet the community, once formed, has the right of eminent domain and can assert it over the lands of Indians who have not voted to join, as well as over white people who have purchased land within the reservation boundaries. With the customary profligacy of the New Deal planners, an annual appropriation of two million dollars is contemplated for the purchase of lands so condemned by the community.

All land of individual Indians will be ceded to the tribal community as a whole. Their communal title is to be subject forever to a trust. At no future time may the land ever be sold or mortgaged. This includes perpetual exemption from any tax levy. Inasmuch as it means the drying up of normal sources of credit, the government is to provide a revolving fund of ten million dollars from which the business operations of the community are to be financed.

Inasmuch, also, as the Indian citizen is permitted to avail himself of all the public resources of the state in which he lives without incurring financial obligation in the way of taxes, the public purse must again be drawn upon and appropriations from the Federal treasury to reimburse the state are contemplated for all time to come. . . .

Indian Opposition

The purposes of the bill, it was remarked by a young Sioux woman listening in on the conference, seems to have been devised by Chief Facing-Both-Ways. The expectation is that the return to communal ownership will cause all the Indians to embark at once upon subsistence farming. At the same time they will be trained in the professions, while reverting to their ancient arts and crafts, which in this region were based almost entirely on the buffalo. To combine Blackstone and the polishing of arrowheads, surgery and weaving, business engineering and the sun dance, seems an arduous undertaking. So far as concerns the subsistence farming, the opinion of the Northern Cheyenne is succinctly stated:

"Work is for mules and women."

Yet these same Cheyennes, admittedly the least advanced of the groups of this region, sent this word as their answer to the Commissioner of Indian Affairs:

"You are putting us back into tribal life and we don't like it."

The communal features of the bill had been introduced to the Indians on January 20 [1934] by a circular from the Indian Bureau calling upon the different tribes to organize for self-government. Replies to this were requested by February 15. In some sections the Indians responded favorably, but from so many tribes came word of divided councils, and often outspoken refusal to enter upon the new plan, that it seemed expedient to take the entire proposition of community self-government plus tribal land ownership and management, directly to the people concerned. The Plains Congress was the first decided upon; its date of March 15 was advanced as protests from other sections came in and other gatherings were indicated. Six were in prospect as the Plains Indians convened, and at the close of the Rapid City gathering two or three more had been added.

From the southwestern Indians, who in most instances have never held individual title to their lands, a more enthusiastic response was expected. Forty-seven years under the allotment system, characterized by Commissioner Collier as "wicked and stupid," have certainly not been as educative as the sponsors of the [Dawes] Act hoped when it was passed in 1887. Yet it has given the Indians a sense of individual ownership which they are by no means ready to relinquish.

The delegate from the Crow Creek Sioux is speaking. "He was Sergeant-at-Arms of the State Legislature last session," says one listener to another:

"I heard you were appointed as a Democrat," states this Indian Sergeant-at-Arms to the Commissioner of Indian Affairs, "and then I was told that you were a Republican. But I believe, Mr. Collier, that you must be a Socialist. Your ideas of community government seem to me socialistic. I lived in Sioux community life as a boy and I certainly wouldn't like to go back to it."

210

Verdict of the Shoshone Tribal Council

The Shoshone (Shoshoni) Indians of Wyoming were among several tribes to express opposition to the Wheeler-Howard bill; their report was placed in the Congressional Record *of June 15, 1934.*

The Indian self-government plan outlined by Indian Commissioner John Collier having been submitted to the Shoshone Indian Council and the members of the tribe, and its provisions having been fully considered and discussed, report, as follows:

No. 1. Whereas we feel that the plan does not create or promote the individual initiative that is necessary to make our members self-reliant and self-supporting.

No. 2. Whereas it had been the policy of the Department for many years to get away from the plan of segregating Indians, which we believe is desirable, and the plan submitted would do away with this policy.

No. 3. Whereas the present policy of handling Indians and their land holdings in our opinion can be made very successful provided, however, that there are some modifications to the present rules and regulations.

No. 4. Whereas we do not favor the unit plan of community government as it is not constructive and not workable to the best interests of the Indians.

No. 5. Whereas in conclusion adjudge that the entire structure of this bill gives or guarantees nothing to the Indian only under the supervising power of the Secretary of the Interior and the Commissioner of Indian Affairs, and we further adjudge this bill as a legalized procedure to acquire the Indian land, absolving the United States Government from any suit for nonfulfillment of treaty. It places the Indian in a position as a landless individual and removes him from the position of a landlord to a no-man by its adoption. Now: therefore be it

Resolved, That we "members" of the Shoshone tribe of Indians residing on the Shoshone Indian Reservation in Fremont County, of the State of Wyoming, request that the Wheeler-Howard bills (H.R. 7902 and S. 2755) be amended so as to entirely exclude the said tribe of Shoshone Indians from the provisions of said bill.

This movement to *de-individualize* the Indian grows out of the theory that the red man's original status was communistic, and that his welfare will best be served by a return to that condition. The facts do not support either assumption completely.

The early attitude of the Plains Indians toward the land was rather that of non-ownership than of communistic ownership. It is true that certain tribes claimed the right to rove and hunt in a certain area, but it was a right which must at any moment be defended against the attack of another tribe. The great council held in 1825 at Prairie du Chien [Wisconsin] was a well meaning attempt on the part of the United States to induce the tribes to set boundaries as between themselves and refrain from fighting about it. The effort was not wholly successful. The Sioux and Chippewa even had a renewal of their habitual warfare on the way home from the council. Least of all did any covet the right to cultivate the soil. Some of them had in their ancient tradition a sort of vague notion that their women once raised a little corn and a few melons. But they had long since forgotten the art, if they had ever possessed it. Wild berries must suffice.

Yet the white men believed these roving buffalo hunters could and should be transformed into tillers of the soil. To that end was devised the allotment act, for which friends of the Indians toiled for many a season before its final passage in 1887. Upon the division of the land so that each person had individual title to a farm, it was expected that the Dakota plains would blossom with corn.

It was a hope frustrated. The women, since the tribe no longer followed the buffalo, began to set up home gardens. The hunter and warrior of the family felt no urge to lay his hand to the plow handle or to grub about with a hoe. Here and there one adopted the new ways, but it could not be said that enthusiasm for agriculture ran high.

For a period of years the severally owned land was held in trust by the government. But when by reason of the expiration of the trust period, or because of his supposed competency to handle business affairs, the Indian received a fee patent, all too often the result was that he sold his land as speedily as he could, or borrowed on it and failed to meet the mortgage payments. Hence, as the years went on, there grew up a body of landless Indians. Practically all are paupers, says the present Commissioner of Indian Affairs.

The fact of pauperism may be established. Many more than the Indians in these days are on the relief rolls. But the possession of land by no means assures escape from such a condition. Pests and drought do not ask whether land is farmed by the Indians or by the white. They certainly do not hold forth any incentive to agricultural endeavor.

Granted that the community is formed as the bill indicates and the land has been thrown into communal ownership; there will be little difficulty in buying out many Dakota white farmers at a price probably far less than they paid for the lands a few years ago. Granted that the revolving fund is at hand and ready to revolve; who will rush to harness the mules to the plow? Will it be the protected Indian whose land has all these years been safeguarded by the government, but has now been taken from him and returned to the tribe? Or will it be the man who has run through the proceeds of his acres and who now joins the community with nothing to give and everything to receive?

Divisions over Land Ownership

Whoever it may be that turns to tillage, it is expected that any Indian pressure for the passage of the bill will come from those who are without lands. It is but natural that those should be willing to accept another helping who have so quickly disposed of their first portion. A man's allotment may have brought him a considerable sum of money. It may have brought him a big automobile and a tour of the country. Perhaps, he thinks, he may have another such windfall. *Forever* is a long word, and a perpetual trust period set up by one Congress may as easily be terminated when the time comes around for the red man's next New Deal. But the willingness to be helped again to a share of the soil by no means indicates that the recipient expects to stir up that soil and scatter grain upon it.

The man whose land has been kept for him has a different slant upon the situation. He is not inclined to grasp the opportunity to give up his individual tenure for the benefit of the community. Kills the Wolf, over there, has had his thousands for the land and has spent them gloriously. Why should Many Voices give up his right to anticipate a future experience of the same sort?

Already, on some of the Sioux reservations, the proposition has brought about bitter dissension between those of mixed white and Indian ancestry and those designated as full bloods. The latter, having been held under guardianship, are unwilling to share with the mixed bloods, who have already eaten their cake with every sign of enjoyment. The landless mixed bloods naturally see greater promise in the idea of community rights to the land.

Resentment of Indians

So far as the Indians of the Plains are concerned, it is from the landless mixed bloods that the Indian Bureau hopes to hear a demand for the passage of the Howard-Wheeler bill. The recent congress at Rapid City has made it plain that acceptance of the plan can come but slowly if at all. A high-pressure campaign may succeed in inducing those who have nothing to lose to shower upon Congress their demands for another cup of coffee and another piece of pie. Those who still have lands will yield only with reluctance, if yield they must. Three times, on three successive days, one Davidson of Pine Ridge [South Dakota] attempted to gain the floor for a speech or a motion. Each time he was firmly ruled out of order.

"Mr. Chairman!" he shouted on the third day. "I am to be a victim of this bill, and as an Indian and an American citizen I claim my right to be heard about it!"

It was in vain. The gavel descended as before.

On the final day of the congress the chairman announced that the gentleman out of order the day before could now be heard. It was too late. Mr. Davidson had gone back to Pine Ridge, where it may easily be assumed that his voice and vote will not be in favor of the Howard-Wheeler bill.

The Blackfeet contented themselves with registering objections to the communal features of the bill. The Sioux of Cheyenne River [South Dakota] mildly pointed out that "the bill will not benefit us in such matters." But Harry Whiteman, speaking for his people, the Crows, and surprisingly enough, also for their ancient enemies, the Northern Cheyennes, voiced the refusal which had brought these two once-warring tribes into agreement:

"We don't want to lose our independence and pride of ownership. We have come to the forking of the ways. We will fight to the last ditch before giving up the land to community ownership.

"Mr. Commissioner, don't cram this bill down our throats!"

And so with considerable resentment in their hearts the Indian delegates left the first general meeting held at Rapid City to return to their various reservations to campaign "for—or against" the proposal. The reaction at other general sectional meetings—the latest was a conference for the Indians of Wisconsin and Minnesota, would leave little doubt as to how most are going to campaign.

Now the tribal meetings are in full swing and the tide of opposition is rising on Indian reservations over all parts of the country. The Klomaths of Oregon are strongly arrayed against. The Kiowahs of Oklahoma. The larger tribes of Oklahoma—the Five Civilized Tribes, knowing something of the white man's ways of legislation, believe their interests can be taken care of "with an amendment." "Have your bill," they say, "but leave us out of this. Merely say the Five Civilized Tribes are exempted." Even among the Pueblos, upon whose way of living the bill was supposed to be based, appear at this writing to be divided about half and half on the proposed program. The Chippewas resent "being driven back to the bush."

Responding to Collier

Commissioner of Indian Affairs Collier, taking cognizance of this rising tide of objection, has issued the following defense of the New Deal for the American Indian:

"The condition of about 150,000 of our Federal Indian wards is forlorn and even desperate. Existing law, which has stripped them of their last acre of land and faithlessly diverted hundreds of millions of their trust funds, likewise has denied them modern educational advantages, has shut them out from access to financial credit, and has withheld from them, individually and as groups, all power to determine their own lives. The legal system of exploitation is complete and the Indians are helpless to extricate themselves. The identical laws are steadily forcing the remaining Indians, who still possess some land, to surrender the use of the actual title to whites. Grafting and exploiting white interests congregate around the dwindling Indian property, and these interests are massed to defeat the Administration's present purpose.

"That purpose is to extend to Indians the traditional American rights and privileges, including the rights guaranteed in the Constitution but as yet denied toward Indians, and to furnish landless Indians new land needed for self-support. The purpose likewise is to stop the further looting of Indian trust funds and lands by whites.

"Muskogee is the center of the Five Civilized Tribes of Oklahoma. Until twenty-five years ago these tribes, numbering 101,000 members, owned fertile and ample lands and were self-supporting, even prosperous. Today, 72,000 members of these five tribes are totally landless. A handful of the remainder are owners in severalty of valuable lands and oil and mineral properties. Disregarding this handful, the members of the Five Civilized Tribes are subsisting on an average annual income of $47 per capita. Of 15,000,000 acres allotted to the Five Tribes twenty-five years ago, only 1,500,000 remain, and these, under existing law will soon pass to white ownership."

Outspoken criticism of Mr. Collier's statement was promptly made by Levi Gritts, a spokesman for the Cherokees. Gritts attended the sectional conference held at Washington. Pretty indignant and quite eloquent he was when he got back to Muskogee, Oklahoma. Referring to Mr. Collier's remark that something must be done with those "poor, starving tribesmen" of eastern Oklahoma, he asserted that it was the first which he had heard that his countrymen were starving. . . .

The Quapaws, it is understood, have already voted secretly against the measure. Proponents of the bill at their tribal meeting made much of Mr. Collier's statement that Congress would appropriate two million dollars annually for the purchase of "reservation lands."

One eloquent Indian then replied, "His $2,000,000 would amount only to twenty dollars per annum per capita. At that rate it would take at least ten years to get money enough to buy each individual of this group ten acres of land. How many tribesmen could survive this length of time?"

215

"In the revivifying of the Indian spirit, the wide-opened benefits of Indian emergency conservation and of other relief work played an important part."

New Deal Reforms Have Helped American Indians

John Collier (1884–1968)

A social worker and anthropologist who first came into close contact with Indians in the 1920s during a visit to New Mexico, John Collier wrote articles extolling the society of Pueblo Indians and became a prominent critic of government policy toward Indians (especially land allotment) and defender of Indian rights. In 1933 President Franklin D. Roosevelt appointed him commissioner of Indian affairs. Collier served as commissioner until 1945; his tenure, the longest of any individual, marked a turning point in U.S. policy toward Native Americans.

As commissioner, Collier implemented several major changes. He employed thousands of American Indians in the Emergency Conservation Work Agency. He reversed the long-standing governmental policy goal of Americanization for Indians, promoted Indian arts and crafts, transferred students from boarding schools to day schools located in Indian communities, and forbade government officials from requiring students to attend Christian worship services. Under his prodding, Congress passed reform legislation such as the 1934 Johnson-O'Malley Act, which authorized the federal government to contract with states and territories to provide education, medical care, and social welfare services for Indians who were under federal supervision. Perhaps the single most important law Collier helped pass was the Indian Reorganization Act of 1934 (also called the Wheeler-Howard Act). The law halted the sale of tribal lands to individuals, restored Indian tribes

From John Collier, "Annual Report," Bureau of Indian Affairs (Washington, DC: GPO, 1935).

as corporate entities with control over their property and powers of local self-government, and provided for a revolving credit fund for the economic development of Indian businesses.

The following viewpoint is taken from Collier's 1935 annual report on the activities of his department. He argues that the passage of the Indian Reorganization Act, as well as other government antipoverty measures, has improved the lives of American Indians. Most Indian tribes, Collier asserts, have approved of the act's provisions in referendum elections. He attributes remaining Indian opposition to "campaigns of misrepresentation" by businesses and missionary groups who do not have the best interests of American Indians at heart.

This annual report is burdened with overcondensed statements of things done and more things yet to do; with urgencies, programs, and life-and-death necessities, all under the compulsion of speed.

It is all true. But the foundations of Indian life rest in a quiet earth. Indian life is not tense, is not haunted with urgencies, and does not fully accept the view that programs must be achieved, lest otherwise ruin shall swiftly befall.

Indian life is happy. Even the most poverty-stricken and seemingly futureless Indians still are happy. Indians have known how to be happy amid hardships and dangers through many thousand years. They do not expect much, often they expect nothing at all; yet they are able to be happy. Possibly this is the most interesting and important fact about Indians. . . .

Reorganizing Indian Life

The Indian Reorganization (modified Wheeler-Howard) Act was approved June 18, 1934. Its passage made mandatory a complete change in the traditional Federal Indian policy of individual allotment of land—which resulted in the break-up of Indian reservations—and of destroying Indian organization, institutions, and racial heritage to the end that the Indian as an Indian might disappear from the American scene with the utmost speed.

The next result of this policy has been the loss of two-thirds of the 139,000,000 acres owned by Indian tribes in 1887, the year when the General Allotment Act was adopted; and the individualization policy has broken up the land remaining on allotted reservations, has disrupted tribal bonds, has destroyed old incentives to action, and has created a race of petty landlords who in the generous Indian manner have shared their constantly shrinking income with the ever-increasing number of their landless relatives and friends.

The Indian Reorganization Act prohibits future allotments, and the sale of Indian lands except to the tribes; it restores to the tribes the unentered remnants of the so-called surplus lands of the allotted reservations thrown open to white settlement; it authorizes annual appropriations for the purchase of land for landless Indians, provides for the consolidation of Indian lands, and sets up a process which enables Indians voluntarily to return their individual landholdings to the protection of tribal status, thus reversing the disintegration policy.

The act also authorizes a ten-million-dollar revolving loan fund, the use of which is restricted to those tribes which organize and incorporate so as to create community responsibility. It is expected that the organization of Indians in well-knit, functional groups and communities will help materially in the creation of new incentives for individual and collective action. The Indian is not a "rugged individualist"; he functions best as an integrated member of a group, clan, or tribe. Identification of his individuality with clan or tribe is with him a spiritual necessity. If the satisfaction of this compelling sentiment is denied him—as it was for half a century or more—the Indian does not, it has been clearly shown, merge into white group life. Through a modernized form of Indian organization, adapted to the needs of the various tribes (a form of organization now authorized by law), it is possible to make use of this powerful latent civic force.

The Indian Reorganization Act was passed a few days before the end of the Seventy-third Congress. None of the authorized appropriations, however, became available until May 1935. For land purchases the authorized appropriation was reduced to one-half, or $1,000,000; the revolving credit fund was limited to a quarter of the authorization, or $2,500,000; for organizing expenses the amount was reduced from $250,000 to $175,000.

Indian Elections

Congress had ordained in section 18 that each tribe must be given the unusual privilege of deciding at a special election whether it wanted to accept these benefits or reject them. Beginning with August 1934 and ending June 17, 1935, a series of 263 elections resulted in the decision by 73 tribes, with a population of 63,467 persons, to exclude themselves from the benefits and protection of the act, and by 172 tribes, with the population of 132,426 persons, to accept the act.

The participation of the Indians in these referendum elections was astonishingly heavy. In national elections, when a President is chosen and the interest of the voters is aroused through a long, intensive campaign, the average number of ballots cast does not exceed 52 percent of the total number of eligible voters; in referendum elections deciding on such matters as constitutional ratifications, bond issues, etc., when no personalities are injected into the campaign, less than 35 percent of the eligible voters participate. The referendum election on the Indian Reorganization Act did not concern itself with candidates and personalities, yet 62 percent of all adult Indians came to the polls and cast their ballots.

This heavy participation becomes even more significant when it is remembered that at least half the Indian voters could not speak the English language, that reading and writing were unknown to many of them, and that most of them had never voted before. Yet so great was their interest that grandmothers and grandfathers past the allotted span of three score and ten walked many miles to the polling places, there to mark and cast their ballots with celerity and dispatch even though some of them had to be instructed which end of the pencil to use.

Except in a single tribe (Isleta Pueblo), not an Indian voice was raised against the participation of women; everywhere the right of the feminine element to take part in the referendums was conceded without question.

Opponents of Reform

The rejection of the Reorganization Act on 73 reservations, most of them very small (but including the largest reservation, that of the Navajos), was due in the main to energetic campaigns of misrepresentation carried on by special interests which feared that they would lose positions of advantage through the applications of the act. Joining hands in this campaign of misrepresentation were stockmen who feared that the Indians would run their own stock on land hitherto leased to white interests; traders who were afraid of losing their business through the competition of Indian consumers' cooperatives; merchants and politicians in white communities on the edge of reservations; a few missionaries who resented the extension of the constitutional guarantee of religious liberty and freedom of conscience to Indians (not an element in the Reorganization Act, but enforced as a policy by the present administration); lumber interests which did not want to see Indian tribes exploit their own forest resources. These interests, working frequently by the historic method of defrauding Indian tribes with the connivance of certain of their own leaders, spread extreme and bizarre falsehoods concerning the effects of the act.

Among the myths spread by adverse interests on various reservations were such as these: Acceptance of the act would cause Indian owners of allotments to lose their land, which would then be distributed among those Indians who had disposed of their allotments; all farm crops would be impounded in warehouses and thereafter would be equally distributed among the population; the Indians would be segregated behind wire fences charged with electricity; all the livestock would be taken from certain tribes; unalloted reservations would be thrown open to white entry; Indian dances and other religious ceremonies would be suppressed; Indians would not be allowed to go to Christian churches; certain Southwestern reservations would be turned over to Mexico, etc. . . .

The Indian Renaissance

Considering the long history of broken treaties, pledges, and promises, the fact that 172 tribes with an Indian population of 132,000 accepted the word of the Government that the fundamental reorganization of their lives would not harm them is evidence of a new, more satisfactory relationship between the Indians and the Indian Service. The referendum elections served a most valuable purpose. They were palpable proof to the Indians that the Government really was ready to give them a voice in the management of their own affairs, and that the period of arbitrary autocratic rule over the tribes by the Indian Service had come to an end.

This evidence of good faith was reinforced by the request that the tribes begin immediately to formulate the constitutions and charters authorized by the act. Reservation committees and groups set to work at the unaccustomed task of drafting constitutions and of making plans and programs for the economic rehabilitation of the tribes. Charters and constitutions under the Reorganization Act, when once adopted, cannot be revoked or changed by administrative action. Personal government of the tribes by the Secretary of the Interior and the Indian Commissioner is brought to an end.

Indian Emergency Work

In the revivifying of the Indian spirit, the wide-opened benefits of Indian emergency conservation and of other relief work played an important part. It must be remembered that on many reservations the kind of depression which struck the Nation in 1929 had been a chronic condition for a long time, becoming acute when land sales dropped off and the revenue from farm and grazing lands leased to whites dropped almost to the vanishing point. Opportunities for wage work had been all but nonexistent on most reservations, and the psychology of the chronically unemployed had prevailed for so long that it was feared that most of the Indians had become unemployable.

This fear proved to be groundless. Indians young and old not merely accepted emergency relief work, but almost fought for the chance to labor. And they labored effectively. Through their effort the physical plant, the land, the water, the forests, have had many millions of dollars added to their use value in the last 2 years. Incalculable benefits have been derived from the improvement of

The Indian Reorganization Act of 1934

The Indian Reorganization Act (or Wheeler-Howard Act), passed by Congress in 1934, included the following provisions that ended the policy of allotting tribal lands to individuals and that provided for limited tribal self-government.

An act to conserve and develop Indian lands and resources; to extend to Indians the right to form business and other organizations; to establish a credit system for Indians; to grant certain rights of home rule to Indians; to provide for vocational education for Indians; and for other purposes. . . .

That hereafter no land of any Indian reservation, created or set apart by treaty or agreement with the Indians . . . shall be allotted in severalty to any Indian. . . .

SEC. 3. The Secretary of the Interior, if he shall find it to be in the public interest, is hereby authorized to restore to tribal ownership the remaining surplus lands of any Indian reservation heretofore opened, or authorized to be opened. . . .

SEC. 5. The Secretary of the Interior is hereby authorized . . . to acquire . . . any interest in lands, water rights, or surface rights to lands, within or without existing reservations . . . for the purpose of providing land for Indians. . . .

SEC. 16. Any Indian tribe, or tribes, residing on the same reservation, shall have the right to organize for its common welfare, and may adopt an appropriate constitution and bylaws, which shall become effective when ratified by a majority vote of the adult members of the tribe, or of the Indians residing on such reservation, as the case may be, at a special election authorized and called by the Secretary of the Interior under such rules and regulations as he may prescribe. Such constitution and bylaws when ratified as aforesaid and approved by the Secretary of the Interior shall be revocable by an election open to the same voters and conducted in the same manner as hereinabove provided. Amendments to the constitution and bylaws may be ratified and approved by the Secretary in the same manner as the original constitution and bylaws.

In addition to all powers vested in any Indian tribe or tribal council by existing law, the constitution adopted by said tribe shall also vest in such tribe or its tribal council the following rights and powers: To employ legal counsel, the choice of counsel and fixing of fees to be subject to the approval of the Secretary of the Interior; to prevent the sale, disposition, lease, or encumbrance of tribal lands, interests in lands, or other tribal assets without the consent of the tribe; and to negotiate with the Federal, State, and local Governments.

20 million acres of range, through the development of springs and wells and the construction of thousands of stock-water dams, through roads and truck trails, through the construction of thousands of miles of fences and telephone lines. There is not one reservation which, as a result of the emergency and relief work, is not a better place to live on, an easier place in which to gain a living from the soil.

A clear gain to the Indians—and to many white communities in the Indian country—accrued out of the grants from Public Works funds for new Indian community-school buildings, hospitals, and sanatoria, many of them built entirely by Indian labor. Yet the pressing need for structures of this kind has not been half filled. Nor is the Indian irrigation program, financed from emergency grants, more than one-third completed.

Benefits of Relief Work

The benefit derived by the Indians from the emergency and relief work has many aspects. Thousands of the Indian workers have, for perhaps the first time in their lives, learned what it means to have sufficient nourishment of the right kind regularly. Other thousands have been able to acquire minimal household goods, clothing, livestock, and farm implements. Thousands of savings accounts have been started at the various agencies out of earnings of $2.10 per day for 20 days in the month during part of the year.

There have been entries on the debit side also. The number of bootleggers on the fringe of many reservations has multiplied; law enforcement has become more and more difficult. Automobile dealers with second-hand wrecks for sale have encouraged the younger Indians to obligate their potential earnings for years ahead; some traders have encouraged credit buying on far too lavish a scale.

But more important than these shortcomings due to the innate generosity of a race unfamiliar with wise consumption habits is the problem that arises from the introduction of a wage economy on reservations which will supply almost no permanent opportunity for wage work. After the depression is over and the emergency grants cease, what will happen to the now-working Indians?

Rehabilitation Emphasized

To prepare for this inevitable crisis additional funds must be obtained for rehabilitation projects, such as land purchase, housing, the construction of barns and root cellars, the development of domestic water and sanitary facilities, the subjugation of land, the financing of purchases of seeds, implements, and livestock, the stimulation and development of Indian arts and crafts, and the organization and financing of sawmills, fisheries, and other industrial enterprises. This amended program would mean a playing down of the wage motive, a playing up of production for use.

If the necessary grants for this program be made, the Indians on many reservations should be able to pass gradually from relief work to subsistence farming, craft, and other supplemental industrial work of their own.

"We should end the status of Indians as wards of the government and grant them all of the rights and prerogatives pertaining to American citizenship."

The Federal Government Should Terminate Its Trust Relationship with American Indians

Arthur V. Watkins (1886–1973)

Following World War II and John Collier's resignation in 1945 from the position of commissioner of Indian affairs, a growing number of government officials sought to end the federal government's role as supervisor of Indian tribes and trustee of their lands. This policy was known as "termination" because it terminated the federal trustee relationship with Indian tribes. Arthur V. Watkins, a Republican senator from Utah from 1947 to 1959, was a leading proponent of termination. The chairman of the Senate's subcommittee on American Indian affairs from 1947 to 1949 and again from 1953 to 1955, Watkins played an important part in the formulation of federal policy toward American Indians.

The following viewpoint is taken from a 1957 article in which Watkins defends this policy. Watkins argues that government interference has not benefited Indians and that termination would help them gain economic self-reliance. Indians need to be treated not as special wards of the government, he contends, but as full and equal citizens of the United States, with the same rights and responsibilities as other Americans.

From Arthur V. Watkins, "Termination of Federal Supervision: The Removal of Restrictions over Indian Property and Person," *Annals of the American Academy of Political and Social Science*, May 1957. Copyright ©1957 by The American Academy of Political and Social Science. Reprinted by permission of Sage Publications, Inc.

From 1953 to 1962, Congress passed acts terminating the legal status of thirteen Indian tribes and numerous smaller bands, thus ending their treaty relationships with the federal government. These laws led to an upsurge of Indian political activism in subsequent decades.

Virtually since the first decade of our national life the Indian, as tribesman and individual, was accorded a status apart. Now, however, we think constructively and affirmatively of the Indian as a fellow American. We seek to assure that in health, education, and welfare, in social, political, economic, and cultural opportunity, he or she stands as one with us in the enjoyment and responsibilities of our national citizenship. It is particularly gratifying to know that recent years of united effort, mutual planning, and Indian self-appraisal truly have begun to bear increasing fruit.

One facet of this over-all development concerns the freeing of the Indians from special federal restrictions on the property and the person of the tribes and their members. This is not a novel development, but a natural outgrowth of our relationship with the Indians. Congress is fully agreed upon its accomplishment. By unanimous vote in both the Senate and the House of Representatives termination of such special federal supervision has been called for as soon as possible. Of course, as with any such major social concern, methods vary in proposed solutions and emotions sometimes rise as to how the final goal should best be reached. A clear understanding of principles and events is necessary. Here the author seeks more to be factual and informative rather than argumentative and dogmatic. . . . After all, the matter of freeing the Indian from wardship status is not rightfully a subject to debate in academic fashion, with facts marshalled here and there to be maneuvered and counter-maneuvered in a vast battle of words and ideas. Much more I see this as an ideal or universal truth, to which all men subscribe, and concerning which they differ only in their opinion as to how the ideal may be attained and in what degree and during what period of time. . . .

A Historic Moment

A little more than two years ago—June 17, 1954—President Dwight D. Eisenhower signed a bill approved by the Eighty-third Congress that signified a landmark in Indian legislative history. By this measure's terms an Indian tribe and its members, the Menominee of Wisconsin, were assured that after a brief transition period they would at last have full control of their own affairs and would possess all of the attributes of complete American citizenship. This was a most worthy moment in our history. We should all dwell upon its deep meaning. Considering the lengthy span of our Indian relationship, the recency of this event is significant. Obviously, such affirmative action for the great majority of Indians has just begun. Moreover, it should be noted that the foundations laid are solid.

Philosophically speaking, the Indian wardship problem brings up basically the questionable merit of treating the Indian of today as an Indian, rather than as a fellow American citizen. Now, doing away with restrictive federal supervision over Indians, as such, does not affect the retention of those cultural and racial qualities which people of Indian descent would wish to retain; many of us are proud of our ancestral heritage, but that does not nor should it alter our status as American citizens. The distinction between abolishment of wardship and abandonment of the Indian heritage is vitally important. I wish to emphasize this point, because a few well-intentioned private organizations repeatedly seek to influence Congress to keep the Indian in a restricted status by urging legislation to retain him as an Indian ward and as a member of a caste with social status apart from others, not basically as what he is—a fellow American citizen.

Freedom Is the Goal

These organizations have presented some proposals to Congress impossible of accomplishment, but likely to produce argumentation and thus to protract debate beyond reasonable limits. In this manner they apparently seek to justify a continued role as presumable spokesmen for Indian tribes. Likewise, it should be noted that in legislative considerations various other private organizations and serious-minded periodicals have been used as devices propagandizing viewpoints based upon assertions known to Congress to be contrary to the facts upon Indian conditions. Special interests are of course involved in other ways; thus commercial companies having specific reservation leases may be reluctant to see terminal programs proceed, feeling that their own economic interests may be jeopardized. And again, state co-operation in the assumption of responsibilities for their Indian citizens has not always been consistent. Historically, however, the Congress, although perhaps more or less ineffectively until recent years, has sought in the nineteenth and early twentieth centuries to free the Indian. A full study of Congressional actions will bear this out. Freedom for the Indian was the goal then; it is the goal now.

Unfortunately, the major and continuing Congressional movement toward full freedom was delayed for a time by the Indian Re-

Freedom for the Menominees

The Menominee tribe of Wisconsin was one of the first Indian tribes to have its federal trust status terminated. Speaking before the Senate on July 18, 1953, Senator Arthur V. Watkins of Utah contends that the Menominee Indians are economically and socially prepared for this course of action.

This is a bill to provide for termination of Federal supervision of the Menominee Indian Tribe of Wisconsin. . . .

For years Indians, Congress, and persons interested in Indian affairs have joined in raising the cry for liberation of Indians, and yet to date nothing has been done—at least, nothing very effective—to get the Government out of the business of being the guardian of Indians. There has been much talk of such a program, but action has been completely nonexistent. For a great number of years certain tribes of American Indians have been recognized to be fully competent and ready to be placed on their own. The Menominee Indian Tribe of Wisconsin is one of the tribes declared most competent in all available surveys on competency and assimilation. . . .

All available evidence of reports on this tribe, and statistics on its economic and social condition, reinforce the conclusion that this tribe is fully ready for removal from Indian Bureau tutelage. In fact most of the available reports put the Menominees about at the top of advancement among the individual Indian tribes. As long ago as 1930 the Menominees were five-sixths assimilated to modern American ways of life, and evidenced the very least of resistance among the various tribes to adopting the ways of civilization. Yet 23 years have passed without substantial steps being taken toward putting these people on their own. . . .

To work out the details of the proposed amendment, I visited the tribal reservation in Wisconsin and met many of the members of the tribe, and was very favorably impressed, not only with their potential, but with their past accomplishment and particularly with their competency both as a tribe and as individuals. During that visit I became more convinced than ever before that they are now being hampered by Federal supervision, and that, once placed on their own, as they have long been entitled to be, they will develop their present potentials much more rapidly to their own betterment.

organization Act of 1934, the Wheeler-Howard Act. Amid the deep social concern of the depression years, Congress deviated from its accustomed policy under the concept of promoting the general Indian welfare. In the postdepression years Congress—realizing this change of policy—sought to return to the historic principles of much earlier decades. Indeed, one of the original authors of the Act was desirous of its repeal. We should recall, however, that war years soon followed in which Congress found itself engrossed in problems first of national defense and then of mutual security. As with many other major projects, action was thus delayed. . . .

We may admit the it-takes-time view, but we should not allow it to lull us into inaction. Freedom of action for the Indian as a full-fledged citizen—that is the continuing aim. Toward this end Congress and the Administration, state and local governments, Indian tribes and members, interested private agencies, and individual Americans as responsible citizens should all be united and work constantly. The legislatively set target dates for Indian freedom serve as significant spurs to accomplishment. Congress steadily continues to inform itself, to seek out, delimit, and assist those Indians most able to profit immediately by freedom from special supervision, and it acts primarily to speed the day for all Indian tribes and members to be relieved of their wardship status. A basic purpose of Congress in setting up the Indian Claims Commission was to clear the way toward complete freedom of the Indians by assuring a final settlement of all obligations—real or purported—of the federal government to the Indian tribes and other groups.

This picture we must keep in mind when considering the steps that will be taken during the Eighty-fifth and succeeding Congresses and in understanding the setting in which the Eighty-third and Eighty-fourth Congresses acted to directly further the freedom program.

Let us now briefly consider the work of these two recent Congresses.

The House Resolution

In 1953 during the Eighty-third Congress the members of the Senate and the House unanimously endorsed a statement on Indian policy that has continued to be in its general terms the guiding course of Congress. This action taken in the first Session, designated as House Concurrent Resolution 108, should be carefully noted in full:

> Whereas it is the policy of Congress, as rapidly as possible to make the Indians within the territorial limits of the United States subject to the same laws and entitled to the same privileges and responsibilities as are applicable to other citizens of the United States, to end their status as wards of the United States, and to grant them all of the rights and prerogatives pertaining to American citizenship; and
>
> Whereas the Indians within the territorial limits of the United States should assume their full responsibilities as American citizens: Now therefore, be it
>
> *Resolved by the House of Representatives (the Senate concurring),* That it is declared to be the sense of Congress that, at the earli-

est possible time, all of the Indian tribes and the individual members thereof located within the States of California, Florida, New York, and Texas, and all of the following-named Indian tribes and individual members thereof, should be freed from Federal supervision and control and from the disabilities and limitations specially applicable to Indians: The Flathead Tribe of Montana, the Klamath Tribe of Oregon, the Menominee Tribe of Wisconsin, the Potawatomi Tribe of Kansas and Nebraska, and those members of the Chippewa Tribe who are on the Turtle Mountain Reservation, North Dakota. It is further declared to be the sense of Congress that, upon the release of such tribes and individual members thereof from such disabilities and limitations, all offices of the Bureau of Indian Affairs in the States of California, Florida, New York, and Texas, and all other offices of the Bureau of Indian Affairs whose primary purpose was to serve any Indian tribe or individual Indian freed from Federal supervision should be abolished. It is further declared to be the sense of Congress that the Secretary of the Interior should examine all existing legislation dealing with such Indians and treaties between the Government of the United States and each such tribe, and report to Congress at the earliest practicable date, but not later than January 1, 1954, his recommendations for such legislation, as in his judgment, may be necessary to accomplish the purposes of this resolution.

Thereafter there were bills introduced and hearings held in 1954 on twelve Indian groups totaling 1,715 printed pages. As a result Congress enacted legislation providing for release of federal supervision over the property and individual members of the Alabama and Coushatta Tribes of Texas, the Klamath of Oregon (Klamath and Modoc Tribes and the Yakooskin Band of Snakes), the Tribes of Western Oregon (Grand Ronde, Siletz), the Menominee Tribe of Wisconsin, and certain tribes in Utah (Shivwits, Kanosh, Koosharem and Indian Peaks Bands of Paiutes; the mixed-blood Uintah and Ouray [Utes]). All of the above except the Utah Indians were specified in House Concurrent Resolution 108.

Approximately ten thousand Indians were thus set on the road to complete citizenship rights and responsibilities. . . .

During the Eighty-fourth Congress legislation resulted in approval of releasing federal control over the property and individual members of three tribes in Oklahoma—the Peoria, Ottawa, and Wyandotte. Each of these tribes voluntarily adopted a resolution requesting the introduction and enactment of terminal legislation. . . .

Secluded reservation life is a deterrent to the Indian, keeping him apart in ways far beyond the purely geographic. By way of preparation for future decontrol programs, the Eighty-fourth Congress . . . passed the Vocational Rehabilitation Act to assist Indians to adapt themselves more readily to off-reservation life. Self-reliance is basic to the whole Indian-freedom program. Through our national historic development the Indian was forced into a dependent position with the federal government more and more, as America advanced westward, tending to sublimate his natural qualities of self-reliance, courage, discipline, resourcefulness, confidence, and faith in the future. Congress has realized this, and has steadily acted more positively to restore to the Indian these qualities. But self-reliance demands opportunity to grow. The Indian must be given the conditions under which—and only under which—self-reliance can be wholeheartedly regenerated. . . .

Experience developed in carrying out the legislation adopted by the Eighty-third Congress for freedom from special federal control over Indians will be a valuable guide in continuing to develop further freedom-program bills. Generally, this experience has shown that other factors being equal, the smaller and rather well assimilated tribes or other groups, having relatively minor and cohesive property or other value interests easily adjustable to individual shares, appear the more likely subjects for prompt release from federal controls. And conversely, rather unassimilated and/or large groups with quite major or intricate property or other value interests require more time, patience, and mutual understanding in moving toward eventual freedom from their federal wardship status. . . .

Voluntary Indian Actions

The Commissioner of Indian Affairs, Glenn L. Emmons, has noted that one of the most helpful and promising courses toward termination is by voluntary request of the Indian groups themselves. In an informal statement on January 31, 1956, at a House subcommittee hearing on appropriations Emmons remarked:

> . . . In a number of areas, tribes have taken the initiative in exploring the means of programming their way toward eventual self-determination, that is, the Sisseton-Wahpeton Tribe in the Aberdeen (S.D.) area, the Makah and Colville Tribes in the State of Washington, several urban colonies in Nevada, the tribes in the Quapaw jurisdiction in eastern Oklahoma, . . .

> . . . in order for projects to be meaningful to the tribal groups, they must be developed at the local level in consultation with the tribal groups affected, and there must be a continuous follow-through in the development and implementation of the program proposals.

On April 12, 1956, in a major memorandum to all of the Bureau area directors and superintendents, Commissioner Emmons again referred particularly to the value of voluntary Indian group action. He said in part:

> A good program is one which results from the desires of and

fits the needs of a particular group of Indians. In whole or in part the program should, if possible, be the work of the Indians themselves.

As to the question of legislation Emmons specifically noted that:

> . . . In some cases, it may develop that special legislation will be necessary to forward a group's basic program. In other cases the Indian group may feel that the group's cultural assimilation and integration into the community life about them has progressed to the point where they desire early congressional consideration of termination legislation. In either case, the Area Director should advise the Commissioner with a view to arranging for special guidance and assistance.

Freedom for the Indians

. . . The basic principle enunciated so clearly and approved unanimously by the Senate and House in House Concurrent Resolution 108 of the Eighty-third Congress continues to be the overall guiding policy of Congress in Indian affairs. In view of the historic policy of Congress favoring freedom for the Indians, we may well expect future Congresses to continue to indorse the principle that "as rapidly as possible" we should end the status of Indians as wards of the government and grant them all of the rights and prerogatives pertaining to American citizenship.

With the aim of "equality before the law" in mind our course should rightly be no other. Firm and constant consideration for those of Indian ancestry should lead us all to work diligently and carefully for the full realization of their national citizenship with all other Americans. Following in the footsteps of the Emancipation Proclamation of ninety-four years ago, I see the following words emblazoned in letters of fire above the heads of the Indians—*THESE PEOPLE SHALL BE FREE!*

VIEWPOINT 4

"Termination bills . . . jeopardize the Indian's very existence."

The Federal Government Should Not Terminate Its Trust Relationship with American Indians

Ruth Muskrat Bronson (1897–1982)

In the 1950s the policy of "termination" became popular in government circles. The term referred to the termination of the federal trust protection over Indian lands and of the governing roles of Indian tribal governments and the Bureau of Indian Affairs. Between 1954 and 1962 (after which termination fell out of favor), laws were passed authorizing the termination of more than one hundred Indian tribes or bands. The twelve thousand Indians affected by these laws then became subject to state jurisdiction. These developments helped spark the rise of Native American political activism. Among the organizations opposed to termination was the National Congress of American Indians (NCAI), which was founded in Denver in 1944 and was one of the first major intertribal Indian organizations.

The following viewpoint is taken from a 1955 article by Ruth Muskrat Bronson, an activist for the NCAI who served as the organization's director and secretary in its early years. A Cherokee, Bronson was the author of *Indians Are People Too*, published in 1944. In her article, Bronson argues that a hasty termination of the federal government's relationship with and responsibilities to American Indians would cause them great harm and would violate past treaties. Moreover, she contends that some of the Indian tribes who have already agreed to termination of federal trusteeship have done so under extreme pressure and duress. State and local governments, she asserts, may not adequately replace the federal government in the provision of social services to Indians. Termination may also force Indians to give up their traditional culture and beliefs, Bronson concludes.

If the official policies of the Federal Government, as reflected by the current policies of the Bureau of Indian Affairs and the actions of the 83rd Congress, continue to be pursued the American Indian (like that other living creature associated with him in history, the buffalo) is likely, similarly, to continue to exist only on the American nickel.

The tragedy is that this may come about through misunderstanding of the issues involved in the proposed termination of Federal trusteeship over the Indian. These issues have been almost completely obscured in a miasma of confusion caused by conflicting financial interests, conflicting opinions on proper psychological solutions, and of justice itself. And, most important of all, caused by uninformed sentiment.

Misconceptions and Misunderstandings

The average American is noted for his sympathy with the underdog. He is also apt to have romantic sentiment for the American Indian. Add to these two admirable qualities a vague sense of guilt for the actions of his forebears in ousting the original inhabitants of the rich land they adopted and for the long and shameful history of broken treaties with these dispossessed, and you have a tendency toward impulsive action based on a desire to make amends. If this action is founded on superficial or inaccurate knowledge rather than on thoughtful study or familiarity with fact and reality the result can be exceedingly serious, even disastrous, for the Indian. This is true in the case of the termination bills since these jeopardize the Indian's very existence and unquestionably would lead to his eventual—literal—extinction.

There is even widespread misconception as to what is involved in the Federal trusteeship. The casually informed citizen, dedicated to fair play, feels there is something definitely insulting in labeling an adult a ward of the government, as though he were being branded as too incompetent to function without a guardian. Actually, today's Indian enjoys all the major rights and obligations of every American citizen: the right to vote, for instance; to move freely about the country (that is, to live on a reservation or not, as he chooses); the right to sue in court and to make contracts, to hold office; the obligation to pay taxes, and to fight and die for his country in the armed forces.

In addition, he has special privileges, which is what trusteeship boils down to, which he gained by bargaining with his conquerors. In the not so distant past the Indians agreed to end their fighting and cede land to white settlers in exchange for certain defined, inalienable lands and specified services which the Indians could not provide for themselves and which are provided by the States and local communities for non-Indian citizens. It is hard to see how benefits make a "second class" citizen out of an

---

Against Termination

Since the 1950s American Indian leaders have generally opposed any proposals to terminate federal trusteeship over Indian tribes. The following passage is excerpted from a 1966 speech directed at government officials by Earl Old Person, then the chairman of the Blackfoot tribe of Montana. He later became president of the National Congress of American Indians.

It cannot be denied that every time the Bureau of Indian Affairs goes to Congress for money, they justify their request for appropriations on the grounds that they are trying to "get themselves out of the Indian business." This means termination to members of Congress and to Indians.

It is important to note that in our Indian language the only translation for termination is to "wipe out" or "kill off". We have no Indian words for termination. And there should be no English word for termination as it is applied to modern day terms regarding the relationship of the U.S. Government and the American Indian. Why scare us to death every year by going to Congress for money and justifying the request on the grounds that the money is necessary to "terminate the trust relationship of the U.S. to the American Indian"?

You have caused us to jump every time we hear this word. We made treaties with the U.S. Government which guaranteed our right to develop our reservations and to develop as a people free from interference. In order to bring about this development, careful planning must be done on the part of not only the agencies of Government, but by the tribes themselves. But how can we plan our future when the Indian Bureau constantly threatens to wipe us out as a race? It is like trying to cook a meal in your tipi when someone is standing outside trying to burn the tipi down.

So let's agree to forget the termination talk and instead talk of development of Indian people, their land, and their culture.

Indian, especially when preferential treatment seems not to jeopardize the status of veterans, farmers, subsidized airlines and steamship companies, manufacturers protected by tariffs, or the businessmen with rapid tax write-offs.

On the contrary, it would seem to be our established political philosophy that the economic well-being of particular groups is a legitimate concern of the Federal government—all this aside from the fact that, in the case of the Indians, it is a matter of solemn treaty.

In addition to the treaties which established reservations as the property and home of the Indian people, the Reorganization Act of 1934 affirmed the partnership of Indian tribes and the Federal Government. Consolidating numerous individual treaties that had been effected with Indian tribes over the years, the Indians were granted by this Act the right to exist as distinct communities, with their own properties, culture, and religion, and the promise of certain services to be furnished by the Federal Government normally furnished [to] other citizens by the states was reaffirmed and enlarged upon.

In the 83rd Congress there was a concerted effort to abrogate this Act, by means of over 100 bills claiming to "free" Indians. Ten of those bills proposed termination of trusteeship over specific tribes. Five of them were passed and signed by the President. All of the bills follow the same pattern. They were introduced by less than a handful of men, but were designed to cut down the Indian on many fronts: the family, the band, the tribe and at State level. They would destroy the tribal organizations, abolish tribal constitutions and corporations formed under the Act of 1934 and void Federal-Indian treaties. Government supervision of the sale of Indian property and expert guidance on the development of natural resources which has been provided up to now would also be cut off, thus exposing the individual Indian, the weak as well as the strong, to exploitation by the unscrupulous and those more knowledgeable in the commercial ways of a highly complex and competitive society. This would take away from him the protection that was preventing further depletion of his last remaining resources. Such a loss would be the country's as well as the Indian's, since conservation along with guided expert development would cease.

In addition, there would be a cessation of education, health and welfare services now supplied by the Federal Government, guaranteed by treaty and sorely needed, without assurance that these would be provided by the States or local communities. . . .

Termination Without Safeguards

Actually very few voices are raised against eventual termination of trusteeship over the Indians. The Indian people themselves, the friends of the Indians, and the authorities on Indian affairs who are deeply concerned about the trend toward termination are frightened and deeply disturbed, not only because of the inequities contained in the legislation proposed in the 83rd Congress, but at the haste, without proper safeguards or study in relation to the conditions of individual tribes.

And most of all, we are deeply concerned that termination is being decided upon *without the consent,* nay, over the protests, of the Indians concerned. Too often when Indian consent is given it has been obtained by unfair pressures amounting to nothing less than administrative blackmail, as in the case of two tribes which accepted termination bills because they were denied their own funds until they consented. This seems to them a shocking violation of faith.

The informed feel that there should be an attack on the major forces that are keeping the Indian from realizing his potentialities: ill health, lack of educational opportunities, widespread poverty. By attacking these problems at the root, they feel the day will be hastened when the Indian people will no longer need the protection of a special relationship with the Federal Government.

Termination of trusteeship, they believe (if it should be undertaken at all), should be carefully planned-for well ahead of the event, after thorough study, with the agreement of the Indians, the Federal agencies involved, the States and local government units, and the other organizations who would assume responsibility for providing the services now given by the Federal Government. Maintenance of the tribal integrity, if this is what the Indians want, must be assured in any program looking toward their future healthy integration into the American way of life. The consent of the Indians, moreover, should not be obtained by pressure amounting to duress such as was used last year in the cases of Menominee and Klamath when it was made clear to these two tribes that they would be permitted to withdraw their own money in the United States Treasury only if that withdrawal was coupled with "termination."

More than one theorist has stated that "the solution to the Indian problem" is the absorption of the Indian into the culture, race and society of the European-oriented American way. Shouldn't the Indian have something to say about this? Should the Indian be forced to give up his beliefs, his way of conducting his affairs, his method of organized living, his kind of life on the land he is a part of, if he chooses not to? Shouldn't the Indians have the same right to self-determination that our government has stated, often and officially, is the inalienable right of peoples in far parts of the world? Do we apply a different set of principles, of ethics, to the people within our own borders?

VIEWPOINT 5

"Visiting the Indians, we saw a normal and happy integration into the community."

Indians Who Have Moved to Cities Have Fared Well

O.K. Armstrong (1893–1987) and
Marjorie Armstrong (b. 1912)

Throughout the twentieth century, many Native Americans left their reservation homes to resettle in U.S. cities. In the 1950s, this urban migration was actively encouraged by the federal government as part of a general thrust to integrate Indians within American society and to reduce the federal government's role in Indian affairs. Supporters of relocation argued that it provided the best way of relieving poverty and population problems on reservations and of helping Indians achieve the lifestyle of middle-class Americans.

The following viewpoint is taken from a 1955 *Reader's Digest* article that depicts the urban relocation of American Indians in positive terms. The article was written by O.K. and Marjorie Armstrong, a husband-and-wife team of journalists whose later books include *Religion Can Conquer Communism* and *The Baptists in America*. (O.K. Armstrong also served one term as a congressman representing Missouri.) The writers describe the experiences of several Native Americans who, with government assistance, chose to seek a new life in America's cities. The government's relocation programs not only help Indians but also benefit American taxpayers by reducing the amount of federal funds spent on Indian reservations, the authors conclude.

From "The Indians Are Going to Town," by O.K. and Marjorie Armstrong. Reprinted with permission from the January 1955 *Reader's Digest*. Copyright 1955 by The Reader's Digest Assn., Inc.

"Sixth floor—Indian Bureau. All Indians off!" sang out the elevator operator at 608 S. Dearborn Street, Chicago. In an aside to us he said, "They all go to the same place."

Off stepped a young Indian couple, the man wearing a red shirt and jeans with a belt of silver circles, she in a print dress with an enormous turquoise necklace. She carried a tiny baby on one arm, and was leading a toddler. They were followed by a tall Indian in cowboy boots.

All were plainly ill at ease and smiled their appreciation when we volunteered to show them to the Indian Relocation Office. In the reception room a neatly dressed young Indian woman spoke to the couple in their own Navajo tongue, calling their names, Hola and Ula Sunrise. Delighted, they responded to her welcome. Then she turned inquiringly to the tall man.

"Me—I'm Charley Gray Fox, a Sioux from Rosebud, South Dakota," he announced with a grin.

During the next hour three other Indians arrived: A Cheyenne from Montana, a Creek from Oklahoma and another Navajo from Window Rock, Ariz. All had been picked by officials at their reservation to begin a new life in the big city, and had suitable homes and jobs waiting for them through the efforts of Kurt Dreifuss, director of the Relocation Office, and his staff.

"Why did you leave your reservation?" we asked Charley Gray Fox.

"Me—I'm tired of little odd jobs around Rosebud. I want a regular pay check!"

"What job will you take?"

He held up his huge bronzed hands. "Anything I can do with these! I like to work with my hands. Mechanics—anything. Just so I'm building something."

We asked the Sunrises why they came to Chicago. The young husband waved expressively toward his baby and the toddler peeping from behind the mother.

"Too many Navajos—not enough to eat," he answered.

The American Indians are on the warpath again. "Operation Relocation," begun in 1952 under former Commissioner of Indian Affairs Dillon Myer, is developing into a major activity of the Indian Bureau under present Commissioner Glenn L. Emmons. Its purpose is to give a helping hand to Indians who want to leave the reservations to find employment. Some 6200 of the estimated 245,000 Indians on reservations had been resettled by late 1954 (of whom 2500 are workers in good jobs), via relocation centers established in Chicago, Denver, Los Angeles and Oakland. Additional centers are being considered for Seattle, St. Louis and Kansas City.

"At long last," says Commissioner Emmons, "we are doing more than keeping the Indian on relief. We are helping him to help himself."

For several weeks last summer we visited reservations—westward from the Dakotas to Oregon, thence southward through California, then east to the great Navajo, Hopi, Apache, Pueblo and other southwestern areas. Everywhere we saw the tragedy of these twin evils: overpopulation in proportion to resources, and underemployment for men and women anxious to work.

When Kit Carson herded the Navajos into their huge, barren tract in 1868, there were only 7800 of them. Today there are 71,000. The grazing lands and other resources won't adequately support more than half this population.

In South Dakota the Indian population has grown from 21,000 in 1930 to 30,000 today—and this is about the proportion of increase in all Indian areas.

A few tribes receive good incomes from their reservations, such as the Klamaths in Oregon from timber and the Arapaho in Wyoming from oil and gas. But the majority of reservations are little better than country slums. Not more than 20 percent of the Crow Indians of Montana or the Shoshoni-Bannocks in Idaho make a living from their own use of reservation lands. Of the 1700 families on the Pine Ridge Reservation in South Dakota, only 200 are self-supporting.

We asked Charles F. Miller, chief of the Indian Bureau's Relocation Branch: "Why haven't more Indians left for better jobs on their own?"

"Suppose you had never been very far from home," he responded. "Suppose your land and money were held in trust by the Government, and you feared discrimination because of your race if you ventured outside. Suppose maybe you had difficulty speaking English. Wouldn't you hesitate to buck a big city looking for work? Well, that's the situation for many reservation Indians."

Success of the relocation program, Mr. Miller feels, is due to three important things: careful selection of applicants, fitting the Indian to the right job, and adjusting him and his family to the new community.

On each reservation a relocation officer makes contact with those who show an interest in resettling. An applicant must be 18 years old or more, in good health and of satisfactory reputation. His fare is paid to the relocation center of his choice, and the center pays his living expenses until he receives his first full pay check. He is told plainly that he will be expected to stand on his own feet after he gets the job.

At the Relocation Office, expert interviewers discuss his experience, ability and interests, take him to visit plants and places of business where jobs are available, help him choose. Housing is found for him—and his family, if he has one. Employees of the Relocation Office follow through with help on getting the children into school, how to shop at department stores and supermarkets. A minister or priest of the family's faith may call and add his words of welcome.

This 1952 photograph of a Navajo family illustrates some of the impoverished conditions under which many Indians on reservations lived—conditions that caused some to advocate urban relocation for Indians.

Several big industrial firms give the relocatees on-the-job training. Many of the Indians attend night school, and the Indian Bureau is now emphasizing manual and vocational training on the reservations.

Why the big cities for Indian workers? Why not small towns near home? Relocation officers give three reasons:

First, unhappily, the greatest discrimination against Indians exists in non-Indian communities near the reservations. But in big cities Indians are readily accepted into school, church and community life.

Second, there are more job possibilities in the cities. Mary Nan Gamble, director of the Los Angeles Relocation Office, pointed out: "Every sort of industry, big and little, is located here. We have 1000 contacts with potential employers in our files, and 375 have already accepted Indian workers. We hope to double those figures in another year."

Third reason is suitability of Indians for industrial occupations. Says Brice Lay, Relocation Director at Oakland: "With proper training, an Indian can learn to do almost anything skillfully. Our underemployed Indians constitute the most needless waste of human resources in America. For these people the relocation program comes as a rainbow of hope."

From many Indians working at their jobs, and from their employers, we learned how bright that rainbow can be. The Stewart-Warner Corp. in Chicago has employed about 30 relocatees. "Indians make good workers," Burt Muldoon, personnel director, told us. "We start them at $1.40 per hour, and after a year many have reached $1.80. Our machines work fast, but nothing is too fast for a well-trained Indian."

Because of the good record made by several Indian employes, the Boeing Airplane Co. in Seattle plans to hire more Indians when that city's Relocation Office opens. North American Aviation, Los Angeles, has employed 200 resettled Indians, finds them particularly skillful at cutting, shaping and riveting sheet metal. "They are intelligent, industrious people," J.M. Wright, employment supervisor, declared. "We plan to continue participating in this program."

Employers are discovering how adept Indian women are as stenographers and machine operators. (About one fourth of all relocated workers are women.) Betty Koester, personnel director of Swimwear, Inc., a plant in Los Angeles which makes women's swim suits and beach towels, walked with us down long rows of sewing machines. Of the 200 employes, 32 were relocated Indian girls. "Navajos, Pueblos, Utes—we like them all," she said. "They are neat, diligent and skillful."

Relocation has a strong appeal to younger Indians. The largest group of relocatees is composed of former GI's from 28 to 33 years old, married, with one or two children. With quiet earnestness, Benny Bearskin, a Winnebago whom we met in Chicago, expressed sentiments we heard echoed by many other young Indians: "They've kept the old folks as museum pieces, through ignorance and idleness, but we young Indians are going to free ourselves by education and work. We can be good Americans, making a decent living, and still keep our Indian culture."

Visiting the Indians, we saw a normal and happy integration into the community. Several were buying their own homes. There were schoolbooks for children of parents who never went beyond the third grade in reservation schools. There were radios and television sets.

Indian centers in Chicago and Los Angeles provide a clubhouse with reading rooms, kitchen for refreshments, and recreation hall. They are usually open day and evening, and every Indian in town is invited to come in and get acquainted with members of all the tribes represented in the city. The Chicago All-Tribes American Indian Center sponsors a baseball team, appropriately called the Braves. Its news sheet, *Tom Tom Echoes*, keeps all tribes informed of Indian doings. Teenage parties are lively affairs. Hearts are never lonely at the Indian Center. Many romances blossom.

In Chicago the center's chieftain is Ted White, whose father was Sioux and mother Oneida. Winnebago Benny Bearskin helps him with dances and pageants. "We do what the Government can't do—we make them feel at home," White told us.

Not all relocatees are readily adjusted. About 30 percent go back to the reservations—mostly because of homesickness. But after seeing the folks an increasing number leave home a second time. Steady work and regular pay have a strong pull. Those who return usually bring a list of names of "relatives" (meaning good friends) whom they want relocated *pronto*.

Average cost of relocating an Indian worker in all areas is about $200. "The best investment the Indian Bureau ever made, both in money and in human values," Mr. Miller calls it. He showed us reports on Indians who had worked at their new jobs for a year or longer. Selecting five Indian families, we found it had cost the American taxpayers only $1156 for relocation expenses, while from their combined incomes of about $15,000 during their first year they had paid income taxes totaling $1418.

Among the Indians relocated by George T. Barrett when he was area relocation director at Billings, Mont., were John Houle and his wife of the Cree tribe. Later Mrs. Houle wrote these words of appreciation:

"We are working and finding friends among those we once feared. The things we work for are ours. We can pass them on to our children. By the work of our hands and the understanding of our hearts we have won back our birthright."

As the relocation program progresses, the existing reservations can better support those Indians who desire to live close to the soil on farm or ranch. The others can find their places in new homes and chosen occupations, and the stream of a truly noble race, so long dammed by tradition and prejudice, will strengthen the current of American life.

Viewpoint 6

"For every former trapper-farmer now adjusted to assembly-line work and city life, there are ninety-nine adrift in a new and hostile environment."

Indians Who Have Moved to Cities Have Not Fared Well

Ruth Mulvey Harmer (b. 1919)

The migration of American Indians from reservations to American cities increased in the 1950s, in part because of federal government programs designed to encourage them to relocate to major metropolitan areas such as Los Angeles, California, and Chicago, Illinois. Pamphlets and articles distributed within Indian reservations touted the advantages of urban living, and relocation was enthusiastically supported by government officials and others who believed that American Indians would benefit by entering mainstream American society. Participants in urban relocation programs were typically provided money for travel and one month's living expenses, job placement assistance, and counseling. However, many of those who made the move to the city faced a variety of problems, including poverty, discrimination, and difficulties of cultural adjustment.

The following viewpoint is taken from a 1956 article by Ruth Mulvey Harmer, a journalist and writing teacher who investigated the conditions of American Indians living in Los Angeles. Harmer asserts that, contrary to claims of the federal government's Bureau of Indian Affairs, most of the Indians who moved from reservations to cities have received little government support and are not adjusting well to urban life. She contends that

From Ruth Mulvey Harmer, "Uprooting the Indian," *Atlantic Monthly*, March 1956. Reprinted by permission of the author.

the government must strengthen its education and preparation programs for Indians who wish to relocate. An even better solution, she proposes, would be for the government to provide greater support for economic development on Indian reservations, enabling residents to stay.

Harmer served for five years on the board of the Indian center she discusses in this article. She later became a professor of English at California State Polytechnic University, Pomona, and a writer of books on various social issues.

Two months ago Little Light, her husband Leonard Bear, and their five children were persons of standing in a Creek Indian community in Oklahoma. They had only eighty acres of poor land and a modest cabin, but except for the hungry seasons they understood their way of life; they were at peace.

Today they are slum dwellers in Los Angeles, without land or home or culture or peace. Leonard Bear and his family have become part of that vast army of displaced persons which has been created by the government's policy of accelerating the "integration" of the Indian. Uprooted from their native soil, many without even the weapon of comprehensible language with which to defend themselves, the 400,000 indigenous Americans still living in reservations and small communities are being turned loose upon the asphalt jungles of metropolitan centers in one of the most extraordinary forced migrations in history.

The Relocation Program being carried out by the Bureau of Indian Affairs was established in 1951 to help the Indians become part of the national economy and part of the national life. However, it did not really become important until August 15, 1953, when President [Dwight D.] Eisenhower signed Public Law 280. That law, which he branded as "most un-Christian," authorizes any state to substitute its own law for federal Indian law and its own codes for Indian tribal codes. It was enthusiastically hailed in the Western states by persons who had long been seeking legal sanction to move in on Indian lands, superficially poor but rich in sub-surface oil and minerals. Further strength was given to the program to dislodge the Indians under the terms of the Watkins Bill (Senate 2670), providing that the 177 pure-blood Paiutes who own 45,000 acres of potentially valuable land in Nevada should no longer receive federal aid protection. Another precedent to weaken the Indians' hold on their whittled-down grants was set by Senate Bill 2745, which forcibly removed from trusteeship status all individually owned Klamath lands in Oregon and which authorized any enrolled Klamath to force the tribe to sell its corporate holdings in order to buy him out.

Other bills now pending promise to end all federal services to Indians, to liquidate all tribal organizations, and to dispose of their holdings.

However, the Bureau of Indian Affairs is accomplishing that end so rapidly through the Relocation Program that additional laws may be simply *ex post facto* legislative items. A remarkably effective sales campaign is prompting thousands of Indians to abandon their lands and interests for the "promised lands" of the relocation centers.

In defense of the program, an officer of the Bureau of Indian Affairs points out that some of the new immigrants to the urban centers have become model citizens and are "enjoying the fruits of Twentieth Century civilization . . . up to and including television sets." That is true. But the Bureau is curiously vague about the number of maladjustments and even the number of returnees, which well-informed welfare and social workers in several of the centers set at 60 per cent.

For every success story, there are a hundred failures. For every former trapper-farmer now adjusted to assembly-line work and city life, there are ninety-nine adrift in a new and hostile environment. Against the optimistic pronouncement of government agents that "with a little proper guidance, Indians have no trouble making the major adjustment from reservation to city life" is the bitter cry of Little Light: "So this is the land of sunshine they promised us!"

Little Light's Story

A damning summary of the program was spoken by a woman in the chairless kitchen-dining-living room of a small shanty on the outskirts of Los Angeles. Five children, black eyes round with wonder in their apricot faces, sheltered against her skirt. The walls were unpainted, the floor a patchwork of linoleum. Through an archway, another room was visible where three beds crowded together. A two-burner gas stove stood on a box, and on the only other piece of furniture in the room—a battered table— rested the remains of dinner: some white, grease-soaked bags which had contained hamburgers and fried potatoes prepared by the restaurant a few blocks away.

She answered our questions in an Indian dialect which the woman beside me interpreted. "No, my husband is not here. He went out with some other men. He does every night. They are drinking.

"Yes, he is working. He makes lots of money. One dollar and

sixty cents an hour in the airplane factory.

"Yes, the children are in school. All but Zena." She indicated one of the girls, about ten years old. "Zena is sick. I don't know what sickness. There is no doctor.

"Yes, the food came from that place. I don't go to the store often. Everybody laughs at me.

"Yes, I want to go back. There is not money. We pay seventy-five dollars a month for this house. We pay for food. We pay for lights. We don't have the money to go back."

Then the patient planes of her face became distorted. "They did not tell us it would be like this."

What had "they" told Little Light and her husband?

A good indication may be found in an article entitled "Relocation News" written by George Shubert for the *Fort Berthold Agency and News Bulletin* of Newtown, North Dakota, for May 12, 1955. Following a glowing account of jobs for young men and women with a large company in Chicago—"skilled, life time jobs . . . with paid vacation, sick benefits, paid pension plan, union membership, protection, etc."—the Indian Affairs officer wrote:—

> This office is presently equipped to offer financial assistance to a large number of qualified persons who have an earnest desire to improve their standard of living, by accepting permanent employment and relocation to one of four large urban areas in the United States; namely Chicago, Illinois, Denver, Colorado, Oakland, California (including the entire Bay Area) and Los Angeles, California.
>
> Our offices in both areas are presently able to place on jobs and render any assistances necessary to practically an unlimited number of families. They also state that there is a good selection of employment opportunities and housing facilities available at the present time.
>
> The rapidly rising waters in the bottom lands of the reservation should remind us of the fact that the Fort Berthold people have lost forever over one-half of the natural resources and practically all of their Class 1 and 2 agricultural lands, comprising one-quarter of the area of the entire reservation and one-half of the agricultural resources, thereby rendering the remaining portions of the reservation inadequate to provide subsistence for the remaining members of the tribes, at a standard comparable to the people adjacent to the reservation.
>
> We feel that a workable solution to the above problem would be to avail yourselves of the opportunities offered by the Relocation Branch of the Bureau of Indian Affairs. It must be at least worthy of serious consideration for persons who have ambitions to advance economically and socially and to provide better opportunity for their children.

Undeniably, the *pitch* is effective. The prospect is given a choice between the nothing of life in Fort Berthold and the glittering something of security and prosperity elsewhere; aid and friendship will be given to those who make the "right" choice. And even if the prospect is reluctant to send in the boxtop for himself, he should think of his children.

For those who cannot be reached by words, there is the poster recently concocted in the Los Angeles Relocation Center picturing a number of pleasant, comfortable houses owned by Indians who are shown demonstrating the wonders of garbage disposals in the assorted kitchens and of television sets in the assorted living rooms.

The salesmanship rates an A plus, but what about the product?

Limited Government Assistance

First of all, the government's financial assistance in connection with relocation is limited specifically to one-way travel costs and a weekly allowance until the first pay check comes in. Those monetary aids are made *only* to persons without any funds; partial grants are given to those who have some reserves. But that even the maximum grant is sufficient is highly debatable: transportation costs and a living allowance for a few weeks might be all that a bright young man moving from San Francisco to New York would need to tide him over the transitional period; it is not enough to cover the period of adjustment needed by a family moving from a pre-Columbian culture into the mechanized twentieth century.

"Accepting permanent employment" is another rather meaningless phrase since absolute job security is almost nonexistent. Moreover, many of the Indians find it impossible to work in foundries or at assembly-line jobs after a history of outdoor experience. The Bureau of Indian Affairs accepts no responsibility for those who wish to transfer from the jobs they took blind when they first arrived.

That the Relocation Offices in the four areas are presently able to "render any assistances necessary to practically an unlimited number of families" is an absurdity. In Los Angeles, where between 150 and 200 new arrivals are pouring in each month under government sponsorship (another 100 are coming on their own), the Relocation Office has a staff of fourteen persons, including clerks, receptionist, secretaries, and others who play no active role in the "integration." Those who do, necessarily confine themselves to receiving the Indians who show up at the office, making job contacts for them, giving them a living allowance and the address of a vacant dwelling.

This sketchy reception is obviously a prologue to disaster for persons whose acquaintance with the American language is painfully new if it exists at all, who are not accustomed to handling money—most of them have lived in an agricultural environment where barter is the approved method of exchange—who are generally more ignorant of urban ways than a six-year-old child reared in a city, and who become unutterably lonely removed from the security of tribal identity.

No Guarantees for Golden Promises

Michael Harris, an urban affairs reporter for the San Francisco Chronicle, *wrote in the March-April 1971 issue of* City *magazine about the continuing problems of American Indians who relocated to large cities.*

The trading off of rural hopelessness for despair in the city is evidence of the successes scored by recruiters from the Bureau of Indian Affairs on reservations in the Southwest, the Dakotas, and anywhere else Indians might be found, including Alaska. The Government agents promise jobs or education, decent housing, and a good life in the city. And then, after the prospects are persuaded to accept the offer, the recruiters issue one-way tickets to Minneapolis, Cleveland, Dallas, or any of several California cities that have imperceptibly become new camping grounds for American Indians.

Later, when the promised new job proves to be only part-time work at substandard wages, when the decent housing fails to materialize, and when the initial living allowance runs out, it is discovered that there are no guarantees to back up the golden promises. For many Indians, the move to the city means a shift from dependence on the Federal Government on the reservation to a place on the welfare rolls in the city. In financial terms, all that has happened has been the transfer of responsibility for part of the Indian population from the Bureau of Indian Affairs to local taxpayers.

Their first glimpse of city life is rarely happy. In Los Angeles, where there has been an acute housing shortage since the beginning of World War II, the Indians have been hard pressed to find decent accommodations. Many of them are sent to antiquated rooming houses and apartments in the Bunker Hill area, which is now being razed with federal and municipal funds. Others are sent to trailer courts and dreary buildings in the southern part of the city near the aircraft plants.

For many, a few days is enough; others leave in a few weeks; some stay, and for most the going is rough. A number of the men—particularly the GIs and those who have taken the five-year training course at Sherman Institute or other government schools—fare rather well. They know English, they have learned a trade, they have had an extended relationship with white men and white men's ways. But most are hopeless and dangerous misfits.

The Indians in Los Angeles—and there are now 10,000 of them, representing 86 tribes—have had a relatively good police record: a one per cent arrest, mostly on charges of drunken driving and "plain drunk." That figure soared in 1955. During the Memorial Day lost weekend, an estimated one out of every four of the men haled into court was an Indian. Not long ago, for the first time in the history of Los Angeles an Indian was picked up by the police for child beating—a crime unheard of among them. Recently, and for the first time, a number have been arrested for sex offenses. Women and children have been getting into trouble, too.

The Los Angeles Indian Center

When a 21-year-old Sioux was brought before a municipal court judge to defend himself on a charge of drunken driving, he apologized: "If I go into a bar and have a couple of drinks, everyone is nice to me. Friendly. I feel good then."

At that point, a small, slim Indian woman rose to intercede. "This boy is not delinquent," she told the judge. "We are."

By "we," Stevie Whiteflower Standingbear meant the Los Angeles Indian Center which she heads and which is doing heroic work to make relocation easier for its victims. The Center began in 1935 when Myra Bartlett, an Indian and a singer on the Orpheum Circuit, decided to establish a meeting place for the Indian women working as housemaids whom she encountered each Thursday afternoon gathered at the streetcar terminal for a "weekly visit." It was a refugee center during the depression and was reorganized under the American Friends Service Committee in 1948 and supported by that group until last October [1955]. Now on its own, with a $20,000 yearly budget and a staff of two persons—Mrs. Standingbear and Mary Buck—the Center has become an island of security for the Indians in Los Angeles.

One of its main functions is to make available to newly arrived and needy Indians the help of those established in the city. More than 200 volunteers render all kinds of services from baby-sitting and practical nursing to loaning or giving money, finding decent living quarters, obtaining medical treatment, and just visiting.

Aside from this emergency work, the Center provides a familiar environment for the 10,000 Indians in Los Angeles. Its dances, dinners, classes, clubs, and activities for all age groups have an average weekly attendance of more than 600. The Center's chapter of Alcoholics Anonymous has rescued scores of men and women. Although the Center itself has little money, it is often able to scrape up a bit to tide destitute persons over a period of immediate want. This is particularly valuable since municipal and state services are not available to persons who have not fulfilled residence requirements. "We can get medical care for some people by taking them—including pregnant women—through the emergency entrance," Steven Standingbear reports. But those who are not specifically emergency cases must either find a creditor or wait until their sickness becomes acute. A small number obtain some help from one of the professional men and women who aid the Center "as a charity." The courts parole to the Center some of the newer arrivals who have been picked up for drunkenness. "If we can only get to them during the first few weeks they are here, we can save a lot of suffering," Mrs. Standingbear feels. . . .

The dedication of the staff and the volunteers has enabled the Center to perform almost incredible tasks. To a large degree, it has permitted the successful integration of hundreds of Indians, and it has minimized the problem of relocation in Los Angeles. Many cities have fared worse. In Minneapolis, Indians, who comprise less than one per cent of the city's general population, make up more than 10 per cent of the inmates at the men's workhouse and almost 70 per cent at the women's workhouse. Judge Luther Sletten of that city's municipal court calls it "one of our gravest social problems."

What Needs to Be Done

Obviously, something must be done with Indian lands inadequate to support the present and fast-growing population. One solution would be a kind of domestic Point Four program which would enable the Indians to make the most of the rich potential of reservation lands. Instead of being hindered, they should be encouraged to start businesses on reservations and in their communities. Young men with trade and technical training have had to leave home in order to utilize their newly acquired skills. One of the recent applicants for help in finding a job at the Los Angeles Indian Center was a former GI who had attended a barbers' school after his discharge. He returned to his reservation with an enthusiastic plan to open a barbershop, but government agents said no. Schools and extension classes should be instituted to help the Indians exploit their resources. If necessary, tribal funds which have been impounded could pay the costs of running them.

If, however, the program to dislodge the Indians is to be an all-out one, some educational program must be established to prevent the creation of another acute minority problem. It is imperative to slow down the relocation until the Indians have been prepared for integration.

The first step would be to institute a comprehensive orientation program in the relocation centers and on the reservations, providing some education and vocational training for the Indians who are to be sent into a mechanized, urban environment.

Secondly, there should be a thorough screening process to make sure that those who are participating in the program are able to make the adjustment physically and mentally. Obviously, a knowledge of the English language is a prerequisite. So is at least fair health. Many of the new arrivals have been women in advanced pregnancy; many have been men with tuberculosis scars and other defects which make them unacceptable to industries.

Instead of being given the rosy picture of the promised land, the Indians who are leaving the security of their old life should have a more realistic picture of what lies before them. Most of them, Mrs Standingbear says, are "woefully prepared." Few bring changes of clothing, bedding, or even cooking utensils—apparently under the delusion that the centers will "take care of everything."

Courses in household management are a must for women who have never seen electric lights and know nothing about shopping and little about cooking anything but the foods they have always eaten, which are rarely available. One woman was severely burned when her little tot tried to light the unfamiliar gas stove in their city dwelling.

A health insurance program is a must since the limited budgets of unskilled workers settling down in a new environment rarely stretch to cover medical and hospital bills. And the municipalities charged with their integration should make exceptions to residence requirements in order to permit the new arrivals to avail themselves of necessary services. The American Indians, that long-suffering and inarticulate minority, have a great contribution to make to our culture. Unless they are permitted to do that, they will become a social and economic burden of magnitude—a shadow on the national conscience.

VIEWPOINT 7

"AIM succeeds because it has beliefs to act on. AIM is attempting to connect the realities of the past with the promises of tomorrow."

The American Indian Movement Has Helped Native Americans

Dennis Banks (b. 1930)

Dennis Banks, a Chippewa born on the Leech Lake Reservation in northern Minnesota, was one of the founders of the American Indian Movement (AIM). Begun in 1968 in Minneapolis, Minnesota, the organization originally focused on improving the conditions facing local Indians, especially their treatment by police. In the early 1970s, while Banks was serving as its executive director, AIM became nationally famous—and controversial—for its militant actions. These included a 1972 protest march in Washington, D.C., during which AIM activists took over the administration building of the Bureau of Indian Affairs and destroyed official documents, and a 71-day violent standoff between Indian activists and federal agents at Wounded Knee, South Dakota, in 1973.

The following viewpoint is taken from a 1974 fact sheet prepared by Banks in which he describes AIM's origins, structure, and goals. He argues that, through its protests and other actions, AIM has succeeded in drawing public attention to the American Indian's struggle for justice and respect.

From "Fact Sheet: The American Indian Movement (AIM)," Exhibit 6 of *Revolutionary Activities Within the United States: The American Indian Movement*, Hearing before the Senate Subcommittee to Investigate the Administration of the Internal Security Act and Other Internal Security Laws, Committee on the Judiciary, 94th Cong., 2nd sess., April 6, 1976.

1. *How? When? Where? did AIM start?*

The American Indian Movement was founded on July 28, 1968 in Minneapolis, Minnesota to unify the more than 20 Indian organizations which were felt to be doing little, if anything, to change life in the Indian ghetto. As it became clear that most of these organizations treated Indians paternalistically, with little incentive to manage their own affairs, AIM, first called the Concerned Indian America (CIA), redirected its attention away from the organizations and toward the Indian people as the means to Indian self-determination.

Police Harassment

A catalyst for AIM in 1968 in the city of Minneapolis was the pervasive police harassment of the Indian people. While Indians represented only 10% of the city's population, 70% of the inmates in the city jails were Indian. To divert Indians from the jails, AIM formed the ghetto patrol, equipped with two-way radios which monitored the police radios. Whenever a call came over involving Indians, AIM was there first, and for 29 successive weekends prevented any undue arrests of Indian people. The Indian population in the jails decreased by 60%. And, out of the patrol evolved the federally funded Legal Rights Center, where established attorneys donated up to 80% of their time to serve poor people.

2. Who founded AIM?

The cofounders of AIM are Dennis Banks, Clyde Bellecourt, and George Mitchell, Chippewas of Minnesota. Banks is from the Leech Lake Reservation and Mitchell and Bellecourt from White Earth. Banks now serves as national director, succeeding Vern Bellecourt, also of the White Earth Reservation.

Among the national coordinators:

Russell Means, Oglala Sioux from Pine Ridge, South Dakota; Clyde Bellecourt, Chippewa from the White Earth Reservation, Minnesota; Eddie Benton, from Lac Court, Oreilles Reservation, Wisconsin; Reuben Snake, Winnebago from the Winnebago Reservation, Nebraska; Carter Camp, Pawnee from Pawnee, Oklahoma.

3. How extensive an organization is AIM?

There are 79 chapters of AIM internationally, eight of which are in Canada. AIM has also developed ties with aboriginal organizations in Australia and continues to grow on and off the reservations.

4. What is the structure of AIM?

Unlike other organizations and agencies dealing with Indian affairs, AIM uniquely begins with the people and pyramids to a national organization. It is the chapters which direct and dictate priorities to the national officers, who in turn create and guide AIM in the long-range strategy to meet those priorities. Each chapter is independent and autonomous. . . .

5. *What are the goals of AIM?*

Recorded history bears witness to the fact that the American Indian has been an oppressed nation since the take-over of their lands which they had inhabited as a native culture. If the present trends in cultural and social suppression are allowed to exist, the Indian, as a nation, as a proud people, and as a cultural nation of people will become extinct. The ultimate goal of AIM is therefore to strive for existence as a people and to shake the bonds of oppression so that the American Indian may return to his culture as a free man. AIM credits forced anti-Indian religious doctrines, the lack of a proper education, and the anti-Indian governmental administration to their probable extinction. AIM feels strongly that these factors must be eliminated if they are to be accorded the right to be a people in a free nation.

6. *What has been the role of AIM in protest demonstrations around the country?*

AIM has played the major role in Indian demonstrations over the last five years; AIM was in evidence in more than 150 demonstrations prior to November 1972; alone. Its role has been a peaceful one, to try to work within the system toward its goals, unless pushed by counterforces into a militant stand. Often AIM's presence is a direct response to a call from the Indian people, and AIM will shoulder the blame, deserved or not, for political actions by the Indian people.

Actions of AIM

For example, AIM was present:

Throughout a nationwide protest in seven major cities in early 1970 against the BIA [Bureau of Indian Affairs] treatment of urban Indians people who leave the reservation under the Relocation Program, secured menial jobs in the city and then abandoned.

On Mount Rushmore, once in the fall of 1970 and again in June 1971, when Sioux Indians claimed ownership of the monument and surrounding land because of the government failure to honor the Treaty of 1868 promising repayment for land in the Black Hills taken by early white settlers. The sit-in also denounced racism toward Indian people and demanded a hearing by Secretary of the Interior on Indian Issues.

On the Trail of Broken Treaties, which culminated in the takeover of the Bureau of Indian Affairs Building in Washington, D.C. on November 1, 1972. The Trail began one year after a caravan of Indians descended on Washington to protest the circumvention of Louis Bruce's authority as Commissioner of the BIA.

Proclamation at Alcatraz

In November 1969, Indians of All Tribes, a group of activists that included Dennis Banks, occupied Alcatraz Island in San Francisco Bay. Claiming the island—the site of a recently closed federal prison—for all American Indians, the group issued the following manifesto. Activists remained on Alcatraz until June 1971, when they were removed by federal agents.

Proclamation to the Great White Father
and to All *His* People, 1969

We, the native Americans, re-claim the land known as Alcatraz Island in the name of all American Indians by right of discovery.

We wish to be fair and honorable in our dealings with the Caucasian inhabitants of this land, and hereby offer the following treaty:

We will purchase said Alcatraz Island for twenty-four dollars (24) in glass beads and red cloth, a precedent set by the white man's purchase of a similar island about 300 years ago. We know that $24 in trade goods for these 16 acres is more than was paid when Manhattan Island was sold, but we know that land values have risen over the years. Our offer of $1.24 per acre is greater than the 47¢ per acre the white men are now paying the California Indians for their land.

We will give to the inhabitants of this island a portion of the land for their own to be held in trust by the American Indian Affairs and by the bureau of Caucasian Affairs to hold in perpetuity—for as long as the sun shall rise and the rivers go down to the sea. We will further guide the inhabitants in the proper way of living. We will offer them our religion, our education, our life-ways, in order to help them achieve our level of civilization and thus raise them and all their white brothers up from their savage and unhappy state. We offer this treaty in good faith and wish to be fair and honorable in our dealings with all white men.

We feel that this so-called Alcatraz Island is more than suitable for an Indian Reservation, as determined by the white man's own standards. By this we mean that this place resembles most Indian reservations in that:

1. It is isolated from modern facilities, and without adequate means of transportation.
2. It has no fresh running water.
3. It has inadequate sanitation facilities.
4. There are no oil or mineral rights.
5. There is no industry and so unemployment is very great.
6. There are no health care facilities.
7. The soil is rocky and non-productive; and the land does not support game.
8. There are no educational facilities.
9. The population has always exceeded the land base.
10. The population has always been held as prisoners and kept dependent upon others.

Seeing no change in BIA policies, despite the Administration's reorganization, Indian organizations across the country called in AIM to help organize and secure a second caravan to Washington, D.C., leaving from three points: Los Angeles, San Francisco, and Seattle. The purpose of the caravan was to set up meetings with representatives of the Administration, BIA, and Congress to negotiate the nine demands of the Trail of Broken Treaties Pan American Native Quest for Justice, including the 20-point solutions papers called for "Renewal of Contracts, Reconstruction of Indian Communities and Securing an Indian Future in America."

At Cass Lake, Leech Lake Reservation in Minnesota, where AIM held a national convention May 10–16, 1972 at the Invitation of the tribal council in order to meet with the townfathers and resort owners of Cass Lake over invasion of Indian fishing rights by the sports fishermen who converge on Cass Lake as the sturgeon capital of the country. A blockade of the reservation was called off after negotiations.

At Custer on February 6, 1973, in protest of the murder of Wesley Bad Heart Bull by a white man who went unpunished, on a three-month suspended sentence.

At the Siege of Wounded Knee, where for 71 days the people of Pine Ridge Reservation, S.D., with the support of people across the country, held the site of the Wounded Knee Massacre of 1890, demanding that the federal government honor the terms of the 1868 Treaty with the Oglala Sioux Nation. (February 27–May 8, 1973)

A Spiritual Movement

7. What is AIM's position of the traditional foundations of Indian life?
AIM is always first a spiritual movement. In the words of Kills Straight, an Oglala Sioux on the Pine Ridge:

> From the inside, AIM people are cleansing themselves. Many have returned to the old religious ways of their tribes, away from the confused notions of a society which has made them slaves of their own unguided lives. AIM is first a spiritual movement, a religious rebirth, and then a rebirth of Indian dignity. AIM succeeds because it has beliefs to act on. AIM is attempting to connect the realities of the past with the promises of tomorrow.

8. What is AIM's relationship with other Indian groups? With the radical left?
AIM stands to represent ALL Indians as a fact of Indian life in a free world.

AIM is regarded as a radical leftist movement; however AIM's goals are to represent itself as a peaceful movement trying to get these things which have been promised to them. Historically it has been proven that the American Indian has been treated inhumanely and now, because of AIM's thrust for equality, the Indian is fighting for honor; ignored until Wounded Knee, AIM is now looked to for direction by Left and Third World groups. In the words of AIM leader Russell Means, "AIM represents the only true revolutionary group, a sovereign people with a land base backed by treaties with the federal government. The Indian people have 24,000–40,000 years experience on the Western Hemisphere. We should be able to tell people with 250 years experience. If the labor movement had looked us in the 30's, perhaps they would not have lost."

"The American Indian Movement has raised good issues through the press, but it has seldom followed through to negotiate."

The American Indian Movement Has Had Limited Effectiveness

Gerald Vizenor (b. 1934)

Gerald Vizenor, a Chippewa Indian novelist, poet, and professor, has taught at the University of Oklahoma and the University of California at Berkeley. In the following viewpoint, taken from Vizenor's 1978 revision of a 1976 essay, he describes a meeting he witnessed between activists of the American Indian Movement (AIM) and local tribal leaders at the Leech Lake Reservation in Minnesota in 1972. Criticizing AIM members' actions at both this meeting and previous events, Vizenor argues that AIM has been more successful in gaining media attention than in securing concrete gains for Native Americans. He concludes that AIM's militant tactics have done little to improve the lives of American Indians, especially compared with the gains that Indians have made through peaceful means such as education, economic development, and legal cases.

Eight years ago [in 1968] Dennis Banks, dressed in a dark suit, white shirt and narrow necktie, strode into the office of the director of the American Indian Employment Center and told him to

From Gerald Vizenor, "Confrontation or Negotiation," adapted by the author from *Growing Up in Minnesota: Ten Writers Remember Their Childhoods*, edited by Chester G. Anderson (Minneapolis: University of Minnesota Press, 1976). Copyright ©1976 by the University of Minnesota Press. Reprinted by permission of the publisher.

stop picketing the Bureau of Indian Affairs.

"Demonstrations are not the Indian way," Banks said then, wagging his finger. The director of the center had organized a peaceful demonstration in front of the Minneapolis area office of the Bureau of Indian Affairs, demanding equal services for urban tribal people.

Since then Banks and hundreds of young adventurers have trouped across the country, from Plymouth Rock to Alcatraz, dressed in century-old tribal vestments, demanding recognition of treaty rights, equal justice and sovereignty. The [1973] occupation of Wounded Knee may be the last symbolic act for the aging militant leaders.

The American Indian Movement is an urban revolutionary movement whose members have in recent years tried to return to the reservations as the warrior heroes of tribal people. . . .

The Confrontation Idiom

In the late 1960s the American Indian Movement became a symbolic confrontation group. The confrontation idiom means punching out the symbolic adversary of racism and oppression at the front door, with the press present, and walking out the back door. Those who followed the ideologies of confrontation were in conflict with those who believed that confrontation should lead to negotiation and institutional changes. The negotiation idiom means punching out the adversary at the front door with the press present, but waiting around for an invitation to return and grind out some changes.

The problem in the differences of approach was not only political ideology, but the response of the press. Journalists seldom reported what happened beyond the symbolic punch-out at the front door. The press presented the heroes of confrontation, but not of negotiation. . . .

Behind the scenes, tribal people have been arguing about the use of violence as a means of change. Some say that violence has only polarized the dominant white society and strained interpersonal relationships. Other tribal people argue that violence has made the job of moderates working within the system much easier. White people listen better after violence. . . .

Consider these changes through education: Hundreds of tribal people have earned high-school equivalency certificates on three reservations in Minnesota in the past three years. Many have gone on to college and have found better-paying jobs. Six hundred tribal people are attending colleges in Minnesota compared with fewer than a hundred fifteen years ago.

Consider these changes through the law: There are legal-services programs on most reservations, and hundreds of tribal people are studying in law schools across the country. There have been several successful treaty-law arguments in federal and state courts, including the hunting and fishing suit won by the Leech Lake Reservation.

Consider these changes through economic development: The Red Lake Reservation has a home-construction business and a new vocational school. The Leech Lake Reservation has a food market and service station and a camping and recreation complex.

In 1973 several hundred armed members and followers of the American Indian Movement (AIM) seized the village of Wounded Knee at the Pine Ridge reservation in South Dakota and made militant demands for the restoration of Indian lands. They were soon surrounded by hundreds of federal marshals and FBI agents, and the protest ultimately resulted in a gun battle that killed two Indians. Although the conflict did prompt the federal government to agree to study its treaty obligations to the Sioux, many people, including other American Indians, questioned or criticized AIM's actions at Wounded Knee.

Now consider the changes through violence and radical ideologies: At Cass Lake the leaders of the American Indian Movement were critical of elected tribal officials for negotiating a legal agreement with the state over the hunting and fishing rights won through a federal court decision. The agreement, ratified by the state legislature, will bring millions of dollars a year to the reservation.

This was the scene:

Thirteen armed leaders of the American Indian Movement, including Russell Means and Dennis Banks, filed into the tribal Headstart classroom on the Leech Lake Reservation and took their seats on little-people chairs. They sat with their knees tucked under their chins, dressed in diverse combinations of Western cowboy clothes and traditional tribal vestments from the turn of the last century. . . .

Simon Howard, then president of the Minnesota Chippewa Tribe, entered the classroom, took his little seat, and twirled his thumbs beneath his heavy stomach while the leaders argued about their places in the chain of command—who would stand next to whom at the next television press conference. Howard wore a nylon bowling jacket and a floral print fishing hat in contrast to the renascence of traditional vestments worn by the militants. Howard was born on the reservation and had lived there all his life. He was at the meeting as an elected tribal official to keep peace between white people and the militants. The militants were there for an armed confrontation with white people on the opening day of fishing. . . .

"All right boys, quiet down now and take your seats again," Howard said. The tribal leaders and militants had agreed to meet twice a day with each other and then with the press. "Now, I don't know everyone here, so let's go around the room and introduce ourselves," Howard said. "Let's start with you over there. Stand up and introduce yourself."

The man stood up, dragging his feet forward and swinging his rifle. "My name is Delano Western, and I am from Kansas," he said in a trembling voice. Western, leaning forward and looking down like a shy school child, was dressed in a wide-brimmed black hat with an imitation silver headband, dark green sunglasses with large round lenses, a sweatshirt with "Indian Power" printed on the front, two bandoliers of heavy ammunition, none of which matched the bore of his rifle, a black motorcycle jacket with military colonel's wings on the epaulets, "Red Power" and "Custer Had It Coming" patches, and a large military bayonet strapped to his body next to his revolver.

"We came here to die," Western said in a loud voice and sat down. He and about six hundred militant followers had come to Cass Lake on the Leech Lake Reservation to fight for the treaty rights to hunt and fish on the reservation, which had already been won by reservation tribal officials in federal court.

When white officials from Cass Lake had refused to pay the money demanded by the militants, who were camping on treaty land given over to a church group by the federal government for a summer camp, the leaders held a press conference on a rifle range to scare the public.

Means, smiling for television cameras, was plinking with his small-caliber "white people shooter," as he called his pistol. Banks . . . was preparing for fast-draw target practice. Dressed in a black velvet shirt with ribbon applique, he stood before a collection of empty food cans . . . dropped to one knee, and attempted to draw his small-gauge sawed-off shotgun. It stuck on the rope holder attached to his belt. He stood up and tried again, but it still stuck. This was the first time the Movement had taken up the use of firearms.

Failures at Negotiation

During the occupation of the offices of the Bureau of Indian Affairs in Washington, radical leaders demanded another investigation and reorganization of the paternalistic bureaucracy that has controlled the lives of tribal people on reservations for more than a century. The militants had a powerful position from which to negotiate their demands: It was an election year and scores of congressional liberals were sympathetic. But rather than negotiate the demands, the leaders of AIM accepted more than $60,000 to leave the building and the city. . . . The leaders were at Wounded Knee voicing the very same demands which they sold out in Washington. . . .

The American Indian Movement has raised good issues through the press, but it has seldom followed through to negotiate. At Custer the militants drew national attention to the wrongful death of Wesley Bad Heart Bull. They said the white man who stabbed Bad Heart Bull should be charged with murder. The fire in the courthouse was a violent stunt that detracted from the issue of legal injustices.

The militant leaders are dedicated men who have given many years of their lives to a cause, but it takes more than a rifle and the symbolic willingness to die to bring about institutional changes that will benefit tribal people.

CHAPTER 6

Two Historians Examine the Indian Removal Policy

Chapter Preface

In 1830, at the urging of President Andrew Jackson, Congress passed the Indian Removal Act. Over the next decade, more than sixty thousand Indians were relocated from their homelands in the eastern United States to western territory. Thousands perished during the relocation. Attempts at resistance by the Indians largely proved futile. For example, the Cherokee Indians lobbied Congress against removal and brought legal action to prevent enforcement of the Indian Removal Act. However, Congress was unmoved by the lobbying efforts, and the Supreme Court ruled that the Cherokee had no legal standing to bring suit. In 1838 those Cherokee who had refused to move were forced to do so by state and federal troops. The Seminole in Florida also fought removal in a war that lasted from 1835 to 1842 and that cost the United States fifteen hundred lives and millions of dollars. In the end, though, the Seminole also lost their struggle. Most of them were moved to present-day Oklahoma; those who remained were forced to hide in the Florida Everglades.

The removal of the eastern Indians was condemned at the time in the New England press as an "abhorrent business"—a judgment in which most historians have generally concurred. Yet scholars have often disagreed in their interpretations and analyses of the events surrounding Indian removal. One point of contention concerns the beliefs of Jackson, the Indian fighter turned president who championed the Indian Removal Act. Some historians strongly criticize Jackson's actions and motives. Irwin Unger, in *These United States*, argues that Jackson pushed for removal because he "shared the western contempt for Indians and lust for their rich lands." Other historians maintain that Jackson was sincere when he stated that westward relocation was in the Indians' best interest. Thomas A. Bailey and David M. Kennedy, for example, write in *The American Pageant* that Jackson "harbored protective feelings toward the Native Americans" and that he believed that the Indian cultures and communities could best be preserved by resettling the tribes away from disruptive white contact.

The Indian removal policies of the 1830s provoked much debate at the time of their enactment and are still controversial today. The following viewpoints present contrasting pictures of Andrew Jackson and U.S. Indian policy in the early nineteenth century.

Viewpoint 1

"From 1812 until the end of the century, official [U.S.] policy [toward Indians], no matter in what euphemistic terms expressed, was simply conquest."

The U.S. Policy of Indian Removal Was Intended to Subjugate Indians

Francis Jennings (b. 1918)

Francis Jennings, a historian, served as director of the Newberry Library's Center for the History of the American Indian from 1976 to 1981. His books include *The Invasion of America: Indians, Colonialism, and the Cant of Conquest* and *Empire of Fortune: Crowns, Colonies, and Tribes in the Seven Years War in America.* The following viewpoint is taken from his 1993 book *The Founders of America*, a broad general history of the native peoples of North America both prior to and following European contact. The excerpted passages from the book focus on early-nineteenth-century history in the United States, especially the forcible removal of Indian tribes from the territory between the Appalachian Mountains and the Mississippi River. Jennings argues that during this period the United States was pursuing a deliberate policy of subjugating and victimizing Indians and taking their land. The removal of the Cherokees and other Indian tribes from the southeastern United States, as implemented by President Andrew Jackson, was simply part of the larger picture of American conquest over Indians, he contends. Much of the writing about this period of American "frontier history" has ignored or understated this central fact, Jennings concludes.

We are at the threshold of the nineteenth century, the epoch of the rise of the empire of the United States, and of the crushing of the Indian tribes everywhere. Let there be no quibbling about calling it an empire. The men who governed it made no secret of their intended creation and its "manifest destiny." Invoking the sacred obligation of democracy, they drove Spain out of Florida, bought France and Russia out of the Louisiana Territory and Alaska, seized Texas, California, and the Southwest from Mexico, and were restrained from taking Canada also only by the power of Great Britain.

A Caste System

They defined democracy as a caste system organized by conceptions called race. In this system, the mixed immigrants from Europe were arbitrarily declared "white" regardless of the multitudes who had hacked and spawned their ways through Europe from Asia and Africa in centuries gone by. Rare is the European, even today, who can pass the test imposed by legislatures in South Carolina and Louisiana which required that if even one of a person's ancestors, no matter how far back, was identifiably Asian or African, that person could not be "white"; he was "colored." (Louisiana recently reaffirmed the rule.) By that rule, most Europeans should be Huns as those raiders had not been chaste. In fact, biology was irrelevant to the system; caste was socially determined, not genealogically. As time would show, the possession of large amounts of money erased the taint of race, but this was not easy to come by.

Democracy meant parity among whites. (South Africans of the twentieth century called the system *Herrenvolk* democracy. This term is not easily translatable. Literally it means democracy among the people of the lords. More freely, democracy among the ruling caste.) Africans were enslaved; later, after manumission, they were segregated from whites as far as was feasible. Indians had been segregated from the days of Jamestown colony, but theirs was separation in tribal communities rather than as individuals, and they liked it that way.

In 1848, the French student Alexis de Tocqueville observed what was happening to Indians. "In its dealings with the North American Indians, the European tyranny weakened their feeling for their country, dispersed their families, obscured their traditions, and broke their chain of memories; it also changed their customs and increased their desires beyond reason, making them more disorderly and less civilized than they had been before. At the same time, the moral and physical condition of these peoples has constantly deteriorated, and in becoming more wretched they have also become more barbarous." (It may be noticed that de Tocqueville said *European* rather than *white.)*

Despite this horrendous bill of particulars, de Tocqueville saw also the inextinguishable survival of the "Indianness" that nobody has been able to define: "Nevertheless, the Europeans have not been able to change the character of the Indians entirely."

The tribes were beaten down and forced or menaced into little islands of territory, enclaves called reservations, within their former lands, and even these were whittled at by various processes, legal and otherwise. Reformers approved transplantation of the peoples against their will "for their own good." Invaders who cared nothing for Indians' welfare seized their lands for the invaders' own good. All this, in the mythology of standard American history, constitutes the "transit of civilization" from Europe.

There could be no doubt about the power of the nation-state-empire as compared to the scattered powers of tribes at odds with each other. Benevolently, the conquerors took the subjected peoples under their wing as wards of the state, and interpreted that high-sounding legal phrase to mean that the wards must henceforth do only what they were told. To assure the success of this magnanimity, the philanthropic empire sold Indian lands and appropriated a small portion of the proceeds for the benefit of its wards. To assure that the money would indeed be used for the benefit of such "childlike peoples, incompetent to manage their own affairs," the appropriations were entrusted to reservation agents who usually identified their own benefit as surrogate for the wards'. This political patronage became so notorious that it aroused a reform movement especially strong among churchmen.

All the while, the empire fattened on hordes of voluntary immigrants from Europe and, during half of the century, of involuntary immigrants from Africa.

In contrast, the Indian peoples dwindled in numbers until nearly the end of the century. Was it more than coincidence that the mythic Frontier was proclaimed dead by its historian inventor at just the moment when Indian populations began to recover from their centuries of catastrophe? Frederick Jackson Turner ended his Frontier in 1890.

Continuing Colonization

The nineteenth century hiving-off of Anglo-Americans to create new communities of their own kind in the trans-Appalachian West was a landborne repetition of the seaborne colonizing of the seventeenth and eighteenth centuries. Continental colonization does not differ in essentials from beachhead colonization. Less controlled and more individualistic, this landborne colonizing nevertheless aimed at the same goals of seizure of the land from Native occupants and transformation of it to the colonizers' uses and possession. In the process the Natives were to be either expelled or subjected. We may properly recognize that that result comes only from colonizing, regardless of whether the colonizers come by land or sea or whether they arrive in a trickle or a flood. That the colonizers surround and overwhelm the Natives instead of forming an island within a surrounding Native population does not change the relations of power and process except in possible implications for the long run.

Distinctions must be made between macrocontact and microcontact phenomena. On the macrocontact scale, many Indian tribes of the trans-Appalachian West preserved their independence and a degree of freedom of mobility well into the nineteenth century, long after most eastern tribes had been brought under political control and forced into reservations. Seen in this perspective, the phenomena of "the moving frontier" lie along a range of the processes of colonizing from initial intrusion to ultimate domination.

The means used by Euramericans for achieving domination were only intermittently violent, often because the threat of force was efficacious in itself. Peaceful intercourse, however, established patterns of social process that led inexorably to the economic and eventually political dependency of Natives upon the colonizers. It hardly mattered that the Europeans understood the effect of these processes and helped them along; the processes worked in consequence of interaction between societies whose technologies were sufficiently alike to create the basis for commerce, and sufficiently different to create a powerful demand, with the advantage in the market on the side of the Europeans.

Historical Myth

Neither the people nor the government of the United States intended to respect treaty contracts with Indians longer than the Indians could enforce them. Recognition of this very plain fact requires some painful revision of the pleasant myths we all learned in grade school. These portrayed an "honest yeomanry" (Andrew Jackson's phrase) bravely setting out with their families to conquer the wilderness and create civilization. Pursuing the destiny of Progress, these sturdy, self-reliant, God-fearing folk endure all the hazards and toil of their mission, standing constantly at arms to fend off attack by savage denizens of the wilderness. Among other things, almost as a matter of course, they create democracy which conflicts with the old world oligarchies of the seaboard States and ultimately overcomes them under the leadership of that inspiring champion of the common man, Andrew Jackson.

Even just to recite it all at once like that sounds like parody. The myth is nationalist and racist propaganda to justify conquest of *persons* who happen to be Indians, and their dispossession. It has the further effect of vindicating bellicosity toward Britain, Spain, and Mexico, and of expressing contempt for the synethnic French heritage in the Mississippi Valley.

It will not be enough to assert the myth's falsity. The myth was an intellectual paradigm that cleared the consciences of persons acting in ways that would otherwise be denounced by their religions as immoral and sinful. Bits and pieces of it have been demonstrated by researchers as irrelevant to reality, but the whole paradigm was highly relevant to the purposes of the people espousing it. A different purpose requires a different paradigm. . . .

The Situation in 1800

By 1800, Indians between the Appalachians and the Mississippi had lost power to resist the advancing Americans unless assisted by other powers, and the incoming Americans understood keenly that their Indian antagonists had help from Britain in Canada, and Spain in Florida. There also were still Spanish colonists effectively ruling in Louisiana despite paper shuffling between Spain and France in Europe. [President Thomas] Jefferson's government managed to keep conflict in the West at the level of scuffles because Jefferson wanted to avoid dangerous involvement in Europe's Napoleonic wars, but . . . he aroused the land-hungry with the Louisiana Purchase.

His successor James Madison was not so fortunate. Caught between Britain's seizures of American ships and seamen, and the importunate demands of western "War Hawks" in Congress, Madison had to preside over the War of 1812 in which a British fleet forced him to flee while it burnt his capital. In the West, however, American arms were more successful.

The War Hawks had planned to conquer Canada. Their thrusts toward Montreal and Niagara failed dismally, but their favored leader William Henry Harrison managed to penetrate Canada as far as Moraviantown on the Thames River where he defeated the British decisively. (Ironically, Moraviantown was so named because founded by missionaries of a "peace" religion.) Shawnee Chief Tecumseh died in that battle. The Americans were obliged to retreat south of the Great Lakes, but they had finally put a stop to British support of Indian raids in the Old Northwest. The region opened wide to floods of immigrants from the East who were not slow in coming. They called their new State "Indiana."

Something similar in effect happened farther south. Tecumseh had preached unity there, and Tenskwatawa's revitalization doctrine had made some headway. Young warriors became Indian

"Red Sticks" whose enemies were the American "War Hawks." Among the Creeks, however, older leaders feared American power. When unrestrainable young men accepted Britain's hatchet, something like a civil war broke out among the Creeks, dividing them regionally between Upper Creek Red Sticks and Lower Creeks who were more temporizing. A rising Tennesseean seized the opportunity and defeated the Red Sticks at the Battle of Horseshoe Bend (1814) as decisively as Harrison had done at the Thames. Andrew Jackson forced the Creeks to cede twenty million acres to the United States, and it would be very strange if some of them had not ended up as possessions of his political patrons and himself.

Jackson has been puffed unrecognizably into an icon of Frontier Democracy. In actuality he had little feeling and less sentiment for common people. Jackson identified himself as a *gentleman* of substance and status above the common ruck. As a young lawyer

---

"Civilization" and Removal

R. David Edmunds, a professor of history at Texas Christian University, maintains in an essay from Indians in American History *that President Andrew Jackson and his supporters wanted all Cherokees removed from their lands despite the tribe's efforts to adopt aspects of white American culture.*

In 1828 Andrew Jackson was elected to the presidency and a spokesman for the frontier entrepreneurs was in the White House. Jackson's election also marked an increase in federal pressure to remove the tribespeople to the trans-Mississippi west. Although previous administrations had counseled the Indians to remove, they had appraised the problem from an ethnocentric rather than a racial perspective. Presidents such as John Quincy Adams believed the Indians to be inferior, but from Adams' viewpoint they were inferior because they had not attained the socioeconomic-political level of Europeans or Americans. If Indians would adopt white ways and become civilized, they could be assimilated into American society.

The Jacksonians had no intention of assimilating the Indians into American society. Regardless of the tribespeople's adoption of American institutions, frontier entrepreneurs wanted them removed from their lands and forced beyond the frontier. The Cherokee's "civilization" program, for example, afforded them little protection from white Georgians. After gold was discovered on Cherokee lands, white Americans ignored the tribe's constitution, newspaper, and pious Protestant congregations. Tribal lands were overrun. Regardless of how "civilized" the Cherokees had become, other Americans still saw them as "Indians" and, therefore, not encompassed in the protection that the Constitution extended to white men.

he sided with creditors against debtors, with property against the poor. He soon acquired slaves. He allied with the richest man in Tennessee politics, Governor William Blount, who had acquired a million acres of land by speculation, and it was Blount who had appointed Jackson commander of the Creek War troops.

Jackson's victory over the Creeks began his rise to glory and power. When the British prepared to attack New Orleans, Jackson was sent in 1815 to organize the defense. Luck served him well. A pirate named Jean Lafitte offered help that included cannon and an intimate knowledge of the terrain, and Jackson shrewdly accepted. He adjusted his defense lines in accordance with Lafitte's advice, and set Lafitte's cannon among them. When British troops advanced, the partners mowed them down. Folklore attributes the victory to Jackson's backwoods sharpshooters, but most British casualties fell before grapeshot from the cannon. Nevertheless, folklore prevailed, and Lafitte dropped out of the picture reported back east.

Though the battle occurred after peace had been negotiated, it was decisive in two ways. It convinced British rulers that sea power could not penetrate the Mississippi, and it projected Andrew Jackson to national fame.

The Mississippi Valley

The War of 1812 guaranteed security to colonizers of the vast Mississippi Valley. What must be stressed now is that the Valley was *not* a wilderness. Before the Anglo-Americans flooded in, a mixed population inhabited and organized the region for their own purposes. "Frontier history" has chosen to ignore their presence and the culture they had created and lived by for more than a century, primarily because those facts are completely at odds with the assumptions and theories underlying racist Frontier history, but a new generation of scholars has arisen.

Among them, Daniel H. Usner, Jr., has identified and explored a "cross-cultural web of economic relations" that extended within "a network of coastal towns and interior [French and Spanish] posts stretching from the Alabama River to the Red River." He calls it a "frontier exchange economy," and its first feature to strike the eye is its complexity. It is an advanced development of the intersocietal exchange so prominent wherever Indians traded with Europeans. This network involved nationals of Spain in West Florida and New Mexico, Frenchmen along the Mississippi, and Afro-Americans, slaves and free, as well as American Indians in a number of tribes. An uncountable number of those "free" Afro-Americans were "maroons" who had escaped from slavery. The network depended heavily upon barter of food—crops and meat provided by Indian and African peasants for military garrisons and commercial and political Europeans. Extra quantities of some foods and many deerskins were produced for European markets.

Far from being the haunts of wilderness, the lower Mississippi Valley of the eighteenth century began to reassert the function it had performed as "main street" of trade under Mexico's earlier Toltec colonists, but only up to the point (geographically) where trading networks of the Great Lakes commercial system took over. (Competition was keen between merchants of Montreal and those of New Orleans.) By the nineteenth century, the southern system had acquired a maturity fully equal (at least) to the culture of backwoodsmen thrusting west from Tennessee. (Young Andrew Jackson did business at Natchez.) Interspersed among a multitude of small holdings were a few large plantations which became more dominating after the export market increased for cotton. Farms were fully agricultural including poultry, swine, cattle, and horses, many of which were imported from New Mexico. Entrepreneurs descended from every ethnic stock and used every traditional commercial device, including pilfering and much smuggling.

In short, when Anglo-Americans broke into the lower Mississippi in the nineteenth century, contrary to Frontier mythology, they brought neither "civilization" nor "democracy" to the region. What they brought must be recognized as conquest and domination which they exerted through imposition of their own system of economics, politics, and government. They strengthened and added to what Daniel Usner describes as a "colonial elite" which "worked steadily to enforce bondage upon black Louisianians and West Floridians, dependency upon Indians, and subordination upon a mixed lot of white settlers." The Anglo-American new social hierarchy and institutions acted to diminish instead of increasing personal freedom while introducing political democracy that functioned as such only for the *herrenvolk*. For lower castes and classes the new systems functioned as colonialism with increased emphasis on chattel slavery.

Jackson and Indian Removal

Before they could take over the lower Mississippi, the expansionists of Tennessee, the Carolinas, and Georgia needed to get rid of several obstacles, mostly Indian. Andrew Jackson increased his reputation as a military hero by seizing Pensacola, the capital of West Florida (1818) under pretext of attacking hostile Seminoles, refugee Red Stick Creeks, and "Maroon" escaped slaves; and he thus deprived hostile Indians of a major source of supplies. Under pressure, Spain ceded all of Florida to the United States, an action that sent Jackson's political stock soaring. Jackson became president in 1828 and was re-elected in 1832. In 1830 his administration picked up a suggestion previously made by Thomas Jefferson. It enacted the Indian Removal law to require the southeastern tribes to move west of the Mississippi.

A series of enforced treaties followed. In 1830 the Choctaws were summoned to the Treaty of Dancing Rabbit Creek. When they objected to the terms presented to them, United States Commissioner John Eaton gave an ultimatum: they must move west or consent to be governed by Mississippi law. Resistance would bring down upon them destruction by American armies. In 1831 the Choctaws started west.

Cherokee leaders considered their options carefully and decided that they could no longer sustain independence on their own terms—they must adopt the civilization of their powerful neighbors. Deliberately, the Cherokees transformed their system of government into a republic. Their genius Sequoyah invented a syllabary that enabled reproduction in writing of all the sounds in the Cherokee language, the people became literate (probably more so than their attackers), they published a weekly newspaper and they adopted the Anglo-American methods of agriculture and capped them with that crowning glory of civilization, plantation slavery.

The Cherokees also accepted missionaries, but chose the wrong kind. The State of Georgia ran their New England Congregationalist missionary off the Cherokees' land and jailed him. Supreme Court Chief Justice John Marshall affirmed the people's right to their territory and was ignored. A story is told, perhaps apocryphal, that President Andrew Jackson remarked, "John Marshall has made his decision, now let him enforce it." Whether or not Jackson actually said that, neither he nor anybody else enforced Marshall's decision.

Pressures on the Cherokees increased instead of lessening, and a party formed within the nation to seek an agreement with their persecutors. Georgians quickly caught on to the division. As Theda Perdue has written, "Governor Wilson Lumpkin of Georgia surreptitiously promised special consideration and some degree of protection to the faltering Cherokees who stood to lose the most in terms of material wealth." Offered this temptation, the "treaty party" signed the treaty of New Echota (29 December 1835) relinquishing all claims to land east of the Mississippi in exchange for five million dollars. The richer Cherokees took their slaves and portable possessions west in the spring of 1836, but the Cherokee nationalists who had had no part in the treaty arrangements stuck fast to their land until rounded up at bayonet point and forced onto the "trail of tears" under hardships and with casualties that few armies have had to endure in combat. Of the 13,000 Cherokees on that trek, at least 4,000 died of privation and exposure.

We may notice in passing that the Treaty of New Echota opened wounds of racism in Cherokee society. Partisans for and against the treaty were genetically mixed, but those in favor appeared to have more Euramerican ancestors than Cherokee, and were culturally the most inclined to accept American ways. Their approval of the treaty won them blame for the subsequent trail of tears and opened a wide gap between social classes and perceived races. The racism of the conquering Americans had the effect, here and elsewhere, of arousing feelings and divisions of race among the conquered peoples.

The Seminole Wars

Like the Cherokees and Choctaws, the Creek Indians were forced west, but the Seminoles of Florida, who included many Creeks, went to war against the United States. Their great war chief Osceola, himself a Red Stick refugee, made the mistake of trusting to negotiations with military commanders who believed in opportunity more than honor. He and eighty-four other Seminoles were seized and imprisoned (October 1837). He died in prison four months later. Although deprived of leaders, the Seminoles fought on in the longest American war before Vietnam. They never accepted defeat though most moved west after being given a cash settlement in 1857.

The Americans were unable to find and remove all the Southeastern Indians, or perhaps they found that troublesome and expensive task not worthwhile. They achieved their main goal by destroying tribal polities and seizing tribal territories, and they ignored the Indians who hid away in mountains and swamps, often with the cooperation of sympathetic American neighbors. Such kindly souls did exist though the spotlight has been given to rampaging imperialists with power.

Nowhere is it clearer that rationalizations of "Frontier history" are irrelevant to plain facts. The conquerors did not bring civilization to the Indians, nor did they bring Christian religion; they actually stopped the mission among the Cherokees. The Indians did not "retire" before the advance of civilization; they were pushed, and pushed hard. The Indians did not require vast territories for their savage way of life; their conquerors wanted and took those territories that had subsisted the Indians from time immemorial. These are all alibis. Southern backwoodsmen had the same motive as German tribesmen forcing their way into the Rhine Valley in ancient times: more recently, the same as the Scots who crossed to Ulster in Ireland; they wanted the land and they had power enough to take it. That was enough for them. The alibis were concocted later by nationalist and racist historians.

Most Southeastern Indians were forced into Oklahoma Territory where they encountered new problems of adjusting to previously resident tribes who did not welcome newcoming competitors for limited resources. Even among the uprooted and transplanted, many survivors successfully regrouped and recovered. Richard Sattler, who has specialized in their history, believes that a minimum of about 10,000 each of Cherokees, Muskogees, and Choctaws preserve their native languages today.

The Turning Point of 1812

Americans of the present day are apt to give undue importance to the mid- and late-nineteenth-century freedom struggles of the trans-Mississippi Indians. Worthy of respect though these are, they amounted in U.S. policy to repetition of patterns tried and tested in the East, and the odds were so great against the far western Indians that they never had a chance, regardless of valor. Some knew that and were careful to come to humiliating terms with the threatening colossus. Others fought on to honorable but foredoomed defeat.

The moment of fateful decision occurred during the War of 1812 when William Henry Harrison in the North, and Andrew Jackson in the South, destroyed the last chance of effective Indian resistance. Anthony Wayne's victory at Fallen Timbers and the subsequent [1795] Treaty of Greenville had established a system by which the tribes could co-exist with the United States, each managing its own affairs on its own side of a recognized boundary. Symbolically, Wayne returned to his estate near Philadelphia. But Harrison and Jackson were men on the make in the West, and they shattered the Greenville agreements.

Shawnee chief Tecumseh was the last hope of Indians to hold the tide of Euramerican advance to bilaterally negotiated agreements. After Tecumseh's death, government officials never had the slightest intention of honoring treaties with the tribes. Such arrangements were regarded as mere conveniences to keep the natives quiet until more resources could be mustered and organized.

Many scholars tend to absolve the government of fault by ignoring its actions in order to exclaim over the "resistless tide" of homesteaders. This is error. The homesteaders were resistless because the government intended them to be and took pains to smash opposition wherever it appeared.

A Policy of Conquest

From 1812 until the end of the century, official policy, no matter in what euphemistic terms expressed, was simply conquest. Its purpose was to reduce Indian persons to dependence and to seize tribal lands.

Whether anything else could have been done, given the circumstances of the century, I cannot even guess, but it seems worth-while to single out individuals who were especially treacherous or brutal. Though history's horrors were widespread, violations of common decency become especially significant as indicators of how racist conceptions negated established standards of morality. Perhaps the most valid reason for penetrating hypocritical facades is just this: that the same racist conceptions, if not exposed and rejected by new generations, will produce the same urge to bloody and disastrous conquest. *Conduct condoned will be conduct repeated.* Anyone familiar with contemporary events can supply examples.

VIEWPOINT 2

"The removal program cannot be judged simply as a land grab to satisfy the President's western and southern constituents."

The U.S. Policy of Indian Removal Was Intended to Protect Indians

Francis Paul Prucha (b. 1921)

Francis Paul Prucha taught history at Marquette University in Milwaukee, Wisconsin. He has also written and compiled numerous books on American Indians, including *The Indians in American Society* and *The Great Father: The United States Government and the American Indians*, winner of the Ray Allen Billington Prize awarded by the Organization of American Historians. The following viewpoint is taken from an article in which Prucha examines American Indian policy in the early nineteenth century. He focuses especially on the actions and motives of Andrew Jackson, who as president from 1829 to 1837 was largely responsible for the policy of Indian removal. Reassessing the argument made by some historians that Jackson's Indian policies stemmed from his anti-Indian sentiments, Prucha criticizes it as being too simplistic. A careful examination of Jackson's record and its social context, he argues, reveals that a case can be made that Jackson sincerely intended to help and protect Indian tribes from being overrun by white settlers by removing the tribes from the southeastern states to territory in the west. Jackson believed that once the Indians were resettled in land free of white encroachment, they would be able to prosper by adopting white civilization and by forming their own territorial government that would "eventually take its place in the Union," Prucha writes.

From Francis Paul Prucha, "Andrew Jackson's Indian Policy: A Reassessment," *Journal of American History*, vol. 56, December 1969, pp. 527–39. Footnotes in the original have been omitted here. Reprinted by permission of the author and the publisher, the Organization of American Historians.

A great many persons—not excluding some notable historians—have adopted a "devil theory" of American Indian policy. And in their demonic hierarchy Andrew Jackson has first place. He is depicted primarily, if not exclusively, as a western frontiersman and famous Indian fighter, who was a zealous advocate of dispossessing the Indians and at heart an "Indian-hater." When he became President, the story goes, he made use of his new power, ruthlessly and at the point of a bayonet, to force the Indians from their ancestral homes in the East into desert lands west of the Mississippi, which were considered forever useless to the white man.

This simplistic view of Jackson's Indian policy is unacceptable. It was not Jackson's aim to crush the Indians because, as an old Indian fighter, he hated Indians. Although his years in the West had brought him into frequent contact with the Indians, he by no means developed a doctrinaire anti-Indian attitude. Rather, as a military man, his dominant goal in the decades before he became President was to preserve the security and well-being of the United States and its Indian and white inhabitants. His military experience, indeed, gave him an overriding concern for the safety of the nation from foreign rather than internal enemies, and to some extent the anti-Indian sentiment that has been charged against Jackson in his early career was instead basically anti-British. Jackson, as his first biographer pointed out, had "many private reasons for disliking" Great Britain. "In her, he could trace the efficient cause, why, in early life, he had been left forlorn and wretched, without a single relation in the world." His frontier experience, too, had convinced him that foreign agents were behind the raised tomahawks of the red men. In 1808, after a group of settlers had been killed by the Creeks, Jackson told his militia troops: "[T]his brings to our recollection the horrid barbarity committed on our frontier in 1777 under the influence of and by the orders of Great Britain, and it is presumeable that the same influence has excited those barbarians to the late and recent acts of butchery and murder. . . ." From that date on there is hardly a statement by Jackson about Indian dangers that does not aim sharp barbs at England. His reaction to the Battle of Tippecanoe was that the Indians had been "excited to war by the secrete agents of Great Britain."

Jackson's war with the Creeks in 1813–1814, which brought him his first national military fame, and his subsequent demands for a large cession of Creek lands were part of his concern for security in the West. In 1815, when the Cherokees and Chickasaws gave up their overlapping claims to lands within the Creek cession,

Jackson wrote with some exultation to Secretary of War James Monroe: "This Territory added to the creek cession, opens an avenue to the defence of the lower country, in a political point of view incalculable." A few months later he added: "The sooner these lands are brought into markett, [the sooner] a permanent security will be given to what, I deem, the most important, as well as the most vulnerable part of the union. This country once settled, our fortifications of defence in the lower country compleated, all [E]urope will cease to look at it with an eye to conquest. There is no other point of the union (america united) that combined [E]urope can expect to invade with success."

Jackson's plans with regard to the Indians in Florida were governed by similar principles of security. He wanted "to concentrate and locate the F[lorida] Indians at such a point as will promote their happiness and prosperity and at the same time, afford to that Territory a dense population between them and the ocean which will afford protection and peace to all." On later occasions the same views were evident. When negotiations were under way with the southern Indians for removal, Jackson wrote "[T]he chickasaw and choctaw country are of great importance to us in the defence of the lower country[;] a white population instead of the Indian, would strengthen our own defence much." And again: "This section of country is of great importance to the prosperity and strength of the lower Mississippi[;] a dense white population would add much to its safety in a state of war, and it ought to be obtained, if it can, on any thing like reasonable terms."

Justice Toward Indians

In his direct dealings with the Indians, Jackson insisted on justice toward both hostile and peaceful Indians. Those who committed outrages against the whites were to be summarily punished, but the rights of friendly Indians were to be protected. Too much of Jackson's reputation in Indian matters has been based on the first of these positions. Forthright and hard-hitting, he adopted a no-nonsense policy toward hostile Indians that endeared him to the frontiersmen. For example, when a white woman was taken captive by the Creeks, he declared: "With such arms and supplies as I can obtain I shall penetrate the creek Towns, untill the Captive, with her Captors are delivered up, and think myself Justifiable, in laying waste their villages, burning their houses, killing their warriors and leading into Captivity their wives and children, untill I do obtain a surrender of the Captive, and the Captors." In his general orders to the Tennessee militia after he received news of the Fort Mims massacre, he called for "retaliatory vengeance" against the "inhuman blood thirsty barbarians." He could speak of the "lex taliones" [law of retaliation], and his aggressive campaign against the Creeks and his [1817] escapade in Florida in the First Seminole War are further indications of his mood.

But he matched this attitude with one of justice and fairness, and he was firm in upholding the rights of the Indians who lived peaceably in friendship with the Americans. One of his official acts as major general of the Tennessee militia was to insist on the punishment of a militia officer who instigated or at least permitted the murder of an Indian. On another occasion, when a group of Tennessee volunteers robbed a friendly Cherokee, Jackson's wrath burst forth: "that a sett of men should without any authority rob a man who is claimed as a member of the Cherokee nation, who is now friendly and engaged with us in a war against the hostile creeks, is such an outrage, to the rules of war, the laws of nations and of civil society, and well calculated to sower the minds of the whole nation against the united States, and is such as ought to meet with the frowns of every good citizen, and the agents by promptly prosecuted and punished as robers." It was, he said, as much theft as though the property had been stolen from a white citizen. He demanded an inquiry in order to determine whether any commissioned officers had been present or had had any knowledge of this "atrocious act," and he wanted the officers immediately arrested, tried by court-martial, and then turned over to the civil authority.

Again, during the Seminole War, when Georgia troops attacked a village of friendly Indians, Jackson excoriated the governor for "the base, cowardly and inhuman attack, on the old woman [women] and men of the chehaw village whilst the Warriors of that *village* was with me, fighting the battles of our *country* against the common enemy." It was strange, he said, "that there could exist within the U. States, a cowardly monster in human shape, that could violate the sanctity of a flag, when borne by any person, but more particularly when in the hands of a superanuated Indian chief worn down with age. Such base cowardice and murderous conduct as this transaction affords, has not its paralel in history and should meet with its merited punishment." Jackson ordered the arrest of the officer who was responsible and declared: "This act will to the last ages fix a stain upon the character of Georgia."

Jackson's action as commander of the Division of the South in removing white squatters from Indian lands is another proof that he was not oblivious to Indian rights. When the Indian Agent Return J. Meigs in 1820 requested military assistance in removing intruders on Cherokee lands, Jackson ordered a detachment of twenty men under a lieutenant to aid in the removal. After learning that the officer detailed for the duty was "young and inexperienced," he sent his own aide-de-camp, Captain Richard K. Call, to assume command of the troops and execute the order of removal. "Captain Call informs me," he wrote in one report to Secretary of War John C. Calhoun, "that much noise of opposition was threatened, and men collected for the purpose who seperated on the approach of the regulars, but who threaten to destroy the cherokees in the Valley as soon as these Troops are gone. Capt. Call has addressed a letter to those infatuated people, with assurance of speedy and exemplary punishment if they should attempt to carry their threats into execution." Later he wrote that Call had performed his duties "with both judgement, and prudence and much to the interest of the Cherokee-Nation" and that the action would "have the effect in future of preventing the infraction of our Treaties with that Nation."

Jackson's View on Indians

To call Jackson an Indian-hater or to declare that he believed that "the only good Indian is a dead Indian" is to speak in terms that had little meaning to Jackson. It is true, of course, that he did not consider the Indians to be noble savages. He had, for example, a generally uncomplimentary view of their motivation, and he argued that it was necessary to operate upon their fears, rather than on some higher motive. Thus, in 1812 he wrote: "I believe self interest and self preservation the most predominant passion. [F]ear is better than love with an indian." Twenty-five years later, just after he left the presidency, the same theme recurred and he wrote: "Long experience satisfies me that they are only to be well governed by their fears. If we feed their avarice we accelerate the causes of their destruction. By a prudent exertion of our military power we may yet do something to alleviate their condition at the same time that we certainly take from them the means of injury to our frontier."

Yet Jackson did not hold that Indians were inherently evil or inferior. He eagerly used Indian allies, personally liked and respected individual Indian chiefs, and, when (in the Creek campaign) an orphaned Indian boy was about to be killed by Indians upon whom his care would fall, generously took care of the child and sent him home to Mrs. Jackson to be raised with his son Andrew. Jackson was convinced that the barbaric state in which he encountered most Indians had to change, but he was also convinced that the change was possible and to an extent inevitable if the Indians were to survive.

The Political Status of Indians

Much of Jackson's opinion about the status of the Indians was governed by his firm conviction that they did not constitute sovereign nations, who could be dealt with in formal treaties as though they were foreign powers. That the United States in fact did so, Jackson argued, was a historical fact which resulted from the feeble position of the new American government when it first faced the Indians during and immediately after the Revolution. To continue to deal with the Indians in this fashion, when the power of the United States no longer made it necessary, was to Jackson's mind absurd. It was high time, he said in 1820, to do away with the "farce of treating with Indian tribes." Jackson wanted Congress to legislate for the Indians as it did for white Americans.

Andrew Jackson, both as a military general and as a U.S. president, played a central role in establishing federal Indian policy in the early nineteenth century.

From this view of the limited political status of the Indians within the territorial United States, Jackson derived two important corollaries. One denied that the Indians had absolute title to all the lands that they claimed. The United States, in justice should allow the Indians ample lands for their support, but Jackson did not believe that they were entitled to more. He denied any right of domain and ridiculed the Indian claims to "tracts of country on which they have neither dwelt nor made improvements, merely because they have seen them from the mountain or passed them in the chase."

A second corollary of equal import was Jackson's opinion that the Indians could not establish independent enclaves (exercising full political sovereignty) within the United States or within any of the individual states. If their proper status was as subjects of the United States, then they should be obliged to submit to American laws. Jackson had reached this conclusion early in his career, but his classic statement appeared in his first annual message to Congress [in 1829], at a time when the conflict between the Cherokees and the State of Georgia had reached crisis proportions. "If the General Government is not permitted to tolerate the erection of a confederate State within the territory of one of the members of this Union against her consent," he said, "much less could it allow a foreign and independent government to establish itself there." He announced that he had told the Indians that "their attempt to establish an independent government would not be countenanced by the Executive of the United States, and advised them to emigrate beyond the Mississippi or submit to the laws of those States." "I have been unable to perceive any sufficient reason," Jackson affirmed, "why the Red man more than the white, may claim exemption from the municipal laws of the state within which they reside; and governed by that belief, I have so declared and so acted."

Jackson's own draft of this first annual message presents a more personal view than the final public version and gives some insight into his reasoning. He wrote:

> The policy of the government has been gradually to open to them the ways of civilisation; and from their wandering habits, to entice them to a course of life calculated to present fairer prospects of comfort and happiness. To effect this a system should be devised for their benefit, kind and liberal, and gradually to be enlarged as they may evince a capability to enjoy it. It will not answer to encourage them to the idea of exclusive self government. It is impracticable. No people were ever free, or capable of forming and carrying into execution a social compact for themselves until education and intelligence was first introduced. There are with those tribes, a few educated and well informed men, possessing mind and Judgment, and capable of conducting public affairs to advantage; but observation proves that the great body of the southern tribes of Indians, are erratic in their habits, and wanting in those endowments, which are suited to a people who would direct themselves, and under it be happy and prosperous.

Jackson was convinced from his observation of the political incompetence of the general run of Indians that the treaty system played into the hands of the chiefs and their white and half-breed advisers to the detriment of the common Indians. He said on one occasion that such leaders "are like some of our bawling politicians, who loudly exclaim we are the friends of the people, but who, when the[y] obtain their views care no more for the happiness or wellfare of the people than the Devil does—but each procure[s] influence through the same channell and for the same base purpose, *self-agrandisement.*"

Jackson was genuinely concerned for the well-being of the Indians and for their civilization. Although his critics would scoff at the idea of placing him on the roll of the humanitarians, his assertions—both public and private—add up to a consistent belief that the Indians were capable of accepting white civilization, the hope that they would eventually do so, and repeated efforts to take measures that would make the change possible and even speed it along.

His vision appears in the proclamation delivered to his victorious troops in April 1814, after the Battle of Horseshoe Bend on the Tallapoosa River. "The fiends of the Tallapoosa will no longer murder our Women and Children, or disturb the quiet of our borders," he declared. "Their midnight flambeaux will no more illumine their Council house, or shine upon the victim of their infernal orgies. They have disappeared from the face of the Earth. In their places a new generation will arise who will know their duties better. The weapons of warefare will be exchanged for the utensils of husbandry; and the wilderness which now withers in sterility and seems to mourn the disolation which overspreads it, will blossom as the rose, and become the nursery of the arts."

The removal policy, begun long before Jackson's presidency but wholeheartedly adopted by him, was the culmination of these views. Jackson looked upon removal as a means of protecting the process of civilization, as well as of providing land for white settlers, security from foreign invasion, and a quieting of the clamors of Georgia against the federal government. This view is too pervasive in Jackson's thought to be dismissed as polite rationalization for avaricious white aggrandizement. His outlook was essentially Jeffersonian. Jackson envisaged the transition from a hunting society to a settled agricultural society, a process that would make it possible for the Indians to exist with a higher scale of living on less land, and which would make it possible for those who adopted white ways to be quietly absorbed into the white society. Those who wished to preserve their identity in Indian nations could do it only by withdrawing from the economic and political pressures exerted upon their enclaves by the dominant white settlers. West of the Mississippi they might move at their own pace toward civilization.

Alternatives to Removal

Evaluation of Jackson's policy must be made in the light of the feasible alternatives available to men of this time. The removal program cannot be judged simply as a land grab to satisfy the President's western and southern constituents. The Indian problem that Jackson faced was complex, and various solutions were proposed. There were, in fact, four possibilities.

First, the Indians could simply have been destroyed. They could have been killed in war, mercilessly hounded out of their settlements, or pushed west off the land by brute force, until they were destroyed by disease or starvation. It is not too harsh a judgment to say that this was implicitly, if not explicitly, the policy of many of the aggressive frontiersmen. But it was not the policy, implicit or explicit, of Jackson and the responsible government officials in his administration or of those preceding or following his. It would be easy to compile an anthology of statements of horror on the part of government officials toward any such approach to the solution of the Indian problem.

Second, the Indians could have been rapidly assimilated into white society. It is now clear that this was not a feasible solution. Indian culture has a viability that continually impresses anthropologists, and to become white men was not the goal of the Indians. But many important and learned men of the day thought that this was a possibility. Some were so sanguine as to hope that within one generation the Indians could be taught the white man's ways and that, once they learned them, they would automatically desire to turn to that sort of life. Thomas Jefferson never tired of telling the Indians of the advantages of farming over hunting, and the chief purpose of schools was to train the Indian children in white ways, thereby making them immediately absorbable into the dominant culture. This solution was at first the hope of humanitarians who had the interest of the Indians at heart, but little by little many came to agree with Jackson that this dream was not going to be fulfilled.

Third, if the Indians were not to be destroyed and if they could not be immediately assimilated, they might be protected in their own culture on their ancestral lands in the East—or, at least, on reasonably large remnants of those lands. They would then be enclaves within the white society and would be protected by their treaty agreements and by military force. This was the alternative demanded by the opponents of Jackson's removal bill—for example, the missionaries of the American Board of Commissioners for Foreign Missions. But this, too, was infeasible, given the political and military conditions of the United States at the time. The federal government could not have provided a standing army of sufficient strength to protect the enclaves of Indian territory from the encroachments of the whites. Jackson could not withstand Georgia's demand for the end of the *imperium in imperio* [nation within a nation] represented by the Cherokee Nation and its new constitution, not because of some inherent immorality on his part but because the political situation of America would not permit it.

The jurisdictional dispute cannot be easily dismissed. Were the Indian tribes independent nations? The question received its legal answer in John Marshall's [1831] decision in *Cherokee Nation v. Georgia,* in which the chief justice defined the Indian tribes as "dependent domestic nations." But aside from the juridical decision, were the Indians, in fact, independent, and could they have maintained their independence without the support—political and military—of the federal government? The answer, clearly, is no, as writers at the time pointed out. The federal government could have stood firm in defense of the Indian nations against Georgia, but this would have brought it into head-on collision with a state, which insisted that its sovereignty was being impinged upon by the Cherokees.

This was not a conflict that anyone in the federal government wanted. President Monroe had been slow to give in to the demands of the Georgians. He had refused to be panicked into hasty action before he had considered all the possibilities. But eventually he became convinced that a stubborn resistance to the southern states would solve nothing, and from that point on he and his successors, John Quincy Adams and Jackson, sought to solve the problem by removing the cause. They wanted the Indians to be placed in some area where the problem of federal versus state jurisdiction would not arise, where the Indians could be granted land in fee simple [unencumbered ownership] by the federal government and not have to worry about what some state thought were its rights and prerogatives.

The fourth and final possibility, then, was removal. To Jackson this seemed the only answer. Since neither adequate protection nor quick assimilation of the Indians was possible, it seemed reasonable and necessary to move the Indians to some area where they would not be disturbed by federal-state jurisdictional disputes or by encroachments of white settlers, where they could develop on the road to civilization at their own pace, or, if they so desired, preserve their own culture.

To ease the removal process Jackson proposed what he repeatedly described as—and believed to be—*liberal* terms. He again and again urged the commissioners who made treaties to pay the Indians well for their lands, to make sure that the Indians understood that the government would pay the costs of removal and help them get established in their new homes, to make provision for the Indians to examine the lands in the West and to agree to accept them before they were allotted. When he read the treaty negotiated with the Chickasaws in 1832, he wrote to his old friend General John Coffee, one of the commissioners: "I think it is a good one, and surely the religious enthusiasts, or those who have been weeping over the oppression of the Indians will not find

286

fault with it for want of liberality or justice to the Indians." Typical of his views was his letter to Captain James Gadsden in 1829:

> You may rest assured that I shall adhere to the just and humane policy towards the Indians which I have commenced. In this spirit I have recommended them to quit their possessions on this side of the Mississippi, and go to a country to the west where there is every probability that they will always be free from the mercenary influence of White men, and undisturbed by the local authority of the states: Under such circumstances the General Government can exercise a parental control over their interests and possibly perpetuate their race.

The idea of parental or paternal care was pervasive. Jackson told Congress in a special message in February 1832: "Being more and more convinced that the destiny of the Indians within the settled portion of the United States depends upon their entire and speedy migration to the country west of the Mississippi set apart for their permanent residence, I am anxious that all the arrangements necessary to the complete execution of the plan of removal and to the ultimate security and improvement of the Indians should be made without further delay." Once removal was accomplished, "there would then be no question of jurisdiction to prevent the Government from exercising such a general control over their affairs as may be essential to their interest and safety."

Jackson, in fact, thought in terms of a confederacy of the southern Indians in the West, developing their own territorial government which should be on a par with the territories of the whites and eventually take its place in the Union. This aspect of the removal policy, because it was not fully implemented, has been largely forgotten.

In the bills reported in 1834 for the reorganization of Indian affairs there was, in addition to a new trade and intercourse act and an act for the reorganization of the Indian Office, a bill "for the establishment of the Western Territory, and for the security and protection of the emigrant and other Indian tribes therein." This was quashed, not by western interests who might be considered hostile to the Indians, but by men like John Quincy Adams, who did not like the technical details of the bill and who feared loss of eastern power and prestige by the admission of territories in the West.

Jackson continued to urge Congress to fulfill its obligations to the Indians who had removed. In his eighth annual message, in December 1836, he called attention "to the importance of providing a well-digested and comprehensive system for the protection, supervision, and improvement of the various tribes now planted in the Indian country." He strongly backed the suggestions of the commissioner of Indian affairs and the secretary of war for developing a confederated Indian government in the West and for establishing military posts in the Indian country to protect the tribes. "The best hopes of humanity in regard to the aboriginal race, the welfare of our rapidly extending settlements, and the honor of the United States," he said, "are all deeply involved in the relations existing between this Government and the emigrating tribes."

Jackson's Political Opponents

Jackson's Indian policy occasioned great debate and great opposition during his administration. This is not to be wondered at. The "Indian problem" was a complicated and emotion-filled subject, and it called forth tremendous efforts on behalf of the Indians by some missionary groups and other humanitarians, who spoke loudly about Indian rights. The issue also became a party one.

The hue and cry raised against removal in Jackson's administration should not be misinterpreted. At the urging of the American Board of Commissioners for Foreign Missions, hundreds of church groups deluged Congress with memorials condemning the removal policy as a violation of Indian rights; and Jeremiah Evarts, the secretary of the Board, wrote a notable series of essays under the name "William Penn," which asserted that the original treaties must be maintained. It is not without interest that such opposition was centered in areas that were politically hostile to Jackson. There were equally sincere and humanitarian voices speaking out in support of removal, and they were supported by men such as Thomas L. McKenney, head of the Indian Office; William Clark, superintendent of Indian affairs at St. Louis; Lewis Cass, who had served on the frontier for eighteen years as governor of Michigan Territory; and the Baptist missionary Isaac Mc-Coy—all men with long experience in Indian relations and deep sympathy for the Indians.

Jackson himself had no doubt that his policy was in the best interests of the Indians. "Toward this race of people I entertain the kindest feelings," he told the Senate in 1831, "and am not sensible that the views which I have taken of their true interests are less favorable to them than those which oppose their emigration to the West." The policy of rescuing the Indians from the evil effects of too-close contact with white civilization, so that in the end they too might become civilized, received a final benediction in Jackson's last message to the American people—his "Farewell Address" of March 4, 1837. "The States which had so long been retarded in their improvement by the Indian tribes residing in the midst of them are at length relieved from the evil," he said, "and this unhappy race—the original dwellers in our land—are now placed in a situation where we may well hope that they will share in the blessings of civilization and be saved from that degradation and destruction to which they were rapidly hastening while they remained in the States; and while the safety and comfort of our own citizens have been greatly promoted by their removal, the philanthropist will rejoice that the remnant of that ill-fated race has been at length placed beyond the reach of injury or oppression, and that the paternal care of the General Government will hereafter watch over them and protect them."

In assessing Jackson's Indian policy, historians must not listen too eagerly to Jackson's political opponents or to less-than-disinterested missionaries. Jackson's contemporary critics and the historians who have accepted their arguments have certainly been too harsh, if not, indeed, quite wrong.

For Discussion

Chapter One

1. Some historians argue that behind Powhatan's plea for friendly relations lie veiled threats of withholding food if the colonists are not cooperative. Do you find evidence of such threats? If so, do you think that they strengthen or detract from Powhatan's arguments? Explain.
2. Does the Virginia Company of London make any distinctions between "good" and "bad" Indians in its description of the 1622 conflict? Do such distinctions, or lack thereof, play any part in its recommendations for future Indian policy? What does this suggest about the colonists' views toward Indians?
3. Both Peter Williamson and Mary Jemison include accounts of gruesome acts of violence committed by Indians. Are there other similarities between the two captivity narratives? In what ways, if any, are Williamson's accounts of violence more condemnatory than Jemison's? Provide examples from the viewpoints to support your answer.

Chapter Two

1. What evidence does Tecumseh cite in arguing that whites are intent on "the annihilation of our race"? What evidence does Pushmataha cite in asserting that his people and whites have enjoyed friendly relations? Whose use of evidence do you find more compelling?
2. The viewpoints of the Cherokee petitioners, Andrew Jackson, and Wilson Lumpkin represent the three-way argument over sovereign authority between the Cherokee nation, the United States, and the state of Georgia. What treaties, legal precedents, and other arguments are used by the three sides in claiming authority over the Cherokee people and land? Do any of the three acknowledge the arguments made by the other two? Explain.
3. All the viewpoints in this chapter except the Cherokee memorial were originally presented as speeches. Compare and contrast the rhetorical styles of the various speakers. Which viewpoints seek to inflame their audience or appeal to emotion? What rhetorical devices do they use to try to achieve such responses?

Chapter Three

1. What "false impressions which exist in the minds of many persons East" about American Indians does Samuel J. Crawford wish to dispel? Are these same impressions evident in the viewpoints of James Henderson or Helen Hunt Jackson? Why does Crawford believe such impressions to be damaging in the formulation of Indian policy?
2. Henderson, Crawford, Jackson, and George Armstrong Custer each arguably represent four distinct segments of white American society with differing views on Indians: the federal civilian government, white settlers, reform advocates, and the military. Based on the viewpoints presented, how would you summarize their respective views toward American Indians and U.S. government policy? Toward each other? Defend your answer, citing examples from the viewpoints.

3. Theodore Roosevelt maintains that war between Indians and whites was inevitable regardless of what policy the U.S. government pursued. On what major assumptions does he base his conclusion? Do Chief Joseph's account and the other viewpoints in this chapter lend evidence in support of Roosevelt's position of inevitable conflict, or do they provide alternative scenarios? Explain your answer.

Chapter Four

1. The congressional authors of the report opposing land reform for Indians contend that the prime motivation for the legislation was to acquire more Indian territory. What evidence do they provide to support their claim? What arguments does Carl Schurz make regarding opponents to land reform and the loss of Indian land? Explain what you think he means with his epigram "there is nothing more dangerous to an Indian reservation than a rich mine."

2. What instructions does Thomas J. Morgan give regarding the operation of government Indian schools? Judging from Luther Standing Bear's accounts of his experiences, did the institution he attend faithfully carry out Morgan's prescriptions? On what point, in your opinion, are Luther Standing Bear and Thomas J. Morgan most at odds? Explain.

3. Luther Standing Bear writes of his father telling him to "try to be like a white man" and of striving to attain that goal. How does he reconcile this goal with that of preserving his identity as a Lakota Sioux Indian? Judging from their respective viewpoints, does Luther Standing Bear take a fundamentally different approach to white culture than does Elias Boudinot, the missionary-educated Cherokee whose speech appears in Chapter Two? Explain.

Chapter Five

1. In presenting their arguments on New Deal reforms, both John Collier and Flora Warren Seymour contend that their opinions have the support of most American Indians. What evidence do they use in arguing that Native Americans agree with their respective positions? Do you find their arguments convincing? Why or why not?

2. Arthur V. Watkins compares his goals for Indians with the Emancipation Proclamation that freed the slaves. Why might this comparison be effective in winning American public support? After reading his arguments and those of Ruth Muskrat Bronson, do you agree or disagree with his analogy? Why or why not?

3. The viewpoints of O.K. and Marjorie Armstrong and Ruth Mulvey Harmer both use stories of specific Indians to illustrate their arguments about the pros and cons of urban relocation for Native Americans. Who do you think makes better use of their respective examples? Does either viewpoint raise issues that the other viewpoint fails to address? Explain.

4. Dennis Banks, in listing the accomplishments of the American Indian Movement, includes a paragraph on the Leech Lake incident also described by Gerald Vizenor. How do the two accounts differ? In your opinion, does Vizenor's version call into question the credibility of Banks's arguments on the accomplishments of AIM? Why or why not?

5. What does Gerald Vizenor mean when he calls the American Indian Movement a "symbolic confrontation movement"? What are the limits of such an approach, according to Vizenor? Do you agree or disagree? Explain.

Chapter Six

1. What "pleasant myths" about American history and Andrew Jackson does Francis Jennings seek to dispel? What viewpoints in this volume could be cited in support of Jennings's views on how Native Americans have been treated in American history? Explain.
2. Does Francis Paul Prucha's essay constitute a defense of Andrew Jackson and his policies? Is he basically accepting Jackson's arguments found in Chapter Two at face value? Explain your answer.

General

1. A recurring theme in discussions about Native Americans revolves around the necessity and possibility of "civilizing" Indians—that is, forcing them to adopt aspects of white society. Among those who address this question directly are Mary Jemison, Elias Boudinot, George Armstrong Custer, and Carl Schurz. What two fundamentally different positions do these authors take on civilizing Indians? What position do other viewpoints in this volume take on this question?
2. In his viewpoint, Carl Schurz argues that Indians face either "extermination or civilization." What alternatives to these two choices appear in the viewpoints by John Collier and Luther Standing Bear? What alternatives can be found in other viewpoints in this volume? Explain your answer.
3. Which viewpoints in this volume view Indian-white relations primarily as a clash of different cultures, with peaceful relations dependent on cultural adjustment by either whites or Native Americans? Which viewpoints consider conflicts in Indian-white relations as stemming fundamentally from economic motives, such as people's desire to keep or acquire land? Which set of viewpoints do you find more convincing? Why?

Chronology

ca. 1500	The Iroquois Confederacy is formed.
1513	Spanish explorer Ponce de León leads an expedition to present-day Florida; he and his men are defeated and driven off by Calusu Indians. A second expedition is defeated in 1521.
1539–1543	Two large Spanish expeditions cross much of the present-day United States. Hernando de Soto leads a Spanish army from Florida to Texas; his army leaves destruction and disease among the native peoples he encounters. Francisco Vásquez de Coronado leads an expedition in the American Southwest from California to Kansas. His expedition destroys many villages of the Pueblo Indians but also introduces sheep and horses to native cultures.
1598	Juan de Oñate enters New Mexico to establish a Spanish colony.
1603	French explorer Samuel de Champlain makes contact with Iroquois and Algonquian tribes and explores part of the New England coast.
1607	The first permanent English settlement in North America is established at Jamestown, Virginia. Powhatan Indians save the colony from starvation by providing food and teaching the colonists how to cultivate corn and tobacco.
1615–1649	The Huron Indians and France establish a profitable arrangement in which the Hurons deliver furs acquired through trade with other Indian tribes to the French in Quebec City and Montreal. The Hurons agree to accept French Catholic missionaries in their villages.
1616–1619	Diseases introduced by European explorers and fishermen decimate the Indian population in New England.
1620	The Pilgrims arrive at Plymouth, Massachusetts.
1622	Powhatan leader Opechancanough leads the first major Indian rebellion against the English in Virginia.
1624	The Dutch West India Company founds Manhattan and Fort Orange (Albany) in what is now New York.

1630	English Puritans found the Massachusetts Bay Colony.
1636	Roger Williams is banished from the Massachusetts Bay Colony, in part because he criticized the colony for illegally taking land from the Indians. Williams purchases land from Narragansett Indians and founds the colony of Rhode Island.
1636–1637	Puritans of Massachusetts and Connecticut wage war against the Pequot Indians.
1638	In perhaps the first instance of the establishment of an Indian reservation in America, Quninnipiac Indians are confined to twelve hundred acres of land in Connecticut and subjected to the authority of an English agent.
1643–1701	The Iroquois Confederacy, in alliance with the Dutch (and, after 1664, the English), launches an extended and successful campaign of warfare that displaces and/or exterminates French-allied Indians, including the Huron, Illinois, and Erie tribes.
1644	The second Powhatan uprising in Virginia is crushed by English colonists.
1661	Chippewa (Ojibwa) Indians, pushed westward by Iroquois, French, and English expansion, invade Sioux territory in what is now Minnesota. The Sioux eventually move west to the Great Plains and adopt a nomadic buffalo-hunting culture.
	Puritan missionary John Eliot's translation of the Bible into the Algonquian language is published.
1675–1676	Wampanoag Indians attack towns across New England in what has become known as King Philip's War. The Indians are eventually defeated and their leader Metacomet (King Philip) is killed.
1677	The Covenant Chain—an alliance between the Iroquois Confederacy and the colony of New York—is formed.
1680	Pueblo Indians drive Spanish colonists out of New Mexico.
1682	William Penn signs a treaty of peace with the Delaware Indians.
	The first captivity narrative is published; it describes Mary Rowlandson's experiences with Indians during King Philip's War.
1689–1697	England, France, and their respective Indian allies fight for control of North America as part of King William's War. The Iroquois generally side with the English, while Algonquian tribes fight with the French.

1691	Virginia passes laws banishing English people who marry Indians or blacks.
1693	Spanish forces reconquer the Pueblo Indians and restore Sante Fe as capital of New Mexico.
1701	The Iroquois Confederacy makes peace agreements with France and Great Britain and their allied Indian tribes.
1701–1704	France establishes new trading missions in Illinois and Michigan and seeks alliances with Indian tribes there.
1711–1712	The Tuscarora War takes place in North Carolina between English slave traders and the Tuscarora Indians.
1729	The Natchez nation on the lower Mississippi River, the last remnant of an advanced mound-building civilization that peaked in 900–1250, is destroyed when its leaders and people are captured and sold into slavery by the French.
1754–1763	The French and Indian War (or Seven Years' War) runs concurrently in Europe and in America, where the majority of the fighting occurs in Pennsylvania and New York. Indians fight on both sides. France is defeated and gives Britain possession of its lands in North America, but many Indians refuse to recognize British authority.
1763	King George III of England issues the Proclamation Line, reserving territory between the Appalachians and the Mississippi River as Indian country forbidden to colonial settlement.
1763–1766	In Pontiac's Rebellion, Pontiac, an Ottawa chief, leads a pan-Indian alliance against British forces who have taken over French outposts in the Great Lakes region. Lacking French support, Indian forces are eventually compelled to surrender.
1769	The first of twenty-one missions in California is established by Spanish missionaries in San Diego. Chumash and other Indians are seized for labor, "Christianized," and forbidden to leave the missions.
1775–1783	The American Revolution is fought. Some Indians side with the British and Loyalists, some fight with American revolutionaries, and some attempt to remain neutral.
1777	The Iroquois Confederacy breaks up over the issue of which side to support in the American Revolution.
1778	The first U.S.-Indian treaty is signed; in it, the Delaware Indians agree to support the colonies

against the British. A Delaware proposal for the creation of an Indian state is ignored by the Continental Congress.

1780–1782	A smallpox epidemic kills large numbers of Indians in the Great Plains.
1783	Great Britain recognizes U.S. independence and cedes British territorial claims to lands from the Atlantic to the Mississippi.
1787–1789	Major documents affecting U.S. Indian policy are adopted, including the Northwest Ordinance, the U.S. Constitution, and various treaties with Indian tribes; the principle of centralized federal control over Indian policy and lands is established.
1790–1791	A confederation of Indian tribes in Ohio inflicts decisive defeats on U.S. Army expeditions; General Arthur St. Clair loses six hundred men in a 1791 battle.
1794	General Anthony Wayne defeats a confederated Indian army in the Battle of Fallen Timbers in Ohio.
	Jay's Treaty, signed by Great Britain and the United States, establishes the border between the United States and Canada and guarantees Indians freedom of movement between the two countries.
1795	Twelve Indian tribes sign the Treaty of Greenville (Ohio), ceding substantial territory with the promise that firm boundaries would be set between Indian lands and those open to white settlement.
1799	Handsome Lake, a Seneca Indian, begins a religious movement among the Iroquois that modifies their society by encouraging men to take up farming and condemning alcohol.
1802	Congress passes a law forbidding the sale of liquor to Indian nations; the law is widely ignored.
1803	France sells its Louisiana Territory to the United States; President Thomas Jefferson proposes that Indians be relocated to the new lands.
1804–1806	Meriwether Lewis and William Clark travel from St. Louis to the Pacific Ocean and back; their expedition brings a number of Indian tribes into first contact with the U.S. government.
1808–1813	Shawnee Indian brothers Tecumseh and Tenskwatawa found Prophetstown in Indiana Territory and attempt to build a political-religious movement of Indian resistance.
1811	William Henry Harrison attacks Prophetstown and defeats Tenskwatawa in the Battle of Tippecanoe.
1812–1815	The War of 1812 between Great Britain and the United States is fought. Many Indians side with

	the British, including Tecumseh, who is killed in battle in 1813.
1814	Tennessee militia troops, led by Andrew Jackson, defeat the Creek Indians at the Battle of Horseshoe Bend, forcing the Creek to cede 20 million acres to the federal government.
1817–1818	Andrew Jackson leads U.S. troops against the Seminole Indians in what becomes the First Seminole War.
1819	Spain sells its Florida possessions (including parts of Georgia and Alabama) to the United States.
1824	The Bureau of Indian Affairs (BIA) is created within the War Department.
	Chumash Indians revolt against Spanish mission rule in Santa Barbara, California.
1827	The Cherokee nation adopts a written constitution at New Echota, Georgia; John Ross is elected president. The Georgia state legislature nullifies the constitution.
1828	The *Cherokee Phoenix*, the first Native American newspaper, is published in New Echota.
1830	The Indian Removal Act is passed by Congress at the urging of the administration of President Andrew Jackson. Tribes of the southeastern United States are to be relocated to land west of the Mississippi River; the Choctaw are the first to be relocated.
1832	The Supreme Court in *Worcester v. Georgia* argues that federal treaties have established the Cherokee's right to self-government and that Georgia laws should not apply to Cherokee territory. The decision is not enforced by President Jackson.
	Black Hawk's War takes place in Illinois and Wisconsin.
	Creek Indians are forced to surrender lands in Alabama and relocate to Oklahoma.
1834–1836	California missions are secularized by Mexico; Chumash Indians enslaved by missions are officially freed.
1835	A minority of the Cherokee agree to move west in the Treaty of New Echota.
1835–1842	The Second Seminole War results from U.S. efforts to remove Seminole Indians from Florida.
1837	Congress passes legislation ending direct payments to Indian tribes for ceded lands, placing the proceeds "in trust" to be used for the Indians' benefit—an arrangement that leads to chronic financial mismanagement and abuse.

1838	The Cherokee are forced to travel on the "trail of tears" from Georgia to Oklahoma.
1846–1848	In the Mexican-American War, the United States acquires land that will become Texas, California, New Mexico, Utah, Nevada, and Arizona.
1846–1886	Apache Indians led by Mangas Coloradus and Geronimo resist confinement on reservations and the incursion of miners and U.S. soldiers into Apache territory in New Mexico.
1848	Gold is discovered in California. Within two years, the state's non-Indian population grows from 14,000 to 100,000; within ten years approximately 70,000 Indians are killed by disease or warfare.
1849	The Bureau of Indian Affairs is transferred from the War Department to the Interior Department.
1851	The first Fort Laramie Treaty between the U.S. government and various Great Plains Indian tribes is signed.
1855–1858	The Third Seminole War is fought. The three wars cost the U.S. government an estimated $40 to $60 million.
1860–1861	U.S. government troops are deployed against the Kiowa, Comanche, and Navajo tribes.
1862	The Santee Sioux under Little Crow revolt in Minnesota.
1863	More than eight thousand Navajo are forced to march 350 miles from their homelands to Bosque Redondo; here they are confined to a reservation until allowed to return to their homelands in 1868.
1864	A Cheyenne village at Sand Creek, Colorado, is attacked and its inhabitants massacred by militia troops under Colonel John Chivington.
1868	Conceding defeat to Sioux Indians under Red Cloud, the United States agrees to withdraw from forts on the Bozeman trail.
	In the Battle of the Washita, U.S. troops under the command of George Armstrong Custer slaughter Chief Black Kettle and his band of Cheyenne Indians, including women and children.
1869	Ely S. Parker, a Seneca Indian, is appointed head of the Bureau of Indian Affairs.
	The nation's first transcontinental railroad is completed.
1870	President U.S. Grant gives Protestant missionary organizations control of Indian agencies.
1871	Congress formally votes to end treaty making with any Indian tribe.

1872–1874	White hunters greatly reduce the buffalo population on the Great Plains.
1874	Custer leads an expedition that discovers gold in the Black Hills in territory promised to the Sioux.
1876	Custer and all of his troops are killed by Sioux and Cheyenne Indians at the Battle of Little Bighorn.
1877	The war against the Nez Percé ends with the surrender of Chief Joseph.
	Sioux resistance on the Great Plains ends; Sitting Bull flees to Canada.
1879	The Bureau of American Ethnology is created under the leadership of John Wesley Powell.
	The Carlisle Indian School is established in Pennsylvania.
1881	Helen Hunt Jackson's *A Century of Dishonor* is published.
1882	The Indian Rights Association is founded.
1886	Geronimo and his band of Apache surrender to General Nelson Miles.
1887	The Dawes Act, designed to break up the tribal system and convert Indians into farmers, is passed.
1889	The Ghost Dance, a religious movement inspired by Wovoka, a Paiute holy man in Nevada, spreads throughout the Great Plains.
1890	U.S. Indian population reaches a low of less than 225,000, according to the U.S. census, which also proclaims "the end of the frontier."
	Sitting Bull is killed on the Standing Rock Reservation, South Dakota.
	Big Foot's band of Sioux is massacred by U.S. soldiers at Wounded Knee Creek.
1893	Provisions of the Dawes Act are extended to the Five Civilized Tribes in Indian Territory (Oklahoma).
1901	The Five Civilized Tribes are granted citizenship by an act of Congress.
1903	The Supreme Court in *Lone Wolf v. Hitchcock* rules that Congress has "plenary powers" to abrogate or ignore past Indian treaties.
1907	The Oklahoma Territory and the Indian Territory are combined in the state of Oklahoma; all Indian tribal governments are dissolved.
1911	The Society of American Indians is founded.
1917–1918	Fifteen thousand American Indian men see active duty in World War I.

1918	The Native American Church is incorporated in Oklahoma.
1924	Congress passes the Indian Citizenship Act, making all Native Americans U.S. citizens.
1928	The Meriam Report, commissioned by the federal government, exposes widespread suffering, high mortality rates, loss of tribal lands, and other problems on Indian reservations.
1933	John Collier is appointed head of the Bureau of Indian Affairs by President Franklin Roosevelt; he serves until 1945.
1934	Congress passes the Indian Reorganization Act.
1935	The Indian Arts and Crafts Board is founded.
1941–1945	American Indian men register for the draft; twenty-five thousand see active duty in World War II.
1944	The National Congress of American Indians is established.
1946	Congress creates the Indian Claims Commission to hear cases regarding compensation for loss of Indian lands.
1950	The BIA begins a relocation program to encourage Indians to move from reservations to cities.
1953	Congress passes a series of bills releasing thirteen tribes from federal supervision and terminating federal payments and services.
1961	Delegates to the American Indian Chicago Conference issue the Declaration of Indian Purpose, which stresses the "right to choose our own way of life."
	The Kinzua Dam in New York floods much of the land promised in perpetuity to the Seneca Indians in a 1794 treaty.
1962	The National Indian Youth Council is created to promote Indian nationalism and intertribal unity.
1964	Tribes of Washington State begin what will become a national campaign to restore tribal fishing rights.
1965	As part of President Lyndon Johnson's War on Poverty, American Indians are given access to federal funds (through the Office of Economic Opportunity) outside of BIA channels.
1968	The American Indian Movement (AIM) is founded in Minneapolis, Minnesota.
	The American Indian Civil Rights Act is passed, extending provisions of the U.S. Constitution to Indian reservations.
	The Supreme Court rules in *Menominee Tribe v. United States* that states cannot invalidate Indian

	hunting and fishing rights established through past treaties.
1969–1971	Indian activists seize and hold Alcatraz Island.
1970	President Richard Nixon announces that federal policies will stress Indian self-determination without a termination of federal services.
1971	Nixon signs the Alaska Native Claims Act, which provides Alaska's native peoples with $962 million in compensation for lost lands.
1972	Activists occupy BIA headquarters in Washington, D.C., for six days.
1973	Members of the American Indian Movement occupy the town of Wounded Knee for sixty-seven days, commemorating the 1890 massacre and calling for radical changes in the administration of the reservation. Two Indians are killed during the standoff against federal marshals and FBI agents.
1978	The American Indian Religious Freedom Act grants free exercise of native religions.
	The Indian Child Welfare Act gives tribes a greater role in the adoption of Indian children.
1980	The Penobscot and Passamaquoddy Indians receive $81.5 million in the settlement of a suit to recover 12 million acres of land in Maine.
	The Supreme Court orders the federal government to pay $105 million to the Sioux for lands illegally seized in 1877.
1982	A federal appeals court in Florida rules that state regulations on gambling do not apply to Indian nations, leading to a national proliferation of Indian-run casinos and bingo operations.
1985	Wilma Mankiller, a Cherokee, becomes the first woman in modern history to lead a large Indian tribe.
1990	U.S. census records an Indian population of over 2 million, five times the number recorded in 1950.
	Congress passes legislation requiring universities and museums to return Indian remains and sacred objects requested by tribes.
	The Supreme Court rules that states can outlaw the use of peyote, part of the religious practices of the Native American Church.

Annotated Bibliography

Stephen Ambrose. *Crazy Horse and Custer: The Parallel Lives of Two American Warriors*. Garden City, NY: Doubleday, 1975. A dual biography of George Armstrong Custer and the Sioux warrior-leader, culminating with the Battle of Little Bighorn.

Stephen Ambrose. *Undaunted Courage: Meriwether Lewis, Thomas Jefferson, and the Opening of the American West*. New York: Simon & Schuster, 1996. A history of the Lewis and Clark expedition that emphasizes the relationship between Lewis and Jefferson and their interest in learning about the Native Americans then living in the Louisiana Territory.

Gary Clayton Anderson and Alan R. Woolworth, eds. *Through Dakota Eyes: Narrative Accounts of the Minnesota Indian War of 1862*. St. Paul: Minnesota Historical Society Press, 1988. A collection of accounts of one of the deadliest Indian uprisings in American history.

Ralph K. Andrist. *The Long Death: The Last Days of the Plains Indians*. New York: Macmillan, 1964. A history of the conquest of the Plains Indians from the rebellion of the Santee Sioux in Minnesota in 1862 to the Battle of Wounded Knee in 1890.

Virginia Irving Armstrong, ed. *I Have Spoken: American History Through the Voices of the Indians*. Athens, OH: Swallow Press, 1971. An anthology of more than two hundred statements and speeches of Native Americans from the early seventeenth century to 1970.

James Axtell. *The European and the Indian: Essays in the Ethnohistory of Colonial North America*. New York: Oxford University Press, 1981. A collection of ten essays on the social and cultural interactions of the French, British, and Indians in the northeast quadrant of colonial North America.

James Axtell. *The Invasion Within: The Contest of Cultures in Colonial North America*. New York: Oxford University Press, 1985. An ethnohistorical examination of educational and cultural interactions among the French, British, and Indians, with an emphasis on the various efforts of the French and British to Christianize and civilize the Indian.

Howard Bahr et al., eds. *Native Americans Today: Sociological Perspectives*. New York: Harper & Row, 1972. An anthology of published articles on the sociology of Indian-white relations.

Gretchen M. Bataille and Kathleen M. Sands. *American Indian Women,*

Telling Their Lives. Lincoln: University of Nebraska Press, 1984. An examination of themes and styles in the autobiographies of Native American women.

Robert F. Berkhofer Jr. *The White Man's Indian: Images of the American Indian, from Columbus to the Present*. New York: Knopf, 1978. An innovative intellectual history of white perceptions of the Indian over the course of American history.

John Bierhorst. *The Mythology of North America*. New York: Morrow, 1985. A consideration of themes from Indian mythological narratives found in eleven discrete cultural regions of North America.

Henry W. Bowden and James P. Ronda, eds. *John Eliot's Indian Dialogues: A Study in Cultural Interaction*. Westport, CT: Greenwood Press, 1980. Primary sources concerning the work of John Eliot, the leading Puritan missionary among the Indians.

Henry Warner Bowden. *American Indians and Christian Missions: Studies in Cultural Conflict*. Chicago: University of Chicago Press, 1981. A historical survey of the ongoing conflict of cultures between Christian missionaries and Native Americans.

William Brandon. *The Last Americans: The Indian in American Culture*. New York: McGraw-Hill, 1974. An excellent one-volume general history that combines sound narrative and provocative interpretation.

Dee Brown. *Bury My Heart at Wounded Knee: An Indian History of the American West*. New York: Holt, Rinehart, and Winston, 1970. A best-selling account of campaigns of extermination waged against the Sioux, Cheyenne, Apache, Nez Percé, and other tribes, written from an Indian point of view.

Larry W. Burt. *Tribalism in Crisis: Federal Indian Policy, 1953–1961*. Albuquerque: University of New Mexico Press, 1982. A history of the efforts of Congress in the 1950s to promote rapid assimilation of Indians by ending federal services to tribes.

Colin G. Calloway. *The American Revolution in Indian Country: Crisis and Diversity in Native American Communities*. New York: Cambridge University Press, 1995. An examination of the response of eight Indian communities to the American Revolution.

Colin G. Calloway, ed. *The World Turned Upside Down: Indian Voices from Early America*. Boston: St. Martin's Press, 1994. A collection of primary source documents representing Native American reactions to the coming of European colonists.

Kenneth Carley. *The Sioux Uprising of 1862*. St. Paul: Minnesota Historical Society, 1961. A dramatic account of the Dakota Sioux revolt in Minnesota that resulted in the death of the greatest number of white settlers of any single Indian uprising.

Leonard A. Carlson. *Indians, Bureaucrats, and Land: The Dawes Act and the Decline of Indian Farming*. Westport, CT: Greenwood Press, 1981. A history of the implementation of the controversial Dawes Act that concludes that this legislation worked against its intended function of cultural and economic assimilation of American Indians.

George Pierre Castile and Robert L. Bee, eds. *State and Reservation: New Perspectives on Federal Indian Policy.* Tucson: University of Arizona Press, 1992. A collection of essays by historians and anthropologists on federal-Indian relations; most contributors share the perspective that Native Americans, unlike other American minority groups, have unique claims to sovereignty.

Alfred A. Cave. *The Pequot War.* Amherst: University of Massachusetts Press, 1996. An interpretation of the first major military conflict between Puritans and Indians in New England.

John Collier. *Indians of the Americas: The Long Hope.* New York: New American Library, 1947. An overview of Indian history written by the former U.S. commissioner of Indian affairs under President Franklin D. Roosevelt.

David H. Corkran. *The Creek Frontier, 1540–1783.* Norman: University of Oklahoma Press, 1967. A history that emphasizes Indian perceptions and institutions over the course of Creek-white relations from colonial times to the American Revolution.

Rupert Costo and Jeannette Henry. *Indian Treaties: Two Centuries of Dishonor.* San Francisco: Indian Historian Press, 1977. A consideration of treaties made between Indian tribes and the U.S. government and their present significance in such issues as tribal jurisdiction, fishing rights, and water and land use.

William Cronon, George Miles, and Jay Gitlin, eds. *Under an Open Sky: Rethinking America's Western Past.* New York: W.W. Norton, 1992. A collection of fourteen essays on a variety of topics seeking to determine the real significance of the frontier in American history.

Angie Debo. *Geronimo: The Man, His Time, His Place.* Norman: University of Oklahoma Press, 1976. A respected biography of the Apache leader.

Vine DeLoria Jr. *Behind the Trail of Broken Treaties: An Indian Declaration of Independence.* New York: Delacorte Press, 1974. The author, an Indian lawyer and activist, argues that the best solution to the "Indian problem" would be to grant what he calls "quasi-international independence" to Native American tribes.

Vine DeLoria Jr. *Custer Died for Your Sins: An Indian Manifesto.* New York: Macmillan, 1969. A classic revisionist view of American Indian history and a presentation of the demands of Native Americans during the late 1960s.

Vine DeLoria Jr., ed. *American Indian Policy in the Twentieth Century.* Norman: University of Oklahoma Press, 1985. A collection of interpretive essays on federal Indian policy that focuses on the work of the Indian Rights Association.

Vine DeLoria Jr. and Clifford Lytle. *American Indians, American Justice.* Austin: University of Texas Press, 1983. A comprehensive history of the federal court system as it relates to American Indians.

William N. Denevan, ed. *The Native Population of the Americas in 1492.* Madison: University of Wisconsin Press, 1976. An anthology of scholarly papers concerning population estimates for the New World prior to Columbus's voyage.

Carol Devens. *Countering Colonization: Native American Women and Great Lakes Missions, 1630–1900.* Berkeley and Los Angeles: University of California Press, 1992. A history of the reactions of Ojibwa, Cree, and Montagnis-Naskapi women to Christian missions.

Henry F. Dobyns. *Their Number Become Thinned: Native American Population Dynamics in Eastern North America.* Knoxville: University of Tennessee Press, 1983. A series of seven essays focusing on the underlying causes of the decline in Indian population from the fifteenth century to the nineteenth century.

Gregory Evans Dowd. *A Spirited Resistance: The North American Indian Struggle for Unity, 1745–1815.* Baltimore: Johns Hopkins University Press, 1992. A history of Native American resistance to white expansion into the trans-Appalachian west.

Richard Drinnon. *Facing West: The Metaphysics of Indian-Hating and Empire-Building.* Minneapolis: University of Minnesota Press, 1980. A critical intellectual and political history of the evolving rationalizations for white westward expansion at the expense of Native Americans.

R. David Edmunds. *The Shawnee Prophet.* Lincoln: University of Nebraska Press, 1983. A biography of Tecumseh's brother, Tenskwatawa, focusing on his founding of a pan-Indian religious movement in the early 1800s.

R. David Edmunds. *Tecumseh and the Quest for Indian Leadership.* Boston: Little, Brown, 1984. A brief and readable biography of this important early–nineteenth-century Shawnee leader.

John Ehle. *Trail of Tears: The Rise and Fall of the Cherokee Nation.* New York: Doubleday, 1988. An account of the Cherokee nation's efforts to resist removal in the 1830s.

Carlos B. Embry. *America's Concentration Camps: The Facts About Our Indian Reservations Today.* New York: McKay, 1956. A spirited attack on the entire Indian reservation system.

Brian M. Fagan. *The Great Journey: The Peopling of Ancient America.* New York: Thames and Hudson, 1987. A panoramic overview of the origins and lifestyles of America's indigenous peoples.

Stuart J. Fiedel. *The Prehistory of the Americas.* New York: Cambridge University Press, 1987. A description and analysis of pre-Columbian societies that stresses the complexity of their evolution.

Donald L. Fixico. *Termination and Relocation: Federal Indian Policy, 1945–1960.* Albuquerque: University of New Mexico Press, 1986. A history of

U.S. Indian policy following World War II that examines efforts to end federal treaty obligations and relocate Indians in urban areas.

Jack D. Forbes, ed. *The Indian in America's Past.* Englewood Cliffs, NJ: Prentice-Hall, 1964. A compilation and analysis of nearly two hundred documents, including examples of European images of Native Americans and of Indian responses to European contact.

Grant Foreman. *The Five Civilized Tribes.* Norman: University of Oklahoma Press, 1972. A study of the Cherokee, Creek, Choctaw, Chickasaw, and Seminole Indians, their adoption of "civilized" European ways, and their removal to Oklahoma in the 1830s.

Henry E. Fritz. *The Movement for Indian Assimilation, 1860–1890.* Philadelphia: University of Pennsylvania Press, 1963. A history of the post–Civil War assimilationist solutions to the "Indian problem," including the competition between Protestants and Roman Catholics for control of Indian policy.

Sam D. Gill. *Native American Religions: An Introduction.* Belmont, CA: Wadsworth, 1982. An introductory survey that both documents and analyzes Native American religions.

Marion E. Gridley. *American Indian Women.* New York: Hawthorn Books, 1974. Biographies of eighteen historical and contemporary Native American women of note, including Sacajawea, interpreter and guide for the Lewis and Clark expedition, and her great-great-granddaughter, Esther Burnett Horne.

Barbara Graymont. *The Iroquois in the American Revolution.* Syracuse, NY: Syracuse University Press, 1972. A detailed history of Iroquois involvement in the American Revolution and their failed efforts to maintain friendly relations with both the British and the Americans.

Bruce Hampton. *Children of Grace: The Nez Percé War of 1877.* New York: Henry Holt, 1994. An account written for the general reader of the war against the Nez Percé and their attempt to flee to Canada.

Howard L. Harrod. *Renewing the World: Plains Indian Religion and Morality.* Tucson: University of Arizona Press, 1987. A comparative study of four tribes of the Great Plains, focusing on Native American myths, rituals, and religious experiences.

Laurence M. Hauptman. *Between Two Fires: American Indians in the Civil War.* New York: Free Press, 1995. An account of the roles American Indians played on both sides of the Civil War.

Hazel Hertzberg. *The Search for an American Indian Identity: Modern Pan-Indian Movements.* Syracuse, NY: Syracuse University Press, 1971. A history of the development of intertribal American Indian political movements.

Arlene Hirschfelder, ed. *Native Heritage: Personal Accounts by American Indians, 1790 to the Present.* New York: Macmillan, 1995. A collection of 120 narratives taken from oral histories, autobiographies, Indian newspapers, and other sources.

Reginald Horsman. *Expansion and American Indian Policy, 1783–1812.* East Lansing: Michigan State University Press, 1967. This history of the evolution of Indian policy in the early years of the United States argues that efforts to "civilize" and assimilate Native Americans were largely a rationalization for white territorial aggrandizement.

Frederick E. Hoxie. *A Final Promise: The Campaign to Assimilate the Indians, 1880–1920.* Lincoln: University of Nebraska Press, 1984. A history of Indian reforms in theory and in practice that criticizes efforts to assimilate Indians into white society.

Frederick E. Hoxie, ed. *Indians in American History: An Introduction.* Arlington Heights, IL: Harlan Davidson, 1988. A collection of thirteen essays written by specialists in various fields of Native American studies.

Lee Eldridge Huddleston. *Origins of the American Indians: European Concepts, 1492–1729.* Austin: University of Texas Press, 1967. A history of European ideas on the origins of the peoples of the Americas.

Åke Hultkrantz. *The Religions of the American Indians.* Berkeley and Los Angeles: University of California Press, 1979. A comprehensive survey of Native American religions, including an overview of beliefs and rituals from pre-Columbian times to the twentieth century.

R. Douglas Hunt. *Indian Agriculture in America: Prehistory to the Present.* Lawrence: University of Kansas Press, 1987. A study of archaeological, historical, and anthropological scholarship on the evolution of Native American agriculture, including a discussion of federal Indian policies regarding Native American agricultural practices.

Albert L. Hurtado and Peter Iverson, eds. *Major Problems in American Indian History: Documents and Essays.* Lexington, MA: D.C. Heath, 1994. A collection of primary sources and analytical essays on various topics in the history of Native Americans.

Peter Iverson. *The Navajo Nation.* Westport, CT: Greenwood Press, 1981. A general history of the Navajo nation that includes much information on Navajo resistance to John Collier's New Deal reforms.

Peter Iverson, ed. *The Plains Indians of the Twentieth Century.* Norman: University of Oklahoma Press, 1985. A collection of eleven articles dealing with modern problems of the Plains Indians, including legal disputes over water and mineral rights, religious issues, and the impact of the New Deal and World War II.

Francis Jennings. *The Invasion of America: Indians, Colonialism, and the Cant of Conquest.* Chapel Hill: University of North Carolina Press, 1975. A history of Puritan rationalizations of what the author regards as their armed conquest of native peoples and how this "cant of conquest" continued to influence American policies and attitudes toward Indians throughout early U.S. history.

Alvin M. Josephy Jr. *Now That the Buffalo's Gone: A Study of Today's American Indians.* New York: Knopf, 1982. An account of contemporary Native Americans' attempts to retain their identity and a chronicle of recent efforts to restore tribal rights.

Alvin M. Josephy Jr., ed. *America in 1492: The World of the Indian Peoples Before the Arrival of Columbus*. New York: Knopf, 1992. An overview of Indian peoples in both hemispheres shortly before European contact, as well as a topical examination of Indian language, religion, and technology.

Alvin M. Josephy Jr., ed. *Red Power: The American Indians' Fight for Freedom*. New York: American Heritage Press, 1971. This collection of articles and speeches from various sources chronicles the rise of the "red power" movement.

Robert H. Keller. *American Protestantism and United States Indian Policy, 1869–82*. Lincoln: University of Nebraska Press, 1983. A detailed history concentrating on the efforts of President U.S. Grant to alter federal Indian policy by placing it in the hands of Protestant reformers.

Lawrence C. Kelly. *The Assault on Assimilation: John Collier and the Origins of Indian Policy Reform*. Albuquerque: University of New Mexico Press, 1983. A biography of the New Deal–era reformer.

Arnold Krupat. *For Those Who Come After: A Study of Native American Autobiography*. Berkeley and Los Angeles: University of California Press, 1985. An analysis of famous Indian autobiographies, including those of Geronimo, Yellow Wolf, and Black Elk.

Karen O. Kupperman. *Settling with the Indians: The Meeting of English and Indian Cultures in America, 1580–1640*. Totowa, NJ: Rowman and Littlefield, 1980. A comparative history of Indian and English technology, religion, culture, and government in colonial times.

James Levernier and Hennig Cohen, eds. *The Indians and Their Captives*. Westport, CT: Greenwood Press, 1977. A collection of important captivity narratives organized into five distinct historical phases.

Patricia Nelson Limerick. *The Legacy of Conquest: The Unbroken Past of the American West*. New York: W.W. Norton, 1987. This major reinterpretation of the history of the American West describes a highly diverse region where many different peoples wrestled for control of land, resources, and cultural and political supremacy.

Peter C. Mancall. *Deadly Medicine: Indians and Alcohol in Early America*. Ithaca, NY: Cornell University Press, 1995. An innovative history of a troubling topic in the history of both Indians and whites in North America.

Calvin Martin, ed. *The American Indian and the Problem of History*. New York: Oxford University Press, 1987. Essays organized around the theme of different cultural conceptions of time and history.

Janet A. McDonnell. *The Dispossession of the American Indians, 1887–1934*. Bloomington: Indiana University Press, 1991. A highly informative history of federal Indian land policy from the 1887 Dawes Act to the New Deal, during which time the Indian land base was reduced from 138 million to 52 million acres.

William G. McLoughlin. *Cherokees and Missionaries, 1789–1839*. New Haven, CT: Yale University Press, 1984. A history of the relationship between various Protestant denominations and the Cherokee nation, as well as an account of the internal Cherokee debate over assimilation.

D'arcy McNickle. *Native American Tribalism: Indian Survivals and Renewals.* New York: Oxford University Press, 1973. A history of the various efforts of American and Canadian Indians to retain their ethnic and cultural identities.

D'arcy McNickle. *They Came Here First: The Epic of the American Indian.* New York: Octagon, 1975. A general history of Native Americans by an American Indian scholar who helped found the National Congress of American Indians.

James Merrell and Daniel Richter, eds. *Beyond the Covenant Chain: The Iroquois and Their Neighbors in Indian North America, 1600–1800.* Syracuse, NY: Syracuse University Press, 1987. A collection of nine essays on the relationship between the Iroquois Confederacy and surrounding tribes.

Christopher L. Miller. *Prophetic Worlds: Indians and Whites on the Columbia Plateau.* New Brunswick, NJ: Rutgers University Press, 1985. A history of Indian and white perceptions of one another, as well as an account of how the arrival of diseases, the rifle, and the horse drastically changed Native American culture.

Steven Mintz, ed. *Native American Voices: A History and Anthology.* St. James, NY: Brandywine, 1995. Contains a brief historical overview and an extensive collection of excerpted speeches, reports, and writings pertaining to American Indians.

Jedediah Morse. *A Report to the Secretary of War of the United States on Indian Affairs.* New York: A.M. Kelley, 1970. A reprint of an 1822 report by a minister who was commissioned by the federal government to travel among and describe the state of American Indians.

Gary B. Nash. *Red, White, and Black: The Peoples of Early America.* Rev. ed. Englewood Cliffs, NJ: Prentice-Hall, 1982. A history of interactions among Indians, Africans, and Europeans in eastern North America during the colonial period.

John G. Neihardt. *Black Elk Speaks: Being the Life Story of a Holy Man of the Oglala Sioux.* Lincoln: University of Nebraska Press, 1961. The classic autobiography of the life of Nicholas Black Elk, Sioux warrior and holy man, with an emphasis on his sacred visions.

Roger Nichols, ed. *The American Indian: Past and Present.* 3rd ed. New York: Wiley, 1985. A selection of twenty-four articles on American Indian history.

James S. Olson and Raymond Wilson. *Native Americans in the Twentieth Century.* Provo, UT: Brigham Young University Press, 1984. An overview of Native Americans and federal policy on Indian affairs.

Donald L. Parman. *Indians and the American West in the Twentieth Century.* Bloomington: Indiana University Press, 1994. An examination of the efforts of Native Americans to preserve and reinvigorate their tribal governments and to reestablish control over natural resources.

Donald L. Parman. *The Navajos and the New Deal.* New Haven, CT: Yale University Press, 1976. This history and evaluation of the New Deal reform efforts of BIA commissioner John Collier describes those reforms as at best a mixed blessing for the Navajos.

Roy Harvey Pearce. *Savagism and Civilization: A Study of the Indian and the American Mind.* Baltimore: Johns Hopkins University Press, 1967. A provocative history that seeks to explain how Europeans embraced the concept of an uncivilized savage and applied the idea to Native Americans.

Theda Perdue. *Slavery and the Evolution of Cherokee Society, 1540–1866.* Knoxville: University of Tennessee Press, 1979. A history of slavery among the Cherokee that seeks to explain how this institution affected the tribe's structure and culture.

Kenneth R. Philp. *John Collier's Crusade for Indian Reform, 1920–1954.* Tucson: University of Arizona Press, 1977. A history of the reform efforts of John Collier before, during, and after the New Deal and of Indian responses to those reforms.

Kenneth R. Philp, ed. *Indian Self-Rule: First-Hand Accounts of Indian-White Relations from Roosevelt to Reagan.* Salt Lake City, UT: Howe Brothers, 1986. An important primary source collection of Indian leaders' commentary on Native American affairs during the fifty years following the passage of the 1934 Indian Reorganization Act.

Francis P. Prucha. *American Indian Treaties: The History of a Political Anomaly.* Berkeley and Los Angeles: University of California Press, 1994. An examination of the treaty-making process and the impact of treaties on Indian life.

Francis P. Prucha. *Documents of United States Indian Policy.* 2nd ed. Lincoln: University of Nebraska Press, 1990. A compilation of 199 official documents concerning major formulations of federal Indian policy, arranged chronologically from the American Revolution to the 1980s.

Francis P. Prucha. *The Indians in American Society: From the Revolutionary War to the Present.* Berkeley and Los Angeles: University of California Press, 1985. Among the best one-volume general surveys of the subject.

George I. Quimby. *Indian Life in the Upper Great Lakes, 11000 B.C. to A.D. 1800.* Chicago: University of Chicago Press, 1960. The prehistory and history of a number of tribes, including the Huron, Ottawa, Chippewa, Sauk, and Fox.

Jon Rayhner and Jeanne Eder. *A History of Indian Education.* Billings: Eastern Montana College, 1989. A study of Indian schools and their role in the effort to assimilate Native Americans, as well as an account of patterns of Indian resistance and cooperation.

Daniel K. Richter. *The Ordeal of the Longhouse: The Peoples of the Iroquois League in the Era of European Colonization.* Chapel Hill: University of

North Carolina Press, 1992. A history of the response of the Iroquois Confederacy to European colonization that maintains that the Iroquois were not passive victims of the colonization process.

Glenda Riley. *Women and Indians on the Frontier, 1825–1915*. Albuquerque: University of New Mexico Press, 1984. A study of the reactions of white frontier women to the American Indians they encountered.

Michael Rogin. *Fathers and Children: Andrew Jackson and the Subjugation of the American Indian*. New York: Knopf, 1975. A strong indictment of the Jackson administration and its Indian removal policies.

Annette Rosenstiel. *Red and White: Indian Views of the White Man, 1492–1982*. New York: Universe Books, 1983. A collection of primary source speeches in which Native Americans express their views on European and American cultures and conduct.

Kirkpatrick Sale. *The Conquest of Paradise: Christopher Columbus and the Columbian Legacy*. New York: Knopf, 1990. An indictment of Columbus that contends that the explorer and those who followed him to the Americas are responsible for the destruction of native cultures and their environment.

Neal Salisbury. *Manitou and Providence: Indians, Europeans, and the Making of New England, 1500–1643*. New York: Oxford University Press, 1982. An ethnohistory of colonial New England that evenhandedly examines not just intercultural relations but intertribal relations as well.

Bernard W. Sheehan. *Savagism and Civility: Indians and Englishmen in Colonial Virginia*. Cambridge: Cambridge University Press, 1980. An examination of the English doctrine of "savagism" and its place in informing English perceptions of native peoples, as well as a history of the permanence of this doctrine in the English and American mindset.

Richard Slotkin. *Regeneration Through Violence: The Mythology of the American Frontier, 1600–1860*. New York: HarperPerennial, 1996. A general history of the frontier, with a particular focus on the violence directed at Native Americans.

David E. Stannard. *American Holocaust: Columbus and the Conquest of the New World*. New York: Oxford University Press, 1992. Surveys the diversity of native peoples as of 1492 and describes the destruction of 90 percent of that population during the ensuing five hundred years.

Stan Steiner. *The New Indians*. New York: Harper & Row, 1967. A study of the rising mood of resistance among Native Americans during the 1960s.

Graham D. Taylor. *The New Deal and American Indian Tribalism: The Administration of the Indian Reorganization Act, 1934–45*. Lincoln: University of Nebraska Press, 1980. Analyzes the reforms of Indian commissioner John Collier and recounts the administration of the 1934 Indian Reorganization Act and the Native American response.

Robert M. Utley. *The Indian Frontier of the American West, 1846–1890*. Albuquerque: University of New Mexico Press, 1984. A historical survey of Indian-white relations in the trans-Mississippi West.

Alden T. Vaughan. *New England Frontier: Puritans and Indians, 1620–1675.* Boston: Little, Brown, 1965. A positive appraisal of Puritan attitudes and behavior toward Native Americans as well as a history of the adjustments both peoples made over the course of the seventeenth century.

Alden T. Vaughan and Edward W. Clark, eds. *Puritans Among the Indians: Accounts of Captivity and Redemption, 1676–1724.* Cambridge, MA: Belknap Press, 1981. An anthology of the accounts of Puritan colonists who had been held captive by American Indians.

Jack O. Waddell and O. Michael Watson, eds. *The American Indian in Urban Society.* Boston: Little, Brown, 1971. A sociological examination of the American Indians who left reservations for the city.

Anthony Wallace. *The Long, Bitter Trail: Andrew Jackson and the Indians.* New York: Hill and Wang, 1993. A history of the Indian Removal Act of 1830, an indictment of Andrew Jackson, and a chronicle of the relocation of the Five Civilized Tribes.

Wilcomb E. Washburn. *The Assault on Indian Tribalism: The General Allotment Law (Dawes Act) of 1887.* Philadelphia: Lippincott, 1975. A narrative and documentary history of the motives, goals, and impact of this important piece of legislation.

Wilcomb E. Washburn. *The Indian in America.* New York: Harper & Row, 1975. This general history of the Indian from pre-Columbian times to the 1970s includes a harsh indictment of the American Indian Movement of the 1960s.

Richard White. *"It's Your Misfortune and None of My Own": A History of the American West.* Norman: University of Oklahoma Press, 1991. This comprehensive history of the American West from the years of Spanish exploration to the 1980s both incorporates the best of recent scholarship and offers major reinterpretations of the relationship between Native Americans and newcomers.

Richard White. *The Middle Ground: Indians, Empires, and Republics in the Great Lakes Region, 1650–1815.* New York: Cambridge University Press, 1991. A thoroughly researched history of the political, social, and cultural forces that shaped this region.

Index

Adams, John Quincy, 270, 286–87
agriculture
  and Cherokee Indians, 73, 101
  increase of, among Indians, 169
  Indians won't practice, 134–36, 139,
    178–79, 212–13
AIM. *See* American Indian Movement
Alabama, Indians in, 75, 86, 92, 94,
  96–97
Alabama Indians, 229
Alcatraz Island, 255, 259
Algonquin Indians, 160
American Board of Commissioners for
  Foreign Missions, 285, 288
American Board of Foreign Missions,
  85, 87
American Friends Service Committee,
  249
American Horse, 140
American Indian Employment Center,
  258
American Indian Movement (AIM)
  goals of, 254, 256
  has had limited effectiveness, 258–62
  has helped Native Americans,
    252–57
  protests by, 252, 254–56, 259–62
American settlers
  Indians should join together against,
    62–66
  Indians should live in peace with,
    67–72
  land taken from Indians by, 30, 34,
    63–66
    Cherokees, 73–74, 84–85, 93, 99,
      101–104
    as inevitable, 157–63
    as unjust, 143–56
  treatment of Indians by, 63–66,
    68–69, 137–42
  see also colonists
Apache Indians, 127, 177
Arapahoe Indians
  income from resources, 239
  treaties with, 118, 127
  war against U.S., 116–17
Arizona Territory, Indians in, 138
Armstrong, Marjorie, 237
Armstrong, O.K., 237
Assiniboine Indians, 119

Bad Heart Bull, Wesley, 256, 262

Banks, Dennis, 252, 253, 255, 258–61
Battle of Horseshoe Bend, 270, 284
Battle of Little Bighorn, 131, 193
Battle of the Thames, 63, 270
Battle of Tippecanoe, 63, 278
Bellecourt, Clyde, 253
Bellecourt, Vern, 253
Benton, Eddie, 253
Blackfoot Indians, 214, 234
Black Hawk, 65
Black Hawk War, 65, 70
Black Hills, 254
Blount, William, 271
Board of Indian Commissioners, 207
Boudinot, Elias, 73, 85, 96
Bronson, Ruth Muskrat, 232
buffalo, 70, 169
Bureau of Indian Affairs (BIA)
  abolishment of, 229, 232
  AIM protest of, 252, 254
  appropriations for, 234
  and Board of Indian Commissioners,
    207
  corruption in, 167
  protests against, 252, 254, 259, 262
  relocation programs, 237–42, 243–51

Calhoun, John C., 281
California, Indians in, 229
Call, Richard K., 281
Camp, Carter, 253
Carlisle Indian School, 187–89, 191,
  194–95
Carson, Kit, 239
Cass, Lewis, 88, 161, 288
Catataugh, 29
Catawba Indians, 178
Century of Dishonor, A (Jackson), 137,
  140
Cherokee Indians
  as agricultural society, 73, 101
  are creating a civilized society,
    73–83, 101, 273
    con, 84–91, 274
  constitution of, 73, 92, 101, 285
  extinction of, 94
  and Five Civilized Tribes, 67, 182
  independent state of, 78–80, 86–87,
    90, 92–94, 105
  land taken from, 73–74, 84–85,
    92–100, 101–104, 265, 270–71, 278,
    285

preservation of language of, 275
relocation of, 74, 84–91, 92–100,
    101–104, 273–74
and reorganization, 215
self–government of, 78–80, 273
system of writing of, 78, 80–81, 273
treaties with U.S., 74, 92, 101–102,
    105–108, 273–74
tribal system of, 182
U.S. government aid to, 87–90, 93,
    98–99, 103
Cherokee Nation, 75–76, 101
Cherokee Nation vs. Georgia, 286
Cherokee Phoenix newspaper, 74
Cheyenne Indians
    and reorganization, 210, 214
    treaties with U.S., 118–19, 127
    war against U.S., 116–18
Chickasaw Indians
    and Five Civilized Tribes, 67, 182
    land taken from, 278
    and Pushmataha, 67–72
    relocation of, 95, 97
    and Tecumseh, 62–66
    treaties with U.S., 97
    tribal system of, 182
Chief Joseph, 143
Chippewa Indians, 65
    as activists, 253, 258, 261
    and American Indian Movement,
        253
    federal supervision of, 229
    and land, 158, 177
    and reorganization, 214
    as self-supporting, 138
    and Sioux, 212
    tribal system of, 182
Choctaw Indians
    extinction of, 94
    and Five Civilized Tribes, 67, 182
    and Indian Removal Act, 67–68
    live in peace with whites, 68–69, 71
    preservation of language of, 275
    and Pushmataha, 67–72
    relocation of, 67–68, 95, 97, 273–74
    and Tecumseh, 62–66
    treaties with U.S., 67–69, 97, 273
    tribal system of, 182
Chu Li-Oa, 79
Civil War, American, 128, 131, 183
Clark, William, 145, 288
Collier, John, 206–15, 216–17, 224
colonists
    attacks on Indian villages by, 30
    captive's account of Indian cruelty,
        35–44, 46–49
    captive's account of Indian

kindness, 45–57
    seizure of Indian land by, 30, 34,
        63–65, 267–68
    should maintain friendly relations
        with Indians, 28–29
    should wage war on Indians, 30–34
    see also American settlers
Colorado Territory, Indians in, 118–19,
    138–39
Colville Reservation, 144
Comanche Indians, 127
Congress of Plains Indians, 207, 210
Cooper, James Fenimore, 131–32, 134
Coushatta Indians, 229
Crawford, Samuel J., 126
Creek Indians
    division in, 270
    extinction of, 83, 94
    and Five Civilized Tribes, 67, 182
    land taken from, 270–71, 278, 280
    and Tecumseh, 62–63
    tribal system of, 182, 244
Crow Indians
    income of, 239
    and reorganization, 214
    and Sioux, 160
    treaties with U.S., 119
culture
    American, should be emphasized,
        183–90, 209, 217
    Indian adoption of European, 67
    preservation of Indian, 191–201,
        216–17, 275
Custer, George Armstrong, 131

Dakota. *See* Sioux Indians
Dakota Territory, Indians in, 138
Dawes Act
    benefits of, 168–74
    as harmful, 176–82, 210, 217–18
    passage of, 168
    reversal of, 206, 210
Delaware Indians, 35, 54, 94, 134

education. *See* Indians, education of
Eisenhower, Dwight D., 225, 244
Emergency Conservation Work
    Agency, 216, 220
Emmons, Glenn L., 230–31, 238–39
*Empire of Fortune: Crowns, Colonies,
    and Tribes in the Seven Years War in
    America* (Jennings), 265
Evarts, Jeremiah, 85, 87, 288

Five Civilized Tribes, 67, 178, 182, 184,
    214–15
Flathead Indians, 229

Florida, Indians in, 92, 160, 229, 274, 280

Fort Berthold Agency and News Bulletin, 246

Fort C.F. Smith, 119–21

Fort Du Quesne, 50

Fort Laramie Treaty, 116, 119–21

Fort Leavenworth, 154

Fort Mims Massacre, 279

Fort Phil Kearney, 115, 119, 121

Fort Pitt, 50, 52

Fort Reno, 119–21

Fort Wallace, 116

Founders of America, The (Jennings), 265

Fourteenth Annual Report of the Bureau of American Ethnology, 140

French and Indian War, 35, 48, 52

Galagina. *See* Boudinot, Elias

game, disappearance of, 70, 76, 79, 159, 169

General Allotment Act. *See* Dawes Act

Georgia

  Indians in

    civilized, 73, 75, 84–91

    land taken from, 92–100, 101–104, 139, 273, 285

Gibbon, General, 152

Grant, Ulysses S., 122, 139

Great Depression, 206, 220, 227

Great Father: The United States Government and the American Indians, The (Prucha), 277

Greeley, Horace, 134

Guess, George. *See* Sequoyah

Hampton School, 188

Harmer, Ruth Mulvey, 243

Harris, Michael, 248

Harrison, Benjamin, 183

Harrison, William Henry, 63, 269–70, 275

Hayes, Rutherford B., 143, 167

Hayt, E.A., 154

Henderson, James, 115

Homestead Act (1862), 115

Howard, Oliver, 150–51, 153

Howard, Simon, 261

Idaho, 138, 143

Indian Office Reports, 137

Indian Peace Commission, 116, 123

Indian Removal Act (1830), 67, 84–85, 93, 97, 273

Indian Reorganization Act. *See* Wheeler-Howard Act

Indian Rights Association, 170

Indian Territory, 127, 138, 143, 154, 178–79

Indiana, 62–63, 269

Indians

  aid from U.S. to, 87–90, 93, 98–99, 103, 127–29, 132–33, 138

  and alcohol problems, 145, 249–50

  as allies of British, 63, 65, 72, 105, 270

  American cruelty toward, 138–42

  and Americans

    should join together in war against, 62–66

    should live in peace with, 67–72

  assimilation of

    federal supervision and, 226–27, 229–31, 236

    impossibility of, 285

    necessity of, 184–86, 190, 270

  as becoming self-supporting, 138–40, 215

    con, 134–36

  beliefs of

    Lakota Sioux, 192, 193, 197–98, 201

    Nez Perce, 144–45, 151–53

    return to, 256

  captives' accounts of, 35–44, 45–57

  character of, 132–36

  civilizing of

    benefits of, 68–69

    Cherokees becoming, 73–83, 101, 273

    con, 84–91, 274

    as harmful, 56, 198–201, 266–67, 274

    impossibility of, 131–36

    and land ownership, 167–74, 210

    necessity of, 34, 93, 168–69, 208

  colonists and

    attack on, 30–34, 36–37, 39

    befriending of, 28–29, 68–69

    should maintain friendly relations with, 28–29

    should wage war on, 30–34

  compared with blacks, 64, 266

  conversion of, religious

    benefits of, 77–80, 188

    as harmful, 56, 216

    necessity of, 31–33

  and crime, 249–50

  culture of

    is becoming Americanized, 183–90, 209, 217

    is becoming Europeanized, 67

    should be preserved, 191–201, 216–17, 275

    con, 186–88

    tribal, 191–93

daily life of, 53–57
description of, 74
discrimination against, 240, 243, 246
education of
  in boarding schools, 185, 186,
    192–96, 199, 216
  Carlisle Indian School, 187–89,
    191, 194–95
  and correct history of Native
    Americans, 200
  costs of, 189
  as harmful, 136
  higher, 186–88, 259
  by Indians, 199–201, 216, 259
  necessity of, 169, 173, 259
  and placement in white homes,
    188
  segregated, 209
  should destroy Indian culture,
    186–88
    con, 191–201, 216
  should emphasize American
    culture, 183–90, 209, 217
  and vocational training, 185, 186,
    187, 221
  and Wheeler-Howard Act, 209
  will improve standard of living,
    184–85, 259
  and women, 188
extermination of, 122, 181–82
extinction of, 63, 94, 97–98, 233, 254
fishing and hunting rights of, 256,
  260
full bloods, 213
government of
  as communistic, 179–80, 207, 210–11
  constitutions of, 73, 92, 101, 207,
    220–21
  by tribes themselves, 78–80, 178,
    208, 210, 217, 220–21
independent nations of, 78–80,
  86–87, 90, 92–94, 103
inferiority of, 184, 270
integration into American society of,
  237–42, 244–50
land taken from
  Black Hills, 254
  Cherokees, 73–74, 84–85, 92–100,
    101–104, 265, 270–71, 278, 285
  Chickasaws, 278
  by colonists, 30, 34, 63–65, 267–68
  Colorado, 139
  Creeks, 270–71, 278, 280
  as inevitable, 157–63
  Ohio, 139
  as unjust, 143–56
and military service, 241, 248, 250

mixed bloods, 213
New Deal reforms harm, 206–15
  con, 216–23
oppression of, 254
police harassment of, 253
political status of, 281–82
population of, 137–38, 184, 239, 244,
  267
  decrease in, 135
prejudice against, 139, 185, 193–94
protection of, 141–42, 171–72,
  177–78, 180–81, 277–89
and racism, 254, 265, 269, 271, 274,
  276
reaction to Wheeler-Howard Act by,
  209–15, 218–19
relocation of
  by Bureau of Indian Affairs
    programs, 237–42, 243–51
  Cherokee, 74, 84–91, 92–100,
    101–104, 273–74
  Chickasaw, 95, 97
  Choctaws, 67–68, 95, 97, 273–74
  to cities
    benefited, 237–42, 245
      con, 243–51, 254
    costs of, 242, 248
    cultural problems from, 239,
      245–48
    health problems from, 246, 250–51
    housing for, 245, 248
    little government help for, 247
    and opening of Indian centers,
      241–42, 249–50
    and poverty, 244, 245–46
    support for, 241–42, 249–50, 254
    and work for, 238, 240–41, 245–46
  Nez Perce, 143
  should not be allowed, 101–10
    con, 92–100, 270
request for independence by, 225–27,
  231
rights of, 233–34
  citizenship for, 141–42, 186, 190,
    226–29, 231
as savages, 30–34, 36–41, 131–36,
  157–58, 162–63
  con, 144, 192–201
segregation of, 208, 211, 266
and taxes, 209
and trading with whites, 271–72
tribal system of, 179–80, 182
and United States
  are victims of, 137–42
  should pursue peace with, 115–25
  should wage war on, 126–30
wars of

cruelty in, 158–63
intertribal, 159
Nez Perce, 151–53
Plains Indians, 115–17, 121–22,
  126–30, 141
profiting from, 141
settlers killed in, 127–28
women
  cultural training for, 251
  education of, 188
  responsibilities of, 188, 210, 212
  voting rights for, 219
  work for, 241
and work
  Emergency Conservation Work
    Agency, 216, 220–22
  and relocation, 238, 240–41, 245–46
  refuse to, 212
  con, 138–40, 168
  see also Native Americans
Indians Are People Too (Bronson), 232
Indians in American Society, The
  (Prucha), 277
Indians of All Tribes, 255
*Invasion of America: Indians,
  Colonialism, and the Cant of Conquest,
  The* (Jennings), 265
Iroquois Indians, 94, 160

Jackson, Andrew
  and Creeks, 270–71, 278, 280
  and Indian removal, 85, 92, 101–103,
    265, 270–73, 277–89
  and justice for Indians, 279–81,
    286–87
  myths of, 268, 270–72, 278
  protection of Indians by, 277–79, 281,
    284, 287–89
  and retaliation toward Indians,
    279–80
  view of Indians of, 281–84, 288
  and War of 1812, 270–71, 275
Jackson, Helen Hunt, 137
Jamestown, Virginia, 28, 30–34
Jefferson, Thomas, 103, 269, 285
Jemison, Mary, 45
Jennings, Francis, 265
Johnson-O'Malley Act, 216

Kansas
  Indian problems in, 126–30
  Indians in, 138, 229
  reservations in, 118–19
Kickapoo Indians, 65
Kiowa Indians, 126–27, 214
Klamath Indians, 214, 229, 236, 239,
  245

Lafitte, Jean, 271
land
  Americans take from Indians, 30, 34,
    63–65
  Black Hills, 254
  Cherokees, 73–74, 84–85, 92–100,
    101–104, 265, 270–71, 278, 285
  Chickasaws, 278
  Colorado, 139
  Creeks, 270–71, 278, 280
  Georgia, 92–100, 101–104, 139, 271
  as inevitable, 157–63
  as unjust, 143–56
  Supreme Court rules on, 101, 273,
    286
  tribal
    community administration of
      as unfair, 206, 209–15
    restoration of, 218
    should be individually owned,
      167–74, 210, 213–14
    con, 175–84
  see also reservations
Land of the Spotted Eagle (Standing
  Bear), 191
Lapwai Reservation, 143–44, 147–49,
  153
Leavenworth, Henry, 127
Leech Lake Reservation, 252–53, 256,
  258, 260–61
Legal Rights Center (Minneapolis),
  253
Lewis, Meriwether, 145
Longfellow, Henry Wadsworth, 134
Louisiana Purchase, 266, 269
Lumpkin, Wilson, 84, 273

Madison, James, 269
Marshall, John, 101, 273, 286
Masquawkee Indians, 65
McCoy, Isaac, 288
McKenney, Thomas L., 288
Means, Russell, 253, 257, 260–61
Menominee Indians, 225–27, 236
Miami Indians, 160
Miles, Nelson A., 143, 153–55
Miller, Charles F., 239
Minnesota
  American Indian Movement in,
    252–53
  Indians in, 138, 177
  reservations in, 252–53, 256, 258–61
Minority Members of the House
  Committee on Indian Affairs, 175
missionaries
  conversion of Indians by, 77–80, 85,
    87, 273–74

and schools, 77, 188
Mississippi, Indians in, 67–68, 86, 96–97
Mitchell, D.D., 119–21
Mitchell, George, 253
Modoc Indians, 229
Mohawk Indians, 63
Mohegan Indians, 94
Monroe, James, 279, 286
Montana, Indians in, 115, 119–20, 138, 229
Morgan, Thomas J., 183
Muskogee Indians, 275
My Life on the Plains (Custer), 131
Myer, Dillon, 238

Narragansett Indians, 63, 94
National Congress of American Indians (NCAI), 232, 234
Native Americans
  American Indian Movement has helped, 252–57
  con, 258–62
  see also Indians
Navajo Indians, 177, 179, 207, 219, 239
Nebraska, 138, 229
Nevada, 138
New Deal
  reforms will harm American Indians, 206–15
  con, 216–23
New Mexico Territory, 138
New York, Indians in, 229
Nez Perce
  beliefs of, 144–45, 151–53
  Chief Joseph, 143
  flight to Canada, 143
  treaties with, 143, 146–49
North Dakota, 229

Ohio, Indians in, 139
Oklahoma
  Cherokee relocation to, 74, 102
  Indians in, 229, 274
  Nez Perce relocation to, 143
Old Person, Earl, 234
Omaha Indians, 177
Opekankanough, 28, 30, 31
Opitchapan, 29
Oregon, Indians in, 214, 229, 239, 245
Oreilles Reservation, 253
Osceola, 274
Ottawa Indians, 65, 158, 229
Ouray Indians, 229
Overland Journey, from New York to San Francisco in the Summer of 1859, An (Greeley), 134

Paiute Indians, 229
Pawnee Indians, 160, 253
Pennsylvania, 36, 45
Penobscot Indians, 94
Peoria Indians, 229
Pequod Indians, 63
Perdue, Theda, 273
Pine Ridge Reservation, 239, 253, 256
Pocahontas, 28, 30
Pocanoket Indians, 63
Ponca Indians, 177
Pope, John, 120
Potawatomi Indians, 65, 70, 134, 158, 229
Powhatan, 28, 30
Powhatan Confederacy, 28, 30
Pratt, Richard Henry, 187, 208
Prophetstown, Indiana, 62–63
Prucha, Francis Paul, 277
Pueblo Indians, 214, 216, 219
Pushmataha, 67

Quapaw Indians, 215

Ramona (Jackson), 137
Red Cloud, 115, 116
Red Lake Reservation, 260
reservations
  development of, 116, 267
  emergency conservation work on, 220–22
  Indians unsuited to, 135–36
  land administered by community benefits of, 216–23
  opposition to, 206, 209–15, 219–20
  land should be individually owned, 168–74, 210, 213–14
  con, 175–82
  and mining, 171
  and overpopulation, 237–39, 250
  poverty on, 237, 240, 246
  resistance to, 116, 143–56
  restoring land to, 218
  cost of, 209, 215, 218
  should be eliminated, 168, 186, 189
  con, 175–82
  unused land should be made public, 169–74, 189
  whites encroach on, 171–74, 178, 181–82, 190, 218, 267
  see also individual reservations
Revolutionary War, 56, 62, 103
Rolfe, John, 28, 30
Roosevelt, Franklin D., 206, 216
Roosevelt, Theodore, 157
Rosebud Reservation, 191
Ross, Edmund G., 126

Ross, John, 87
Rushmore, Mount, 254

Sattler, Richard, 275
Sauk Indians, 65
Schurz, Carl, 167
Seaver, James E., 45
Seminole Indians
    and Five Civilized Tribes, 67, 182
    tribal system of, 182
    war with U.S., 274, 280
Senachwine, 70
Seneca Indians, 45, 50–51
Sequoyah, 78, 90, 273
Seymour, Flora Warren, 206
Shawnee Indians
    taking captives, 35, 45, 48, 50
    Tecumseh, 62–66
Sheninjee, 54–55
Sheridan, Philip, 129
Sherman, William T., 117–18, 121–22,
    127–29
Shoshone Indians, 211, 239
Shubert, George, 246
Sioux Indians
    as activists, 253
    beliefs of, 192, 193, 197–98, 201
    and Chippewa, 212
    culture of, 193, 196–97
    and reorganization, 207, 210, 213,
        214
    Sitting Bull, 169
    treaties with U.S., 119–20
    tribal system of, 182
    war with U.S., 115, 120–22, 160
    Wounded Knee Massacre, 140, 256
Sitting Bull, 169
Six Nations, 94
Smith, John, 28
Snake, Reuben, 253
Snake Indians, 229
Squaxin Indians, 138
Standingbear, Stevie Whiteflower,
    249–51
Standing Bear, Luther, 191
Sturgis, General, 153

Tecumseh, 62, 68, 71–72, 269, 275
Tennessee, Indians in, 75
Tenskwatawa, 62, 269
Texas, Indians in, 229
To-Cha Lee, 79
Tocqueville, Alexis de, 266–67
Trail of Broken Treaties, 254, 256
Trail of Tears, 102, 273
treaties, U.S. government
    with Arapahoes, 118, 127

with Assiniboines, 119
    breaking of, 116–18, 120–21, 139–40,
        153–56, 220, 233, 254, 268, 275
    with Cherokees, 74, 92, 101–102,
        105–108, 273–74
    with Cheyenne, 118–19, 127
    with Chicasaws, 97
    with Choctaws, 67–69, 97, 273
    with Crows, 119
    legal termination of
        Indians benefit from, 225–31
        Indians harmed by, 232–36
    with Nez Perce, 143, 146–49
    with Sioux, 119–20
    violation of, 232–33
Treaty at Fort Laramie, 116, 119–21
Treaty of Dancing Rabbit Creek, 273
Treaty of 1804, 65
Treaty of 1825, 118
Treaty of Greenville, 275
Treaty of Holston, 105–106
Treaty of Hopewell, 105–106
Treaty of New Echota, 74, 101, 273–74
trusteeship
    government should terminate,
        224–31
    con, 232–36, 244–45
Turner, Frederick Jackson, 267

Uintah Indians, 229
United States
    aid to Indians, 87–90, 93, 98–99, 103,
        127–29, 132–33, 138, 218
    and Canada, 266, 269
    Committee on Indian Affairs, 84, 116
    Dawes Act, 168–74, 175–82, 206, 210,
        217–18
    government
        should pursue peace with Indians,
            115–25
        con, 126–30
    Homestead Act (1862), 115
    Indian Removal Act (1830), 67,
        84–85, 93, 97, 273
    Indian treaties. See treaties, U.S.
        government
    Johnson-O'Malley Act, 216
    Public Law, 280, 244
    railroad construction, 116–18, 123,
        124, 126–27, 130
    relocation of Indians by, 67–68, 74,
        84–91, 92–100, 102, 104–108, 273
        as successful, 237–42, 245
        con, 243–51, 254
    removal policy of
        to protect Indians, 277–89
        to subjugate Indians, 265–76

Supreme Court
  decision on Indian land, 101, 273,
    286
  trusteeship of Indians
    should terminate, 224–31
      con, 232–36, 244–45
  Wheeler-Howard Act, 206–15,
    216–23
Usner, Daniel H., Jr., 271, 272
Utah, Indians in, 138, 229
Ute Indians, 138, 229

Virginia, Indians in, 28, 30–35
Virginia Company of London, 28, 30
Vizenor, Gerald, 258
Vocational Rehabilitation Act, 229

Wahunsonacock. *See* Powhatan
War of 1812, 269
  Andrew Jackson in, 270–71, 275
  ended Indian resistance, 275
  Indians allied with Americans in, 67
  Indians allied with British in, 63
  and security for colonizers, 271
Washington, George, 52, 103

Washington, Indians in, 138, 144
Watkins, Arthur V., 224, 227
Wayne, Anthony, 275
Wheeler-Howard Act
  benefits of, 216, 221
  Indian reaction to
    affirmed, 218–19
    opposed, 209–15, 218
  opposition to, 206–15, 219–20, 227
  provisions of, 221, 235
White Earth Reservation, 253
Williamson, Peter, 35
Winnebago Indians, 65, 253
Winnebago Reservation, 253
Winning of the West, The (Roosevelt), 157
Wisconsin, Indians in, 225, 227, 229
Worcester vs. Georgia, 101
Wounded Knee, South Dakota
  massacre at, 140, 256
  protest at, 252, 256–57, 259, 260
Wyandotte Indians, 229
Wyatt, Sir Francis, 31
Wyoming Territory, Indians in, 138

Yellow Bull, 155